DOWN THE GLORY ROAD

DOWN THE GLORY ROAD

HERB BOYD

AVON BOOKS ▲ NEW YORK

DOWN THE GLORY ROAD is an original publication of Avon Books. This work has
never before appeared in book form.

"I'm In The Mood for Love," by Jimmy McHugh and Dorothy Fields. Copyright © 1935
(Renewed 1963) EMI ROBBINS CATALOG INC. All Rights Reserved. Made in USA;
Lonely House (Kurt Weill, Langston Hughes) Copyright © 1946 (Renewed) TRO-HAMP-
SHIRE HOUSE PUBLISHING CORP. and CHAPPELL and CO. All Rights Reserved.
Used by Permission; Permission for *Booker T. and W. E. B.* granted 1994 by Dudley
Randall; Permission for *My Soul's High Song* granted by the Estate of Ida Cullen, James
Rhone, Administrator, © 1925; "Strange Fruit"—Lewis Allen © 1939 Edward B. Marks
Music Company (Copyright Renewed). Used by permission. All rights reserved; Sonia
Sanchez. From "elegy (for MOVE and Philadelphia)," in UNDER A SOPRANO SKY,
by Africa World Press, Inc., 1987. All rights reserved. Reprinted by permission of the
publisher; *If We Must Die*. Permission granted by the Archives of Claude McKay, Carl
Cowl, Administrator. Published in *Selected Poems of Claude McKay*, Harcourt Brace, ©
1957; *Black Arts*. Reprinted by permission of Sterling Lord Literistic Inc.

AVON BOOKS
A division of
The Hearst Corporation
1350 Avenue of the Americas
New York, New York 10019

Copyright © 1995 by Herb Boyd
Cover art by Jeff Potter
Published by arrangement with the author
Library of Congress Catalog Card Number: 94-32027
ISBN: 0-380-77523-9

Library of Congress Cataloging in Publication Data:

Boyd, Herb, 1938–
    Down the glory road / Herb Boyd.
        p.   cm.
    Includes bibliographic references and index.
    1. Afro-Americans—History. I. Title.
E185.A793   1995   94-32027
973'.0496073—dc20   CIP

First Avon Books Trade Printing: February 1995

AVON TRADEMARK REG. U.S. PAT. OFF. AND IN OTHER COUNTRIES, MARCA REGISTRADA, HECHO
EN U.S.A.

Printed in the U.S.A.

OPM   10 9 8 7 6 5 4 3 2 1

To Elza and my students,
who in their desire to learn taught me

ACKNOWLEDGMENTS
-

On the inner ring of my tree of knowledge and acknowledgment there is my immediate family—Katherine, EZ, Cat, and the cats.

The next circle of intimates include my agent Marie Brown, Don Rojas, Robert Van Lierop, Ron Lockett, David Ritz, Charles Moore, Malik Chaka, Clarence Atkins, Playthell Benjamin, Seneca Turner, Akinshiju Ola, Dan Aldridge, Gene Cunningham, Geoffrey Jacques, Jules Allen, Rod Williams, Eli Fountain, Ken Cox, Mac and John Binion, Robert Allen, Ron Williams, Bill Johnson, Bob Belden, and Cleophus Roseboro.

My ring of mentors and colleagues is so extensive I hesitate to begin, but at the risk of missing a few let me name Stretch Johnson, John Henrik Clarke, Gordon Parks, Harry Haywood, Manning Marable, Ernie Allen, Earl Ofari Hutchinson, Frank McCoy, Bob Mast, James Forman, David Levering Lewis, Elombe Brath, Marion Brown, John Sinclair, Ernest Kaiser, Max Roach, Ron Daniels, Harold Neal, Bill Katz, Rita Griffin, Monroe Sharp, Michael Tabor, Dudley Randall, Paul Robeson, Jr., Quincy Troupe, Preston Wilcox, Abdul Alkalimat, Bill Sales, Sam Anderson, Adrienne Ingrum, Michael Dinwiddie, Fred Beauford, Donald Bogle, Terry Johnson, Gerald Horne, Gloria House, Hilly Saunders, Gerald Gladney, Bert Johnson, Rae Alexander-Minter, Ron Milner, Bill Harris, Michele Gibbs, Louis De Salle, Ken Jones, and Steve Chennault.

Among the folks in the outer ring belong my new friends and writers—Kenny Meeks, Yusuf Salaam, Kevin Powell, Tonya Bolden, Sonia Alleyne, Connie Weaver, Ed Enright, Thom Jurek, Denolyn Carroll, Albert and Allen Hughes, Michael Bennett, David Brisbin, Kris Martin, Michael Adderley, Michael Eric Dyson, John Ewing, Paul Washington, Arne Ashwood, and my editor, Tom Colgan.

We've woven ourselves into the very warp and woof of this nation.
—W.E.B. DU BOIS

INTRODUCTION

IN DOUGLASS TURNER Ward's play, *A Day of Absence,* a small town awakens to discover that all the black people have vanished. A similar act of disappearance occurs in William Melvin Kelley's *A Different Drummer,* when black residents of a fictitious state pack their belongings on wagons and decamp en masse.

Derrick Bell gives this metaphor an intergalactic spin in his fable "The Space Traders." A contingent of aliens from a distant planet lands on Earth with enough gold to eradicate the national debt, a special chemical capable of unpolluting the environment, and a totally safe nuclear engine and fuel, to relieve the nation's all-but-depleted supply of fossil fuel. In exchange for these precious items the aliens request only one thing: to take back to their home star all the African-Americans who live in the United States.

The offer is too tempting to reject, and after some soul-searching, referendums, and a national vote, government officials meet with the aliens and the deal is sealed. When the day of departure arrives, on the last Martin Luther King holiday they will ever enjoy in the United States, some twenty million black Americans, forced to strip off all but a single undergarment, are filed to the holds of spaceships. "The inductees looked fearfully behind them, but, on the dunes above the beaches, guns at the ready, stood U.S. guards," Bell writes at the story's conclusion. "There was no escape, no alternatives. Heads bowed, arms now linked by slender chains, black people left the New World as their forebears had arrived."[1]

These imaginative flights of fancy, however, where blacks, exasperated by the persistence of racism, take leave of their town or state (or senses), or where whites, seeking ways to rid the country of a once vital necessity, now a nuisance,

1

formally relinquish any hold on their darker neighbors, are in sharp contrast to reality. To be sure, the historical record is replete with moments when black Americans—the nationalists, emigrationists, and others of the "back-to-Africa" movement—called meetings and laid plans about getting out of Dodge. And there are more than a few instances when white Americans were convinced (witness those bumper stickers "America—Love It or Leave It") that it would be easier to live without "them." And we know this "them" included more than bearded anti-Americans with dope on their breath! Even old Abe Lincoln spent some sleepless nights mulling over the possibility of sending blacks out of the country since he could see no way to bring about harmony between the races.

Emigrationism and Lincoln's quandary aside, black and white Americans are stuck with each other, for better or worse. What all of us need to know—the task of the following pages—is the extent to which we are, and have been, bound together Down the Glory Road. Deny it though we may, black and white Americans have experienced such a seamless relationship during nearly four hundred years of contact in this land that it is often difficult to determine where European culture ends and African culture begins.

We have been carefully taught, to borrow a phrase from Oscar Hammerstein, the white portion of this mutual experience, whether we learned those lessons or not. But few of us, black or white, know much about the African-American contribution to the shaping of this culture, to the building of this nation.

The essential mission of this book, then, is to disclose a few truths, a few things many of you did not know or refused to acknowledge about our collective coming of age and growing up in America. That "thing" you talked about being in the woodpile, well, it is not only there but imbedded in the blood and sinew of our common history, literature, music, dance, religion, and philosophy; our very ethos, and particularly the bulk of its spiritual essence, is permeated and irrevocably stamped (and inked) with the African presence. We have been more than the spook at the door; we've been in every room in this sometimes house of bondage, even in the "cabinets" (ask FDR), and some of us are the skeletons in the closet.

Check out the underbelly of America, its social, political, and economic infrastructure, and you will discover black ingenuity. No claim is made here, though, for any more than we have contributed or have coming to us. (Too much of what has gone down in the name of the good old American way ain't worth claiming anyway.) "Tell no lies and claim no easy victories," an African patriot once said, and these are our watchwords. We derive no benefit from outrageous assertions of conquest and innovation, or that some white man was actually black, like those rumors about President Harding having black blood in his now very dead veins. First of all, we have accomplished quite enough—there's no need to boast or to manufacture achievements. Furthermore, if we have to claim somebody, why a scalawag like Harding, albeit a benign, compassionate soul, if we accept the conclusions of Marcus Garvey? No need to muddy our legacy with his malfeasance. And if he had a little black ancestry, he sure didn't act like it. Cat had no rhythm whatsoever, according to one musician of his day. There is a body of knowledge, then, that all fully educated Americans ought to possess, and it consists of more than the typical catechism of Eurocentric male icons. Hold on! There is no intention here to throw the works and genius of Shakespeare, Socrates, George Washington, Ernest Hemingway, and others on the pyre, despite the multicultural decal on the sweatband and the sneakers. Any mention of diversity, which is our national treasure, should signify inclusion, not exclusion.

If you are not interested in seeing the light, then there is no need to hear the story about Lewis Latimer, who assisted Thomas Edison, or about Granville Wood's third rail, or Dr. Charles Drew's development of plasma, or what the Ronettes owe to Darlene Love and the Blossoms, or York's importance to Lewis and Clark, or what Estevanico meant to the Spanish conquistadores, or Will Vodery's lilting musical arrangement for the Ziegfeld Follies and *Showboat,* or those last few yards across thin ice by Matthew Henson, or how the black cavalry saved Theodore Roosevelt's hide at San Juan Hill, or the indefatigable black lumberjacks who cleared the path that became the Great White Way, or the way in which "black English" has enlivened the nation's language—and much more than "dese" and "dos," or Crispus Attucks, or all the folks Stevie Wonder evokes on *Talking Book*—talkin' bout that "thing" in the woodpile, y'all!

As Ralph Ellison noted, it is time "to change the joke and slip the yoke," to own up to the fact that all Americans share a dual culture, an indivisible history. It is time to set aside the ignorance and bigotry that would discount any part of the whole, the proverbial nose job to spite the face. It is time to banish forever those who contend that African-Americans have no history and culture, no past or tradition (or nothing to look forward to). For black Americans to suggest this is tragic, for white Americans to do so is merely to revive a denunciation once made of them by the elitists of Europe. "The African-American stamp is indelibly etched on the United States," Benjamin Quarles wrote, "both in the rich and varied contribution of the blacks, and in the depth and scope of the white response to the black presence."[2]

It is time to recognize and honor our dual past or we may never realize the full potential of our dual future. And now, dear Americans, it is time to stop moralizing and to see how truly deep and tangled our lives have been, how vitally linked we are as we trudge down the road to glory. No, this is not a Black Thang, just a book about all we should have known—and probably wanted to know—about each other, but were ashamed, afraid, or never thought to ask.

WE DISCOVERED
CHRISTOPHER COLUMBUS
—

BEFORE WE SET out on this odyssey, there's one thing we have to get straight from jump street. It's about departure and arrivals. Who were the first Africans to arrive in the so-called New World? And when? And from where did they embark?

Like 1492, 1619 is a date that, to mock Franklin Delano

Roosevelt, has lived in infamy. The "twenty Negars" hustled ashore from a "Dutch man of warre" at Jamestown that fateful day in August are often cited as the first meaningful presence of Africans in what was to become the United States. It might be more accurate to say they were the first African captives to land at an English settlement. As with so many colonial achievements, to coin my first oxymoron, the Spanish own this distinction.

Practically every caravel from Spain that landed in the Americas had several Africans aboard. Even Columbus was said to have an Afro-Spanish helmsman (Pedro Alonzo Niño) on his flagship, which would make sense since much of what he knew about crossing the Atlantic, he had learned in part from the African sailors of Guinea and from conversations with Don Juan, the king of Portugal. It is often noted how Columbus studied the documents of Ptolemy, Marco Polo, and Aristotle, but save for Ivan Van Sertima, in his book *They Came Before Columbus*, little mention is given to his conversations with the Guinean mariners. But let's not open the Columbus case; his explorations have been recounted *ad absurdum* with little resolution.

As Jan Carew observes, "On the morning of October 12, 1492, a gathering of Arawakian Lucayos *discovered* Christopher Columbus and his sailors on the eastern shore of their homeland of Guanahani."[3] I think this puts the word "discovered" in the right context. It's hard to discover something when it has already been found. And let's be honest, Columbus discovered he was lost, and to cover up his mistake he resorted to the "dozens," calling folks all out of their name!

The Africans associated with Columbus may have been of mixed ancestry, but those who traveled with Hernando Cortés were indubitably African. One of these Africans found grains of wheat in his ration of rice, planted them, and thereby became the first wheat farmer in the New World. In 1513 thirty or more African captives helped Balboa hack his way through tropical undergrowth to reach the Pacific Ocean. And most significant is the escapade of Lucas Vasquez de Ayllon in 1526, a Spanish judge who attempted to found a colony at San Miguel de Gualdape, the site of the celebrated

Jamestown. (There is some discrepancy whether this incident occurred in Virginia or South Carolina, or if there might have been two separate colonies founded by Vasquez de Ayllon. The decision here is to rely on the work of Richard Robert Wright [and hope he's right] since this was his field, and his research is closer to the primary sources.)

Vasquez de Ayllon was already dead when his dream of a colony turned into a nightmare after a combined uprising of Native Americans and African captives decimated the conquistadores. It was under Ayllon's brutal successor that the insurrection occurred, and the rebels burned nearly everything in sight. Those conquistadores who survived the rampage packed their armor and returned to Haiti, from whence they came. Now in control of the fort, these Africans and indigenous people later intermarried and became the first permanent mixed settlement in what is now the United States, and several decades before John Rolfe, secretary and recorder of the Virginia colony, made that entry about a "Dutch man of warre" landing at Jamestown in the summer of 1619.

BETCHA DIDN'T KNOW

That three of the explorer De Soto's slaves, two Africans and a Moor, were so enamored with their new environment, they escaped and found refuge with the Native Americans. They resided among the Cutifachiqui of South Carolina, and one of the escaped Africans married the woman who headed this Indian nation.

LITTLE STEVIE
THE CONQUISTADOR,
OR LUCKY ESTEVANICO
—

ABOUT THE SAME time Judge Vasquez de Ayllon's successor grabbed his helmet and took off for parts unknown, the most illustrious Afro-Spanish contact was taking place when Estevanico, a slave who belonged to Donates de Carranza, joined the Pamphilo de Narvaez expedition. Estevanico was a tall, well-built, midnight-black man of Moroccan heritage who had been trained as a medicine man. This training would come in handy later.

His name was Estevanico or Little Stephen, which is strange since he was comparatively tall, but they should have called him Lucky Estevanico, given the dangerous episodes he survived. The first narrow escape occurred as the soldiers scurried from Florida. Encountering storms, attacks from the natives, disease, desertions, and incompetent leadership, the expedition found it expeditious to build some vessels and to beat a hasty retreat. While navigating across the Apalachicola Bay, toward the Texas coast, the small armada was swept up in a raging storm. When it was over, the six hundred men of the Narvaez contingent had been reduced to four, including Lucky, who couldn't even swim. One of the other survivors was the treasurer of the expedition, Cabeza de Vaca, who also kept an extensive diary of his adventures. A few hipsters over fifty with a penchant for jazz and avant-garde poetry may recall that imaginative raconteur Lord Buckley and his bebop recitation of this odyssey.

After a harrowing journey of 2,500 miles from Tampa Bay to the Pacific, during which the four survivors became separated, they reunited and triumphantly entered Mexico City. Throughout the separation Estevanico had lived among the natives, whom he dazzled with his power to heal, exorcise, and otherwise bamboozle his captors. "The black explorer . . . became familiar with the Indian dialects and characteristics," writes Richard Robert Wright, "and the experience gained in these eight years of wandering afterward proved valuable to him."[4]

Because they had been given up for dead, the four were viewed as demigods and lauded with extended ceremonies. Estevanico, a gifted storyteller, regaled his hosts with fantastic tales, and they were especially excited about the Seven Golden Cities of Cíbola, which old Lucky may have thrown in as a survival tactic, once the partying was over. The viceroy of Mexico was impressed by the tales and, eager to acquire a portion of the munificence at Cíbola, dispatched Estevanico with three hundred men to find the golden cities and bring back the booty. Lucky Estevanico, a slave in 1527, was by 1539 an envoy for the Mexican empire.

His travels took him across great expanses of the Southwest, making him the first nonresident from Africa or Europe to trod through the region now known as New Mexico and Arizona. But Estevanico's luck and cunning finally ran out upon reaching the land of the Zunis. It is unclear what provoked the natives; it may have been Estevanico's arrogance or the fact they found it incredible that a black man could be the emissary of white men. In any case, he was captured by the Zunis and, after three days of torture, was put to death. It may have been a fitting end for a man who, despite his valor in the face of danger, was in effect nothing more than a mercenary, a collaborator, and a shameless self-promoter. We will meet more of his kind later.

AFRICANS IN THE DIASPORA
—

THE SPANISH EXPLORERS, along with the Portuguese, particularly those legions under the jurisdiction of Prince Henry the Navigator, were leagues in front of the other Europeans in the colonial race to the West. What should not be overlooked, a source of much controversy, is the presence of Africans in the West two hundred years before the Europeans. That there is argument on this issue, in the face of nearly incontrovertible proof, may have as much to say about the scholars who challenge the evidence as the evidence itself.

Ivan Van Sertima has amassed an impressive arsenal of artifacts and research that are all but conclusive in supporting the theory of an African presence in the Americas as early as 1500 B.C. among the Olmecs who lived along Mexico's Gulf Coast. In *They Came Before Columbus*, Van Sertima asserts that the colossal Negroid heads, six to nine feet high, weighing up to forty tons each, found at the sacred center of the Olmec culture were obviously the creations of African sculptors.

There is no denying their Africanness, Van Sertima insists:

> The ancient Americans who sculpted them have been shown to be absolutely masters of realistic portraiture, and did not arrive at these distinctive features through accidental stylization. The features are not only Negro-African in type but individual in their facial particulars, canceling out the possibility of ritual stereotypes of an unknown race produced by some quirk of the sculptor's imagination.

Moreover, why would any sculptors go to such ends to create these deities in someone else's image? It could be argued that a Picasso, for example, certainly didn't look like any of the African-like images populating many of his paintings and sculpture. But Picasso confessed his identification with and fascination for African iconography. If the sculptors along the Gulf Coast were not African, to what then do we attribute the influence—*National Geographic?* There appears to be a kind of veiled racism at the core of these postulates, intending to deny the product of African genius. What is most puzzling about the stone heads of La Venta is not who created them, but where is the rest of the body? You may recall that just the opposite occurred with the uncovering of "Lucy," the 3.5-million-year-old hominid fossil. The skeletal remains of Little Lucy were all body and no head.

When Van Sertima's book and thesis appeared in the late

seventies it caused quite a stir, and recently there has been a similar eruption of controversy around the findings of Martin Bernal. Bernal, in his two volume study *Black Athena: The Afro-Asiatic Roots of Western Civilization,* boldly asserts that the foundation of Western culture, the glory that was Greece, the grandeur that was Rome, stems largely from ancient Egypt, and by extension to Sudan and sub-Saharan Africa. Such a proposal naturally disturbed the old-guard Egyptologists, right down to their mummies. Startling as Bernal's conclusions were, there was nothing new about them. A coterie of black scholars—George James, Dr. Yosef ben-Jochannan, Jacob Carruthers, Asa Hilliard, John Jackson, James Spady, Larry Williams, et al—has been championing this position for years. Bernal's nod to their pioneering work amounts to a knowing wink, as if the formulation were essentially his.

While these black scholars have done the basic spadework, so to speak, Bernal has erected the provocative edifice. Of course, whether from a theoretical or practical standpoint, the contributions in this field of endeavor by the late Senegalese scientist Cheikh Anta Diop are indispensable. Diop not only delved deeply into the Egyptian dynasties, where in his opinion the most dramatic and productive periods occur during the reign of the black pharaohs and their queens (the illustrious dynasties from XVIII to XX), he linked the culture of East Africa with West Africa via the trans-Saharan trading routes, thereby showing an uninterrupted link between Egyptian civilization and the ancestors of African-Americans. Rather simply, this is shown linguistically by seeing the association between the names of Tenkhamenin, the great ruler of ancient Ghana, and Tutankhamen, the legendary King Tut of Egypt, or noting the phonetic correspondences between the Wolof language of Senegal and Egyptian Coptic.

And Diop's research extended into prehistory, boldly asserting anthropological theories that are now commonly accepted. It was Diop's contention that humankind emerged in Africa near the Mountains of the Moon, that the hominid *Homo erectus,* an immediate precursor on the evolutionary chart to *homo sapiens sapiens,* emerged from

Africa and was undoubtedly black, and that white people probably resulted from mutations of Grimaldi Man, who migrated from Africa somewhere between 20,000 and 35,000 years ago. Diop's suggestion of an African woman as the mother of us all is to some degree confirmed by recent studies by molecular geneticists. According to these scientists, somewhere between 100,000 and 150,000 years ago there was a woman, a "Mitochondrial Eve," from whom all people of the world are descended. What it boils down to is that Africans have the deepest genetic roots, which means that an African population was the source of all other populations. Thus, this black Eve was literally the mother of us all, although it is not the kind of genetic information our white supremacist friends would like to know. And it should come as no surprise, then, that the Egyptian mummies that Diop observed all had black skin.

THE NILE VALLEY AND BEYOND

BEFORE WE PUT the mummies and the vistas of Egypt (Kemet) behind us, it should be remembered that, for the most part, we are talking about dynasties, particularly of the Old Kingdom, dependent on slave labor and the work of millions of commoners, despite the otherwise seminal role the Egyptians had on the Greeks and the Romans. And often the magnificent contributions of Egypt, its lavish wealth and influence, are inseparable from the widespread exploitation of the masses. Witness this splendid account of the coronation of Ptolemy II (285–247 B.C.) from John Jackson's *Introduction to African Civilizations*:

> From morn to dusk of a mild November day a stupendous procession paraded broad, marble-lined avenues ... Fourteen lions led a train of panthers, leopards, lynxes, and a rhinoceros. Nubian slaves carried 600 tusks of ivory, 2,000 blocks of

ebony and gold and silver vessels filled with gold dust ...
Hundreds of slaves carried strange birds in cages or on boughs
of trees, and trays of perfume and spices, or led thousands
of Indian dogs on the leash.[5]

Many of us who rave about the greatness of Akhenaton,
Rameses, Imhotep, Nefertiti, Nefertari, Hatshepsut, Cleopa-
tra, and others would probably sing a different tune if we
were to be transported back to those times. Chances are you'd
land smack-dab in the middle of a quarry, consigned for the
rest of your life to chip and ship stone along runners to a
building site. Given the relative achievement of ancient Egypt,
there is still a need for a good class analysis. Much as it is
today, save for the anxiety created by Islamic fundamentalists,
ancient Egypt may have been a nice place to visit, but unless
you were among the royalty, the priestly caste, or the elite,
you might want to consider taking the next boat down the
Nile.

A relativity is also demanded when summoning the glorious
kingdoms of West Africa, where very little archeological exca-
vation has occurred. While it is important to know that we
are descended from fabulous empires that stretched geo-
graphically from Mali to Monomatapa, we should keep in
mind the wholesale despotism so often suffered by commoners. Ghana, Mali, and Songhay are the three most referenced
kingdoms from West Africa, and they occupied the same eco-
logical niche, though increasingly expanded with each new
succession of rule. Located between the enormous salt depos-
its of Western Sahara and the endless supply of gold in the
Senegambia region, the kingdoms were ideally situated to
tax the flow of both commodities through their territory.
With enriched coffers, such renowned leaders as Tenkhamenin of Ghana, Mansa Musa of Mali, and Askia Muhammad of Songhay were able to build powerful armies or to
take lavish trips to Mecca, a pilgrimage required of devout
Muslims, to flaunt their splendor and wealth. We have no
record of the trickle-down effect the lucrative treasuries
had for the lowly villagers. If they were anything like we

are today, the most they could expect was to vibe vicariously from the exploits and ventures.

But despite their financial clout, there was clearly not enough capital or juju available to stop the invasion of the Muslims, which had begun as early as the eighth century, or the European invaders, who by the fifteenth century were on the march across land and sea. Whether motivated by God or gold, the European hordes gradually superimposed their dominance on Africa from Cairo to Cape Town, with the Berlin Treaty of 1884–85 and the Atlantic slave trade with its brutal middle passage as the cornerstone to the African holocaust.

BLACK GOLD

To TRACE THE ancestry of black Americans to their African roots, it is necessary to take a deep breath and examine the horrors of the slave trade. Most of the early Africans who found themselves in the diaspora, unless they were able to secure a one-way ticket on Abubakari's fleet in 1311 (Abubakari, the brother of Mansa Musa, the great leader of Mali, reputedly sailed to the West almost two hundred years before Columbus, albeit on a one-way trip since he was never heard from again) or were fishermen who strayed too far from the African coast and were slung to the West courtesy of the Gulf Stream and a relentless storm, had to endure the middle passage, that corridor of hell from Africa to the Americas. The majority of the merchants and slavers who plied the Atlantic had one thing in mind, and that was to maximize their profits. Thus, they were "tight packers" who believed in getting as many captives in the holds as humanly (or inhumanly) possible.

John Hawkins, captain of the slave ship *Jesus*, and John Newton (later the Right Reverend) were noted tight packers. In *Black Cargoes*, by Daniel Mannix and Malcolm Cowley, Newton provides a graphic description of this process:

The cargo of a vessel of a hundred tons or a little more is calculated to purchase from 220 to 250 slaves. Their lodging rooms below the deck which are three (for the men, the boys, and the women) besides a place for the sick, are sometimes less; and this height is divided toward the middle for the slaves to lie in two rows, one above the other, on each side of the ship, close to each other like books upon a shelf . . .

The poor creatures, thus cramped, are likewise in irons for the most part which makes it difficult for them to turn or to move or attempt to rise or to lie down without hurting themselves or each other. Every morning, perhaps, more instances than one are found of the living and the dead fastened together.[6]

In 1764 Newton, repentant of his former life, left the sea and entered the clergy. Over the succeeding years he would become an ardent foe of slavery and make a name for himself as a composer. Among the hymns he wrote is "Amazing Grace," and the classic line "that saved a wretch like me" is unmistakably autobiographical.

Unfortunately, however, far too few slave captains and merchants felt pangs of conscience and repented. Captain Luke Collingwood was more typical of the breed, in behavior and longevity. Faced with imminent catastrophe during a voyage, though land had been sighted, Collingwood gave the order to jettison 133 Africans since the provision of water was nearly depleted. "If the slaves died of thirst or illness," Collingwood told his crew, "the loss would fall on the owners of the vessel; but if they were thrown into the sea, it would be a legal jettison, covered by insurance." And Lloyd's of London, who charged sky-high premiums because of the prevalence of mutinies, was probably the insurance company of record.

It is not certain if Gustavus Vassa (Olaudah Equiano), best known for the slave narrative he authored in 1788, was an eyewitness to this heartless, uncalled-for action, but he brought it to the attention of the abolitionist movement in England. Vassa, like another African captive, Venture Smith, who wrote a narrative of his life in slavery, experienced the middle passage under Captain Collingwood. Smith recalled a sales transaction that included Collingwood:

I and other prisoners were put aboard a canoe, under our master, and rowed away to a vessel belonging to Rhode Island, commanded by Captain Collingwood and the mate Thomas Mumford. While we were going to the vessel, our master told us all to appear to the best possible advantage for sale. I was bought on board by one Robertson Mumford, steward of said vessel, for four gallons of rum, and a piece of calico, and called Venture, on account of his having purchased me with his private venture. Thus I came by my name. All the slaves that were bought for that vessel's cargo, were two hundred and sixty.[7]

SOUNDBITE

"When I was an infant, Old Myners died (the slave master), and there was a division of the slaves and other property among the family. I was brought along with my mother by old Captain Darrel, and given to his grandchild, little Miss Betsey Williams."

—MARY PRINCE,
THE FIRST BLACK WOMAN FROM THE
DIASPORA TO ESCAPE FROM SLAVERY AND
PUBLISH A RECORD OF HER EXPERIENCES

The Slave Auction

The sale began—young girls were there,
Defenceless in their wretchedness,
Whose stifled sobs of deep despair,
Revealed their anguish and distress.

And mothers stood with streaming eyes,
And saw their dearest children sold;
Unheeded rose their bitter cries,
While tyrants bartered them for gold.

And woman, with her love and truth—
 For these in sable forms may dwell—
Gaz'd on the husband of her youth,
 With anguish none may paint or tell.

And men, whose sole crime was their hue,
 The impress of their Maker's hand,
And frail and shrinking children, too,
 Were gathered in that mournful band.

Ye who have laid your love to rest,
 And wept above their lifeless clay,
Know not the anguish of that breast,
 Whose lov'd are rudely torn away.

Ye may not know how desolate
 Are bosoms rudely forced to part,
And how a dull and heavy weight
 Will pass the life-drops from the heart.

—FRANCES ELLEN WATKINS HARPER (1825–1911)

A SOUL FOR SALE

AS A TERMINAL point, the auction block must have seemed a
cruel joke to African captives who had survived the brutalities
of the rounding-up process and the coffle line or being shack-
led by chain slave-to-slave and endured the dread of barra-
coons (holding forts) at Goree, Cape Coast Castle, and
Elmina Castle, withstood the ravages of dengue, the bloody
flux, and smallpox, and overcome the menacing whips of
fiendish caboceers and first mates. It was as if they were victims of an awful trick, like the jaybird who was asked by the
fox to pick a bone out of his mouth, and once inside, was

devoured by the fox. And the more religious among them must have surely wondered why their gods had forsaken them; to have shepherded them past the fire only to deliver them to the pot.

And this pot was more than a metaphor for those who were convinced their captors were cannibals, and that all the recent grooming and feeding, after weeks of virtual starvation, was merely to make them a more delectable meal. Many of them must have winced or trembled in anticipation when they heard the cannon blast signaling the beginning of the mad dash into the warehouse by potential buyers. Many of the Africans obviously heaved a sigh of relief when they discovered they were only being tagged and marked by merchants, prior to the bidding process.

If the first twenty African captives who were delivered to Jamestown in 1619 felt such trepidation, it escaped the diaries of John Rolfe and the other settlers. In fact, we know very little about these mysterious Africans who somehow got their fates entangled with the Dutch and then the English. Who were they, from where did they come, where were they destined, and what happened to them after that eventful day in August? Two of them, Antony and Isabella, did leave some tracings behind. From their union came William Tucker, the first African child born in English America. After this birth, which occurred in 1624, the shroud once more descends and these first Africans fade from view.

But they provided the crack in the dam, and behind them came the flood of Africans that would make it necessary for the early colonists to determine promptly the status of these dusky newcomers. They were the odd men and women in the margins of history; they had not come on the *Mayflower*, nor were their relatives waiting on the shore to greet the Pilgrims, to tamper with a Will Rogers remark. Were they slaves, indentured servants, or free? By the time William Tucker was a year old, the blacks residing in Virginia were classified as servants, if we can trust the census, which was—as it is today—not the most reliable source. When young Tucker turned eighteen, presuming he was still alive, his status probably changed again—at least it did for most Africans in Virginia.

This status shift resulted from an incident involving a black man, John Punch, who, along with two other servants, a Dutchman and a Scot, fled from Virginia, seeking, we must assume, a kind of early form of political asylum in Maryland. They were immediately apprehended and the Dutchman and the Scot were ordered to serve their masters an additional year, and the colony for three more, but Punch got the book thrown at him and was sentenced to serve his "master or his assigns for the time of his natural life here or elsewhere." Thus, in 1640, that bugaboo of America's criminal justice system called the double standard was officially launched. Later in the year, in another Virginia court, the double standard debuted for black women. A white man slept with a black woman and impregnated her. The woman was flogged for her indiscretion; the white man did penance before the church. No explanation was offered by the court in either case for the disparity in the sentences.

Another case also indicated a drift toward enslavement in Virginia. John Casor, a black indentured servant, was brought to trial by his master, Anthony Johnson. Casor claimed that he had served Johnson for fifteen years as an indentured servant and should be set free. The court decided that Casor should be assigned to Johnson as a servant for life. This case is significant historically in that Johnson, the master, was also black.

If there was any doubt about the legal distinction between black and white servants, the Punch case set the record straight. The Casor case placed the issue within a class context. Some twenty years later in 1661, Virginia passed a statute recognizing slavery. It sent a chilling effect through the small but vocal black community. And this statute, given the increasingly large black population, was quickly followed by others as the colony sought measures to stifle the possibility of revolt. Gradually slave codes were introduced with the intention of controlling mobility, possession of weapons, assembly, and association. In the Carolinas these codes were even harsher since many of the plantation masters were veterans of the Caribbean and knew what it took to keep things in check. Things were not much better "up South." Even in the so-called bastion of liberty, Massachusetts, blacks were denied their equal rights and slavery seeped more virulently into the body politic. By 1664, New York City, having gone through several stages of transformation since old Peter Menuit swiped it from the natives "for twenty-four dollars and a bottle of booze," was well on the road to slavery. The profitability of slavery in Virginia was too enticing for the New Yorkers, and it wasn't long before Wall Street merchants were screaming like they do at the Stock Exchange, only this time the commodity was breathing and possessed a soul.

But to compare slavery in the North with the southern "peculiar institution" is not only odious, it is ludicrous. The enterprise of slavery in the North, albeit lucrative, had neither the economic clout nor the widespread prevalence. There existed in the South the climate, the soil, and the ethos to make the system exceedingly expansive and productive. "I am of the same opinion now as I was two years ago," bellowed General Charles Cotesworth Pinckney to the Constitutional Convention in 1787, "that while there remained one acre of swampland uncleared of South Carolina, I would raise my voice against restricting the importation of Negroes (slaves). I am as thoroughly convinced as that gentleman is, that the nature of our climate, and the flat, swampy situation of our country, obliges us to cultivate our lands with Negroes, and that without them South Carolina would soon be a desert waste."[8]

There is no way to confirm if General Pinckney was a student of Aristotle, but his rationality seems only one step removed from the philosopher's contention that some men were "slaves by nature." We can deduce from the general's remarks that there is a land perfectly suited for certain workers, and South Carolina was created for "Negroes" to develop. To suggest that blacks were born to be slaves is really to place the cart before the horse, that is, to extrapolate from one's social status some notion of inherent character, as Winthrop Jordan concludes in his book *White Over Black*, to impute to individuals characteristics suited to their social roles.

South Carolina's first "natural slaves" arrived in 1670. As A. Leon Higginbotham, Jr., asserts, "Blacks were not imported in large numbers into South Carolina until the late 1690s with the development of rice as a profitable staple.'' In many respects, South Carolina, like the other American colonies, first relied on white indentured servants as a labor force, but this option was fraught with several liabilities, most significant, the insufficient numbers. A similar problem hampered the use of the indigenous population. By 1708, with the formal recognition of black slave labor, the issue was resolved forever, and soon blacks outnumbered whites. And throughout the colonial period—and South Carolina alone had this distinction—blacks would be the majority of the population.

Because of its direct connection with the island of Barbados, South Carolina had a useful prototype upon which to base its slavery system. Slavery evolved in South Carolina practically unimpeded by the possible mitigating circumstances of neighboring colonies. Virginia was too remote to have any real impact, and North Carolina was essentially an extension of Virginia with a different economy that produced such staples as tobacco, corn, and livestock. Most crucial, though, to the colony's unique growth was the severity of the slave codes and the complete absence of any challenge to the draconian legalities. As the legal noose slackened about the necks of white indentured servants, it tightened around the necks of black slaves.

LET YOUR MOTTO
BE RESISTANCE!

GIVEN THE SEVERE limitations of freedom and the brutal application of the slave codes, it was only a matter of time before the colony's worst nightmare—the insurrection—disturbed the relative serenity. The proverbial crap hit the fan in 1739, not once but three times. The most serious uprising took place at Stono, a plantation about twenty miles west of Charleston. Led by a slave named Cato, the rebels killed two guards at an arsenal, took the weapons, and struck a westerly course toward the Edisto River.

Their objective was to escape into Spanish-held Florida, where the governor had promised liberty to all fugitive English slaves.

As they marched along toward the river with their colors flying and two drums beating, they were joined by other slaves. Like General Sherman's "scorched earth campaign" across the South to Atlanta—some 125 years in the future—the slaves destroyed and burned everything in their path. About thirty whites were killed, and one kindly master was spared. Alerted to the rampage, the white militia took out after the rebels, devised a surprise attack, and killed fourteen blacks. In two more days of fierce fighting, twenty more rebels were killed and forty captured. The remaining twenty rebels took a stand in a final battle and ten were killed, and the "other ten made good their bid for freedom," Herbert Aptheker reported.

Nearly one hundred slaves were involved in this uprising, which makes it one of the largest in American history. Before the Civil War, South Carolina would witness countless revolts and conspiracies, including the often-discussed plot by Denmark Vesey in Charleston in 1822. We should note two other celebrated rebels of Virginia: Nat Turner and Gabriel Prosser. But the fulcrum of revolt was in South Carolina, and nothing captures the spirit of insurrection and the desire for freedom more than this song written by a slave:

> *Arise! arise! shake off your chains!*
> *Your cause is just, so Heaven ordains;*
> *To you shall freedom be proclaimed!*
> *Raise your arms and bare your breasts,*
> *Almighty God will do the rest.*
> *Blow the clarion's warlike blast;*
> *Call every Negro from his task;*
> *Wrest the scourge from Buckra's hand,*
> *And drive each tyrant from the land!*

> *(Chorus)*
> *Firm, united let us be,*
> *Resolved on death or liberty!*
> *As a band of patriots joined,*
> *Peace and plenty we shall find.*

Within two years of Cato's revolt at Stono, a plot of similar magnitude was taking place in New York City. When a fort on what is now the Battery went up in flames on March 18, 1741, and was followed by a succession of other fires, rumors were afloat of a slave conspiracy to destroy the city and massacre all the whites. Blacks were arrested and imprisoned whether under suspicion or not.

A month or so after the destruction of the fort, Mary Burton, a white indentured servant to John Hughson, an innkeeper, was called before a grand jury to testify about an alleged robbery planned in her master's place. Pressured by the jury, Burton sang like a canary, and when she was through, she had implicated three blacks, Caesar, Prince, and Cuffe, in a plot not only to rob but to burn down the town, kill all the whites, and make themselves rulers of the city. She also implicated her master, his wife, Sara, and another white woman, Peggy Kerry, known as the "Irish beauty," in the conspiracy. Kerry had a child by Caesar and was his mistress. There are accounts, too, that suggest Burton had an affair with Caesar, which may have prompted her accusations.

Shortly thereafter, a trial was held in an atmosphere reeking with apprehension and terror. Fresh in most minds was the revolt of 1712 when a band of black insurgents laid siege to the town before they were captured and executed. The case was followed with great interest, particularly by slaveholding communities. At the completion of the trials, eighteen were hanged and fourteen were executed, one in slow torture by fire. Some seventy blacks were transported out of the country. John Hughson, his wife, Sara, and Peggy Kerry, as well as an English priest, John Ury, were among those hanged.

That such extreme retribution was administered may have derived from the nature of the plot and its multiracial character. Never before had blacks and whites unified in such a manner. Apparently the law enforcement agency and city officials wanted to send a clear, unmistakable message to future plotters that they would prosecute such actions with the fullest extent of the law, and some.

While blacks were seemingly everywhere striking blow after blow for freedom—and their quest would receive additional

impetus by 1805 when the great Toussaint L'Ouverture led
a successful Haitian revolution—white America had liberty,
fraternity, and equality on its list of priorities. The cry was a
familiar one, and that it was meant ostensibly for whites only
did not dissuade thousands of blacks from participating in
the American Revolution.

BETCHA DIDN'T KNOW

In 1641 Mathias De Sousa was chosen as a representative to the Maryland colonial general assembly, becoming the first black elected official in American history.

WE, TOO, HOLD THESE TRUTHS

IN FACT, AND it may be the only bit of information widely
known about the role of blacks prior to and during the Revolutionary War, a black man, Crispus Attucks, was the first to
fall for freedom. (In 1692 when the Salem "witch" trials were
the source of intolerance, Tituba, a slave, was the first woman
to be tried. She confessed after being severely flogged, impli-
cating two other women. Only by admitting she was a witch
was Tituba spared execution.) Who Attucks was and what his
motives were remain troublesome facts. What seems indisput-
able, however, is that he was not a drunken sailor who accidentally became a martyr and stumbled onto the pages of
history.

Attucks's father, Prince, was born in Africa, and his mother,
Nancy, was an indigenous Natick. When he was eleven years
of age, Attucks was tired of being shuttled from one slave

owner to another. Unhappy with his situation, he ran away to become a sailor and a whaler. Somewhere over the course of years he had learned to read and write, and to comprehend the basic principles of freedom and equality. He was present at several meetings with other patriots where the burdensome taxes levied by England were discussed; he may have been incensed, too, by the stiff restrictions of the navigational acts and their impact on seamen. Later, in his mid-forties, Attucks wrote a letter of protest to Tory Governor Thomas Hutchinson, expressing with keen insight his devotion to freedom. So his position in the ranks of protesters at Boston Commons was not coincidental; he just happened to be out front. Others were gunned down at this massacre in March 1770, but ironically, only this fugitive slave has achieved immortality.

Five years later when the Revolutionary War would begin in earnest, Attucks's sacrifice was not forgotten as hundreds of free blacks enlisted to fight against British tyranny. Obviously many of them joined the fray hoping this struggle for freedom and independence would ramify beyond the immediate cause to reach their brothers and sisters still laboring in bondage. Much like their motivations in future wars, blacks carried a dual purpose into battle—America's freedom first and then their own. Indeed, many blacks heeded the call of drum and fife, but many more continued to petition for their freedom through whatever legal means were open to them. In concert, then, with picking up the gun was a number of black citizens picking up the pen and waging their own battles for the antislavery cause.

Tick off the names: Lexington, Concord, Bunker Hill or Breed's Hill, Ticonderoga, Brandywine, and Valley Forge— blacks distinguished themselves on nearly all the major battlegrounds, and at sea. No single black soldier, among the 5,000 who fought alongside the patriots, was as ubiquitous as Barzillai Lew. Lew, a native of Groton, Massachusetts, joined the war right from its inception in 1775 and served seven years, drumming and fifing his way throughout New England, including the famous Battle at Bunker Hill, where he must have witnessed the heroic deeds of black patriots Peter Salem,

Salem Poor, and Prince Hall. After the war Hall would play a key role in the founding of the Black Masonic movement as well as in the abolitionist movement. Lemuel Haynes, who would later become a noted theologian and minister for white congregations in New England, was also seemingly everywhere, joining two blacks—Epheram Blackman and Primus Black—of Ethan Allen's Green Mountain Boys at Fort Ticonderoga, and in the thick of things at Lexington and Concord. Haynes was also quite a poet, and this is the last stanza from his poem "The Battle of Lexington":

> *This motto may adorn their Tombs*
> *(Let Tyrants come and view):*
> *"We rather seek these silent Rooms*
> *Than live as slaves to you."*

Look closely at the famous painting of George Washington crossing the Delaware on Christmas Day 1776. The black man in the commander's boat is either Prince Whipple or William Lee, Washington's trusted valet, who was by his side for seven years during the war. Oliver Cromwell was another black with Washington during that surprise attack on the Hessians at Trenton. That they were there at all, or that blacks were allowed to fight in the war, was due to a strange turn of events and proclamations, some of them authored by Washington himself. John Rutledge, a delegate from South Carolina to the Continental Congress, probably a colleague of the previously mentioned General Pinckney, introduced a resolution in 1775 barring blacks as soldiers; a resolution restricting the use of slaves had already been approved ten days earlier. General Washington complied with the decisions.

But soon a reversal of the trend emerged. Prompting this reconsideration was the large number of slaves reportedly lured by Lord Dunmore's decree to free all those who fought for the British. Washington, urged on by legislators and military advisors, amended his resolution. "Free Negroes who have served in this army," Washington announced in a letter sent to Congress, "are very much dissatisfied at being discarded" and he was thus allowing them to be enlisted, but only those who had fought with the army previously, no others. There has been speculation that Washington changed his mind after a meeting with the black poet Phillis Wheatley. If Wheatley had any influence on him, it probably had less to do with her skillful use of words than with her stunning intelligence. In any case, the exigencies of the war soon outran any stern reservations, and states passed their own laws permitting the limited participation of blacks as soldiers and sailors.

Yes, blacks served in the nascent navy. They were aboard such brigs as the *Trumbull*, the *Julius Caesar*, the *Alliance*, and the *Morning Star*. One black sailor, James Forten, a powder boy, would later become a notable entrepreneur, and acquire fame and wealth as the inventor of an improved mechanism for handling sails. He would also make a mark as an outstanding abolitionist. Like the African pilots with the Spanish explorers, blacks were the helmsmen of several ships that plied the waters of the Hudson River, Chesapeake Bay, and along the Atlantic seaboard.

Many blacks were spies, too. Pompey, a slave belonging to a Captain Lamb, obtained the British password that facilitated General Anthony Wayne's surprise attack and capture of Stony Point, New York. For this act Pompey was given his freedom. Quaco Honeyman of Rhode Island also gained his freedom by supplying the patriots with important tactical information.

It should also be noted that among America's allies were about seven hundred Haitian free blacks who formed what was known as the Fontages Legion. Christophe, who would succeed Toussaint L'Ouverture as Haiti's leader, served in this unit and possibly carried home the bug of liberation.

Blacks who put their lives on the front lines were certainly pleased to know that their commitment may have been instrumental in the abolition of slavery, albeit gradual, north of Maryland. It was, perhaps, too much to expect that it might lessen the shackles in the bowels of slavery. For that, another war, even more destructive and shattering, would be necessary.

"He (the king) has waged cruel war against human nature

itself, violating its most sacred rights of life and liberty in the persons of a distant people who never offended him, captivating and carrying them into slavery in another hemisphere, or to incur miserable death in their transportation thither ... determined to keep open a market where MEN should be bought & sold he has prostituted his negative for suppressing every legislative attempt to ... restrain this execrable com merce ...'' If you've never read this portion of Thomas Jefferson's Declaration of Independence, it stands to reason since it was deleted from the original version. Jefferson's attempt to pin the slavery rap on King George III was as disingenuous as other parts of his great rhetoric proved to be hypocritical. (Of course, Jefferson was not alone in his hypocrisy! Most of the "founding fathers" and eight of the first twelve presidents were slaveholders.) All the talk about holding certain truths to be self-evident and "that all men are created equal and endowed by the creator with certain inalienable rights" had nothing to do with black people, though they embraced the spirit and the letter of the words, often citing them in the numerous petitions they delivered to state legislatures.

Not until you reach the bottom of the famous document and examine the list of grievances the patriots had against the king is there anything remotely pertaining to blacks, and there King George is accused of fomenting "domestic insurrection" in the colonies. This is evidently a reference to the various decrees put forth by Lord Dunmore and others attempting to entice slaves to join the royal fighting forces.

Jefferson's excised passages, his high-sounding principles, were also contradicted by his practice. An ardent advocate of the "natural rights of man," he nonetheless enjoyed a life of privilege on a plantation consisting of more than two hundred slaves, including a woman, Sally Hemings, putatively the mother of several of his children, and part of his "Congo harem," as his detractors put it. This controversy, despite two recent books, rages on with no resolution in sight. (Willard Randall in his recent biography *Thomas Jefferson: A Life* contends that Hemings was only eight years old when Jefferson last resided at Monticello.) For each black descendant claiming ties to Jefferson, there are three white descendants refuting them. Curiously, there are very few white people named Jefferson. All of this is reminiscent of the argument often heard in the black community some years ago over whether Phoebe Fraunces, a black innkeeper's daughter, actually saved George Washington from being poisoned one evening when he stopped at the inn for a farewell drink with his fellow officers. The issue will be forever moot because of the absence of conclusive evidence. And why anyone would want to be associated with a man like Jefferson, who was never courageous enough to admit his affair with Hemings, if there was one, or who chose to wait on the next generation to free his slaves, is baffling.

That other great document from the revolutionary period, the Constitution, was equally flawed. Sojourner Truth, the famed abolitionist who had a talent for getting to the meat of an issue, summed up the Constitution with this story:

> "Children," she said. "I talks to God and God talks to me. I goes out and talks to God in de fields and de woods. Dis morning I was walking out, and I got over de fence. I saw de wheat holding up its head, looking very big. I goes up to it and takes holt to it. You b'lieve it, dere was no wheat dere. I says, 'God, what is de matter wid dis wheat?' and he says to me, 'Sojourner, dere is a little weasel (weevil) in it.' Now I hears talkin' bout de Constitution and de rights of man. I come up and takes holt of dis Constitution. It looks mighty big, and feels for *my* rights, but dere ain't any dere. Den I says, 'God, what ails dis Constitution?' He says to me, 'Sojourner, dere is a little weasel in it.' "[9]

A far more telling example of the Constitution's imperfection is readily seen by the number of amendments added since its first appearance. The Thirteenth, Fourteenth, Fifteenth Amendments are the ones most black Americans can cite with ease. It was a pact made with the devil, the renowned abolitionist William Lloyd Garrison often said of the Constitution. While blacks were granted a three-fifths designation in the document, Native Americans were virtually omitted, get-

ting a mention on tax exclusion and a mere five words otherwise—"and with the Indian tribes"—which were tacked as an
afterthought to the commerce clause.

BETCHA DIDN'T KNOW

According to the Constitution of 1787: "Representatives
and direct Taxes shall be apportioned among the several States which may be included within this Union,
according to their respective Numbers, which shall be
determined by adding to the whole number of free
persons, including those bound to Service for a Term
of Years and excluding Indians not taxed, *three fifths
of all other persons.*" (*my emphasis*)

BANNEKER

THE CONTRIBUTIONS OF blacks to an emerging nation extended beyond the war effort. Writers, poets, painters, arti-
sans, teachers, scholars, ministers, and others were
enriching America's intellectual and artistic life. Phillis
Wheatley, as was mentioned earlier, had demonstrated her
genius on many occasions, and to the most eminent of
hosts. Characteristic of black writers of her day, Wheatley's
poetry rarely reflected her African heritage. She was
brought from Africa when she was ten, and by the time she
was seventeen, she published her first book of poetry. Her
poem "On Being Brought from Africa to America" is typical of her style and content:

Twas mercy brought me from my pagan land
Taught my benighted soul to understand
That there's a God, that there's a savior too;
Once I redemption neither sought nor knew,
Some view our sable race with scornful eye,
Their color is a diabolic dye.
Remember, Christians, Negroes, Black as Cain,
May be refined, and join th' angelic train.

Less beholden to the amenities of white society was Benjamin Banneker. Born free in the slave colony of Maryland in 1731, he received his education from a Quaker school. His ability with math and science was a source of amazement, and by 1761 he made a clock out of wooden parts that kept perfect time, striking on the hour for more than twenty years. Of course, white America paid little attention to the innovation—and still doesn't know what time it is. His mastery of astronomy was at the basis of his annual almanacs. A skilled draftsman and surveyor, he was assigned by President Washington to work with French major Pierre-Charles L'Enfant and Andrew Ellicott III to plan the new federal capital in the District of Columbia.

Were it not for an exchange of letters with Thomas Jefferson, Banneker may not have received a wider celebrity. Previously, in his "Notes on Virginia," Jefferson had stated emphatically his belief in black inferiority. "Comparing them by their faculties of memory, reason, and imagination," Jefferson said of blacks, "it appears to me, that in memory they are equal to the whites; in reason much inferior, as I think one could scarcely be found capable of tracing and comprehending the investigations of Euclid; and that in imagination they are dull, tasteless, and anomalous ... Never yet could I find that a black uttered a thought above the level of plain narration; never see even an elementary trait of painting or sculpture."

Of the existing black artists of the day—Wheatley, Ignatius Sancho, et al—Jefferson dismissed them without qualification. That Banneker knew of Jefferson's pronouncements by 1791 is obvious from a letter sent to him, along with a manuscript copy of his almanac.

Suffer me to recall to your mind that time, in which the arms of the British crown were exerted, with every powerful effort, in order to reduce you to a state of servitude; look back, I entreat you ... You were then impressed with proper ideas of the great violation of liberty, and the free possession of those blessings, to which you were entitled by nature; but sir, how pitiable is it to reflect, that although you were so fully convinced of the benevolence of the Father of Mankind, and of his equal and impartial distribution of these rights and privileges which he hath conferred upon them, that you should at the same time counteract his mercies, in detaining by fraud and violence, so numerous a part of my brethren under groaning captivity and cruel oppression, that you should at the same time be found guilty of that most criminal act, which you professedly detested in others.[10]

Jefferson's reply was courteous, but he relinquished none of his belief. "I can add with truth," Jefferson wrote ambiguously, "that nobody wishes more ardently to see a good system commenced for raising the condition both of their [blacks] body and mind to what it ought to be, as fast as the imbecility of their present existence, and other circumstances which cannot be neglected, will admit."

He may have been slow and ambivalent conceding the fact of Banneker's genius, but Jefferson did forward his manuscript to the Marquis de Condorcet with a note therein that commended Banneker for his mathematical deductions. Whether Banneker responded to any of this is inconsequential; his comprehension of spherical trigonometry spoke volumes. Plus, indirectly, the retorts to Jefferson's derogations would come from a number of Banneker's contemporaries—Richard Allen, Absalom Jones, John Chavis, James Derham, Jupiter Hammon, James Forten, Paul Cuffe, Prince Hall, to name a few accomplished blacks who were living proof that Jefferson was either a confused humanist or a troubled racist.

The years following the Revolutionary War witnessed remarkable growth in practically every area of American life. And the roots of America's intellectual, artistic, social, religious, philosophical, and cultural life were never before as tangled with black and white expression. For every Thomas Jefferson there was a Benjamin Banneker (and the ultimate

irony of their lives would occur by 1806 when Jefferson entered the White House in a city Banneker helped to design),
and Banneker's almanacs certainly bore some relationship to
Benjamin Franklin's *Poor Richard's Almanac;* there was
Wheatley's poetry, her couplets evoking Alexander Pope, her
"General Washington" matching Phillip Freneau's "General
Gage." And when Richard Allen and Absalom Jones were
restricted to "Nigger pews" in the Methodist Church, their
answer was to extend the reach of the gospel, first through
the Free African Society and then with the founding of the
African Methodist Episcopal Church. Prince Hall reacted creatively when he was denied entry into the white Masonic halls
and he established one for his sable brothers.

Dr. Benjamin Rush, the benevolent white physician and a
signer of the Declaration of Independence, was effusive in his
praise of Dr. James Derham, with whom he communicated
for years on various diseases, their treatments, and new medicines. The American grain has a confluence in the world of
art, but while we can point with pride at a Gilbert Stuart and
his famous portrait of George Washington, no one knows of
Joshua Johnson, the most successful black painter of the late
eighteenth century. And there is no way in the world Eli Whitney could have perfected his cotton gin without expropriating
the crude developments of slaves who worked at the point of
production. Much has been written, too, about the American
Colonization Society, whose first president was Bushrod Washington, George's brother, but what about Paul Cuffe, of African and Native American blood, who, as early as 1811, was
negotiating with the British African Institute for permission
to trade with Sierra Leone, and a few years later, at his own
expense, took thirty-eight blacks back to Africa? Indeed, there
have been extensive encomiums to Lewis and Clark and their
daring trek across the western frontier from 1803 to 1806,
but what of the slave York, whose linguistic skills and natural
diplomacy facilitated his master's odyssey through western
badlands and wilderness?

YORK AND BLACK HAWK

YORK HAD ALREADY become fairly fluent in French and some Indian words—and much more than "kemo sabe"—before Lewis and Clark mapped their trip to the West. By the time the expedition embarked, he was able to help Sacagewea, the Shoshone woman, in translations. As an interpreter, he was no less skilled than "Negro Abraham," who was the translator for the Seminole nation during its bloody confrontations with the U.S. Army under Andrew Jackson in the 1830s. York and Sacagawea were instrumental in convincing the Native Americans they encountered that the expedition was a peaceful one.

This merger of disparate strands, the interlacing of three cords—the African, the European, the Native American—was immediately necessary as yet another war loomed on the horizon. Young America was in trouble once more, and blacks rolled up what sleeves they had and rushed to the call. There was still some residue to sweep up from the last encounter with the British, and perhaps after this one, the cockeyed black optimists thought, we can really sit down to the table of brotherhood. It was a futile notion, and it would not be the last time black America was willing to sacrifice a few lives for a piece of the liberty pie.

The War of 1812, which in effect was a continuation of the Revolutionary War and an attempt by the British to blockade the American shipping enterprise, was almost a year old when the Battle of Lake Erie occurred. For the Americans it was a significant victory, and there was no lack of black heroism. According to some estimates, nearly a tenth of the sailors who served on the Great Lakes during the war were black. At first Captain Oliver Hazard Perry, though he accepted them, was not happy when he was assigned a contingent of black sailors; the Battle of Lake Erie would change his mind about the blacks' courage under fire. "They were absolutely insensible to danger," Perry said, saluting the blacks' gallantry. With no pun intended, Commander Nathaniel Shaler of the privateer *Governor Thompkins* lauded his black crew members by stating that "while America has such tars, she has little to fear from the Tyrants of the ocean."

However, it was at the Battle of New Orleans where black volunteers were to truly shine. The war was officially over, the Treaty of Ghent had been signed, when things erupted in New Orleans. British regulars massed and mounted a sustained drive to take New Orleans when they were met by two regiments of black volunteers led by Majors Vincent Populus and Joseph Savory. The regiments held their ground, checking the advance and routing the invaders. When the dust had settled, Andrew Jackson congratulated the black units for their bravery, noting that "the two corps of colored volunteers have not disappointed the hopes that were formed of their courage and perseverance in the performance of their duty." Major Savory was singled out for his valor and exemplary behavior in the face of danger. All the colorful ceremonies ringing with praise were fine, but the one thing the volunteers hoped for was not to be: "Uncle Sam" (which during the war had come to personify the federal government) failed to recognize the contribution they made at New Orleans, and only the white volunteers were allowed to join the army's ranks.

Having soundly spanked an aggressive and coercive parent, America was now in position to resume its plans of Manifest Destiny; the dreaded sibling rivalry was still a generation away. A decade or so earlier the gateway to the West had been appreciably enhanced when Toussaint L'Ouverture and his forces nullified Napoleon's great dream of establishing a beachhead in the Western hemisphere. No longer able to count on Haiti and its laborers as an anchor to his North American scheme, Napoleon was ready to cede the Louisiana Territory as much of it had been ceded to him by the Spanish. A good portion of the land transacted belonged to the Pawnees, but these original owners had no say in the matter. The Louisiana Purchase was completed in 1803 at an agreed-on price of $15 million. At a rate of approximately fifteen cents a acre, the United States had acquired most of the land between the Mississippi River and the Rocky Mountains. Old Peter Menuit would have turned green with envy. The Pawnees looked to the land beyond the Great River.

The purchase, however, presented a paradox. In one sense, as an extension of the Haitian Revolution, it helped to stem the importation of slaves. On the other hand, it opened a vast territory for the further spread of slavery. The cotton and sugar planters watched the entire development with avarice, awaiting an opportunity to leap into the mad scramble for land and possibility.

They did not have to wait long. In fact, the starting gun had sounded some years before as Red Cloud and his warriors were powerless to stop the advance of the settlers, which began with a few drops, and soon became a torrent. Resistance was a common, if mostly futile, resolve held by the indigenous people. Sac Indian Chief Black Hawk and his allies are symbolic of the early stance made to block the inevitable onslaught of white cavalry and settlers to occupy their land. A treaty signed by several Sac and Fox leaders under dubious circumstances in St. Louis in 1804 was the source of immediate concern for Black Hawk. Although the treaty provided for the sale of their lands, one proviso, writes Herman Viola in *After Columbus,* "allowed the tribe to continue using it until the federal government needed it, certainly a confusing arrangement at best. A quarter of a century later, the government called upon the tribe to honor its commitment."[11]

Black Hawk refused to comply. And in his autobiography he addressed the situation: "What do we know of the manners, the laws, and customs of the white people? They might buy our bodies for dissection, and we would touch the goose quill to confirm it and not know what we are doing. This," he admitted, "was the case with me and my people in touching the goose quill the first time."

In 1831, as the massive forced removal of natives—the Trail of Tears—from the South to the West was launched, Black Hawk and his followers returned to their village on the Rock

River in Illinois for the spring planting season. White settlers occupied the land and claimed ownership. Scared settlers confronted angry Indians, and the outcome was fairly predictable. It was a lopsided encounter. Seventy whites perished in the skirmish, and nearly all of the five hundred natives were decimated.

Black Hawk survived the battle and would later be lionized as the so-called noble savage, with artists and writers vying to paint his portrait and to tell his story. Meanwhile, the Sac and Fox were caught in a deadly pincer between the settlers and their traditional enemies, the Sioux. "The whites ought not to have permitted such conduct," Black Hawk remonstrated, "and none but cowards would ever have been guilty of such cruelty, which has always been practiced on our nation by the Sioux."

Broken promises, broken spirits, and broken bodies occurred with unerring consistency for the natives. Between 1789 and 1825, Native Americans signed thirty treaties with the United States, surrendering lands or agreeing to new boundaries. They had practically given away the company store when they realized what was happening. When they were not duped, they were the victims of treaty violations and general usurpation of their rights and dignity. The victims of guile and deceit, they learned in due time who the real "Indian givers" were.

SOUNDBITE

"The Cherokee nation is our country; there we were born and reared; there are our homes made by the sweat of our brows; there are our wives and children, whom we love as dearly as though we were born with red, instead of black skins."

—A GROUP OF BLACK CHEROKEES, 1879

TAKE A RIDE ON THE
UNDERGROUND RAILROAD
—

WHETHER BLACK OR red, the 1830s were not a good time for people of color, but what year had been since the arrival of the whites? By now the institution of slavery was firmly entrenched, domesticated, and cotton, among the four leading staples produced by slave labor, was on its way to becoming "king." It's rather ironic that some 160 years later a black man will be singing a commercial about cotton being "the fabric of our lives." There were well over three million slaves in the country, with the bulk of them tied to owners who possessed fewer than twenty slaves. The notion that most slaves lived on sprawling Tara-like plantations, popularized by films and novels such as *Gone With The Wind*, was as far from the truth as *Birth of a Nation* was for the previous generation.

Although there were slave statutes in all the states, enforcement of the codes would vary, depending on one's master and mistress, as well as the temperament of their drivers and overseers. It was universally understood, though, that slaves had no rights in the eyes of white folks; by the 1850s with the passing of the Fugitive Slave Act and the imposition of the Dred Scott decision (blacks have no rights that whites are bound to respect), the linchpin of slavocracy was secured. Generally, slaves were chattel, a piece of property listed on an inventory right next to the mule and the plow. An example of this is seen on a property list of Thomas Jefferson's in 1815 that he offered for tax purposes. He listed the big items first:

> 5,640 acres of land
> 90 slaves of or above the age of 12 years
> 12 do [ditto] of 9 and under 12 years
> 73 head of cattle
> 27 horses, mares, mules and colts[12]

As property, then, slaves could not very well possess any property; to be sure, to have in your possession a weapon, particularly a gun and ammunition, was tantamount to insurrection. Slaves could not leave the plantation without permission, it was unlawful in most states to assemble in groups of more than three after certain hours of the day, and there were strict prohibitions against teaching slaves to read or to write.

These draconian features were rigidly enforced by a court system in which slaves could not bring a suit against a white man, and bolstered by "paddyrollers" or patrollers whose job it was to make sure slaves did not stray too far from their work stations and to intimidate the more foolhardy and recalcitrant from running away. For a slave to strike a white man was to invite the full state militia into the region. For such a rash action the offender could expect one hundred lashes on the bare back, Josiah Henson recalled, "and to have the right ear nailed to the whipping post, and then severed from the body."

It was a system that spared neither man, woman, nor child, said Harriet Jacobs, an escaped slave whose pen name was Linda Brent. "I would ten thousand times rather that my children should be the half-starved paupers of Ireland than to be the most pampered among the slaves of America," she wrote in her highly acclaimed slave narrative.[13] And it is from the numerous narratives, these primary sources or primal screams, that some idea of the day-to-day existence on the plantation is discerned. Unfortunately, there is a scarcity of narratives from the "deep South" and from the smaller farm units where the majority of the slaves were confined. But the narratives of Frederick Douglass, Harriet Tubman, Sojourner Truth, Charles Ball, Henry Bibb, and countless others leave very little to the imagination. They are stark reminders of man's inhumanity to man, bloody records of defilement and abuse, raw accounts of a heroic people bent by oppression and degradation but unwilling to release their claim to the human family, and they had allies who were no less determined to see them walk out of the shadow of death, or be smuggled out, as accomplished by Henry "Box" Brown.

Brown, of Richmond, Virginia, had prayed regularly to God for some relief from slavery. At last, one day God told him to go get a box, to get in it, and mail himself to freedom.

Brown was obedient, and with the help of a friend, was placed in a box addressed to Philadelphia. After a series of mishaps in which the box fell from a wagon and was repeatedly stood wrong side up, Brown reached his destination; it was a most harrowing trip. When the box finally arrived at the correspondent's house, several folks surrounded it but were hesitant to open it. Finally someone rapped upon it, and with a trembling voice asked, "Is all right within?" Brown said he was all right. He then described that next epiphanous moment. "The joy of these friends was excessive, and like the ancient Jews, who repaired to the rebuilding of Jerusalem, each one seized hold of some tool, and commenced opening my grave," Brown said in a narrative published in 1849. "At length the cover was removed, and I arose, and shook myself from the lethargy into which I had fallen; but exhausted nature proved too much for my frame, and I swooned away." When he recovered, Brown, as he had promised to do if his escape was successful, began to sing: "I waited patiently for the Lord, and He heard my prayer."[14]

At the end of his torturous twenty-six-hour journey, Brown was relieved to learn that one of the men prying open his "coffin" was William Still. There may have been more daring and tireless abolitionists then Still, but few matched his fervor and determination to compile records of the fabled Underground Railroad. No, there were no tracks, ties, engines, or boxcars on this line of escape from bondage; its paths or routes, as one bounty hunter noted, were all but invisible, except to the many wary conductors and agents who knew exactly when and from where the next shipment of "passengers" would arrive. It was "a secret avenue to freedom taken by an increasingly large number of daring runaways from the beginning of the nineteenth century through the frenzied rush in the decades between the Fugitive Slave Act and the Civil War," Charles Blockson writes in his collection of first-person narratives on the Railroad.

You would stand a better chance sneaking the dawn past a

rooster than locating the actual points of departure for the Railroad. They were nowhere and everywhere, and anywhere a slave decided he or she had had enough and was ready to risk it all for a slice of freedom. It is also difficult to say when and who started this method of escape. A few historians have assigned the initial efforts to the Quakers, but recent research shows that while the Quakers were critically involved in the enterprise, other religious groups such as the Methodists, Jews, and Roman Catholics were more than passive observers.

But if there is a "chief engineer" of this legendary Railroad, it was the indomitable Harriet Tubman. Having escaped from slavery herself in 1846, Tubman returned to the land of bondage nineteen times, shepherding more than three hundred slaves to freedom. For these brave exploits she was called the "Moses" of her people. Her dedication helps to shed light on the hundreds of blacks who worked on the Railroad, providing direction, temporary stops in "safe houses," money and provisions, or merely inspiration to those weary travelers fleeing down the glory road for the "promise land."

Many of the loyal employees of the Railroad were white, and John Fairfield is among the most notable of those who served without pay or reservation. Like Tubman, Fairfield was a "hands-on" deliverer, not just someone at a safe house or terminal, but one who risked his neck. "He posed as a slaveholder, a Negro trader, or a peddler of eggs and poultry," John Hope Franklin observed, in states throughout the South, including the hellholes of Mississippi and Alabama. "His greatest triumph," Franklin continued, "was in conveying twenty-eight slaves to freedom by organizing them into a funeral procession." His imagination, apparently, had no limitations when it came to liberation.[15]

Railroad men working at terminal points, such as David Ruggles in New York City, William Lambert in Detroit, Henry Highland Garnet in Troy, New York, Lewis Hayden in Boston, and Robert Purvis in Philadelphia, were also outstanding abolitionists. Far too many books on the history of the antislavery movement fail to include the role blacks played in their own quest for freedom. And the names of Sarah and Charles

Lenox Remond, Charlotte Forten, Samuel Ringgold Ward, Sojourner Truth, Francis Grimke, and William Nell would top a long roster of black abolitionists. Certainly admiration must be extended for the devotion of Levi Coffin, William Lloyd Garrison, Wendell Phillips, the great orator, Lucretia Coffin Mott, the Tappan brothers, Harriet Beecher Stowe, Prudence Crandall, Parker Pillsbury, and Thaddeus Stevens, whom we will meet again, but their commitment only helped to embolden those already drawn to the fire.

I'LL STAY WITH THE OLD MAN

RADICAL ABOLITIONIST JOHN Brown was also a fiery source of audacity. And while his bold action at Harper's Ferry in 1859 has been rightfully heralded as an example of the ultimate sacrifice in the fight to emancipate the slaves (and in the tradition of Nat Turner, who in 1831 led a bloody revolt killing sixty whites), the white insurrectionist and martyr was not alone in this memorable bid. Five blacks figured conspicuously in the raid, which was to take control of the federal arsenal and distribute the arms to slaves in the region as part of a massive uprising. Among the ten killed were Lewis Sheridan Leary, a free black from North Carolina, and Dangerfield Newby, a former slave from Virginia, both at that time residing in Oberlin, Ohio. Newby, the first to fall, had his ears cut off as souvenirs. He had hoped by joining Brown to liberate his wife and children from a Virginia plantation. Two of the seven hanged with Brown were Leary's nephew, John Anthony Copeland, a free man from Raleigh but recently transplanted to Oberlin, and Shields Green, a fugitive from Charleston, South Carolina, allegedly a protégé of Frederick Douglass. Green, when given a choice about his fate, told his captors, "I'll stay with the old man." Osborne Perry Anderson, a printer from Fallowfield, Pennsylvania, was among the five who escaped. He would serve with distinction in the Civil War and write an account of the venture entitled *A Voice from Harpers Ferry*. Mary Ann Shadd, a staunch abolitionist and one of the most notable black women of her day, edited the book.

Copeland went bravely to his death without uttering a plea in his own behalf, but not before writing these words to his family in Oberlin: "I am not terrified by the gallows, which I see staring me in the face, and upon which I am soon to stand and suffer death for doing what George Washington was made a hero for doing . . . Could I die in a manner and for a cause which would induce true and honest men more to honor me, and the angels more ready to receive me to their happy home of everlasting joy above?"[16]

Brown, too, went to the gallows with nary a word, although he passed a note to a guard that read "I am quite certain that the crimes of this guilty land will never be purged away but with blood." Little did he know his actions would be the impetus for the Civil War that would fulfill his prophecy.

IT'S A WHITE THANG
—

WHEN THE PURGATIVE blood came, it came profusely as America's war with itself opened a wound that in many ways we are still trying to heal. And some of that blood was black. More than 186,000 African-Americans served in the Union army, and some 29,000 served in various capacities in the Union navy. Nearly 40,000 black soldiers and sailors lost their lives in the war, an exceedingly high mortality rate compared to white casualties, which can be attributed to the reckless way black troops were rushed into battles without decent matériel and proper training, and the slowness with which their wounds were treated.

As in the previous wars, the U.S. government was at first reluctant to conscript blacks into this "irrepressible conflict," which was the culmination of several eddies of sectional strife. This was a war between gentlemen, it was stressed, and had nothing to do with "Negroes." Or with slavery, for that matter, since the official word from newly elected President Lincoln insisted that the conflict was waged to hold a fractious Union together. Lincoln would maintain this line for several months as the war progressed, but the hour was drawing nigh when something had to be done to settle the issue of "contrabands," the slaves set adrift by the war and seeking protection in Union camps.

An additional problem was emerging militarily: The Union forces were up against the wall. They had not won a major battle, and the defeat at Bull Run sent a message that even the lowliest slave understood—the vast reserves of black power could make a difference. On the question of using black troops, Harriet Tubman put an optimistic spin on Lincoln's quandary: "God won't let Massa Linkum beat de South till he do de right ting. Massa Linkum he great man, and Ise a poor nigger; but dis nigger can tell Massa Linkum how to save de money and de young men. He do it by setting de niggers free. S'pose dar was awfu' big snake down dar, on de floor. He bite you. Folks all skeered, cause you die. You send for doctor to cut de bite; but he bite you agin. De doctor cut out dat bite; but while he dwine it, de snake he spring up and bite you agin, and he keep dwine, till you kill him. Dat's what Massa Linkum orter know."

In the spring of 1862 "Massa Linkum," as if heeding Tubman's advice, sent a message to Congress recommending passage of a joint resolution offering federal compensation to any state "which may adopt gradual abolishment of slavery." It was a step in the right direction, black newspaper editorials announced, but only a step. "He has steadily refused to proclaim, as he had the constitutional and moral right to proclaim, complete emancipation to all the slaves of rebels who should make their way into the lines of our army," cried Frederick Douglass, assailing Lincoln in a Fourth of July speech at Himrod's Corners, New York. "He has repeatedly interfered with and arrested the antislavery policy of the Administration. To my mind that policy is simply and solely to reconstruct the union on the old corrupting basis of compromise, by which slavery shall retain all the power it ever had, with the full assurance of gaining more, according of its future necessities."

Douglass seemed to reserve his most memorable rhetoric for the Fourth of July. Time and again the ex-slave from Tucahoe County, Maryland, who had no match as a orator and statesman, used these patriotic occasions to chide and challenge America to live up to its vaunted claim of democracy and freedom for all. With the same vigor and conviction he had demonstrated as a youth when he defeated the notorious slave breaker, Covey, Douglass let the president know he was not about to stand idly by while a mockery was made of his brethren still locked in bondage.

Part of Lincoln's dilemma in issuing full emancipation, which would create the possibility of blacks joining the fray, was connected to the war itself. To issue such a decree before the Union forces scored a decisive victory would appear to be a sign of desperation, Lincoln concluded. On September 17, 1862, the Union army finally won a victory at the Battle of Antietam. Five days later Lincoln issued a preliminary Emancipation Proclamation, which declared that on January 1, 1863, all slaves in "states of rebellion" were forever free. Of course, in these states Lincoln was powerless to enforce the decree. But in the climate of celebration that rippled from one black community to another, the conditional clause in small print was ignored. "De Lord has heard de groans of de people," an ex-slave rejoiced, "and has come down to deliver."

BETCHA DIDN'T KNOW

During the Civil War, Charlotte Forten, from Salem, Massachusetts, spent eighteen months in South Carolina teaching freed slaves.

HANG THE NIGGERS!
—

THERE WAS NO joy in the Irish section of New York City, though. Nor was the news of the Proclamation a time for cheer among white workers in parts of Illinois, Pennsylvania, Indiana, and Ohio. Job security was the first concern of the white workers, who believed the presence of blacks would drive down wages, or worse, replace them in the various plants. An incident at Lorillard and Watson's tobacco factory in Brooklyn, which employed twenty-five blacks, most of them women and children, typified the growing animosity between the races. A mob of Irish workers forced their way into a factory and set it afire, hoping to burn down the building where the blacks worked. A similar attack occurred in Detroit in March 1863, when a mob of white men marched into the black section of the city, destroyed thirty-two houses, killed several blacks, and left more than two hundred people homeless.

Faced with an end to the two-year enlistments and the realization that it might not fill the ranks with volunteers anymore, the Union ordered a military draft. In the draft notice there was a provision that allowed the draftee to send a substitute or to pay $300 to avoid that round of the draft. These options were pointless to the poor or the working class, and in New York City all of the Irish fell into this category. Therefore the draft exacerbated the festering hatred between blacks and Irish, particularly at the work site, where blacks were often replacing the drafted Irishmen.

On July 13, 1863, all of the simmering discord reached a boiling point and for four days New York City experienced the worst race riot in the nation's history. One hundred thirty years later, New Yorkers would clamor about the disturbance in Crown Heights, Brooklyn, but that was a family reunion compared to this race riot. The hostile differences between brothers from the North and South had now ignited the differences between blacks and whites. At the center of this disturbance was a brutal scene in which a white mob, mostly Irish, hung a black man from a lamppost and cheered for Jefferson Davis, the president of the Confederacy. After the police cut the body down, a mob dragged it by the genitals through the streets of New York. In another act of destruction on the east side of New York, not too far from the present site of the Empire State Building, the Colored Orphan Asylum was burned to the ground.

By the time the army gained control of the city, some 150 people were dead, 119 identifiable. There was an ironic twist to this bitter contention between blacks and the Irish. While the newspapers had fanned the flames about the Emancipation Proclamation "releasing hordes" of blacks to replace Irish workers, in reality blacks had occupied most of the servant and waiter positions in New York, and when the potato famine swept across Ireland, the Irish immigrants arrived and took those jobs away from blacks. This paradoxical scenario would be played out in a larger context at the close of the war in the South when the white southerners, desperate for any kind of work, would take over the jobs that belonged traditionally to black skilled and semiskilled workers.

BLOOD, GRAY, AND BLACKS

As EVER, BLACKS were struggling on two fronts. Their resolve in the northern cities was matched by their valor on the gory battlefields. A chance to serve was all blacks were asking, and that opportunity came in deadly succession from New Orleans to Mississippi to Virginia to South Carolina. What remaining doubt there was about the ability of blacks as soldiers was dispelled in battles at Fort Wagner and Port Hudson. William Wells Brown, whose book *Clotel: The President's Daughter* was the first novel published by an African-American (though it was actually printed in England), exercises some of that literary ability in his description of the attack by two black regiments on Port Hudson, a Confederate stronghold on the lower Mississippi.

On the 26th of May, 1863, the wing of the army under Major-Gen. Banks was brought before the rifle pits and heavy guns of Port Hudson. Night fell—the lovely southern night—with its silvery moonshine on the gleaming waters of the Mississippi, that passed directly by the entrenched town. The glistening stars appeared suspended in the upper air as globes of liquid light, while the fresh soft breeze was bearing such sweet scents from the odoriferous trees and plants . . . The line officers of this regiment were all colored, taken from amongst the most wealthy and influential of the free colored people of New Orleans. It was said that not one of them was worth less than twenty-five thousand dollars . . . One of the most efficient officers was Captain Andre Callioux, a man whose identity with his race could not be mistaken; for he prided himself on being the blackest man in the Crescent City . . . At last the welcome word was given, and our men started. The enemy opened a blistering fire of shell, canister, grape, and musketry . . . At every pace, the column was thinned by the falling dead and wounded . . . The last charge was made about one o'clock. At this juncture, Captain Callioux was seen with his left arm dangling by his side—for a ball had broken it above the elbow—while his right hand held his unsheathed sword gleaming in the rays of the sun; and his hoarse, faint voice was heard cheering on his men. A moment more, and the brave and generous Callioux was struck by a shell, and fell far in advance of his company.[17]

Relentless charge after relentless charge was to no avail and the Confederates held their ground.

At Fort Wagner—and who can forget the scene in the movie *Glory* in which Colonel Robert Gould Shaw's lifeless body lies entangled with his black troops?—the courageous black regiments would also be repelled, but in defeat these black troops earned an immortality that might not have been theirs had they succeeded. To these setbacks, thankfully, a number of victories can be appended. There were individual feats of heroism such as the spying successes of Harriet Tubman that supplied the Union with logistical information on troop deployment and possible targets of attack; Robert Smalls's commandeering of a Confederate transport steamer by sailing it past the Confederate fortification into the hands of a Union fleet that lay outside the harbor; and Private James Gardner's actions in which he ran ahead of his brigade and shot a Confederate officer leading his troops.

And so it had been throughout the nation's history. At the Revolution blacks had been on hand as a sort of midwife, the servants providing comfort and succor, and they were there when the "shot was heard 'round the world," never hesitating, but demanding to fight for and with the patriots. In 1812 came another call to arms, and blacks rushed to battle. And when the young nation was unraveling, a house divided into two wings, blacks were once again equal to the challenge, throwing caution to the wind as they made a mockery of Johnny Reb's joke about "Sambo's right to die." The tangled roots of America were now thoroughly soaked and toughened by black and white blood. But yet another test of the deepening merger came into view as the smoke cleared from those final volleys. It was time again to see if "the better angels" of white America's nature would prevail and embrace their sable sisters and brothers.

FORTY ACRES AND A MULE
—

BEFORE "FORTY ACRES and a mule" was appropriated by Spike Lee, it was a phrase closer to Robert E. Lee, at least chronologically speaking. Moreover, as Spike and others mistakenly suggest, it had nothing to do with Abe Lincoln. Right after the Civil War there was a concerted effort by some fifty relief agencies and the federal government to both repair the war-torn South and to stabilize the lives of the recently emancipated slaves. This stabilization plan for blacks, whose needs would be administered by the Freedmen's Bureau, could not be done without allocating them plots of land to tend, argued two radical Republicans, Senator Charles Sumner of Massachusetts and Representative Thaddeus Stevens of Pennsylvania. In this regard they proposed that each ex-slave be given forty acres of land and a mule. General William Tecumseh Sherman had proposed a similar alternative during his "scorched earth" campaign to Atlanta when his regiments were overtaken by slaves from the plantations he had demolished.

Stevens and Sumner's plan to parcel out land was shot down along with their other radical call to abrogate Andrew Johnson's government and replace it with one based on equality before the law and male suffrage. "Forty acres and a mule," W. E. B. Du Bois contended, was a righteous aim, but it was destined for bitter disappointment. "If by 1874 the Georgia Negro alone owned three hundred and fifty thousand acres of land," Du Bois wrote, "it was by the grace of his thrift rather than by bounty of the government."[18] The land question, insofar as it applied to black tenants in the South following the Civil War, was never answered. This part of the Reconstruction plan—as was most of it save for the educational endeavors—was a miserable failure.

UNPOPULAR POPULISM
—

BLACK FARMERS NEVER got those forty acres and a mule, nor did black politicians dominate the Congress or state legislatures in the South, Griffith's *Birth of a Nation* notwithstanding. In this film made in 1915, Griffith celebrated the restoration of white rule over African-Americans in the Reconstruction era. The picture he painted of blacks dominating state governments was vastly overdrawn. Rather than getting to the heart of the race problem in the South following the Civil War, the movie unmasked Griffith, disclosing his racism and his allegiance to white supremacy. The film also helped revive and embolden the moribund Ku Klux Klan. Even when blacks constituted a majority of the population, as they did in South Carolina, they never controlled any state's political machinery. Only twenty-two blacks served in Congress from 1868 to 1901; black politicians held office in southern states for a few years, and for the most part, their tenure in Congress was brief and largely ineffective.

For all the relative achievements of Reconstruction in the political arena, the end of Reconstruction found very little reconstructed, certainly not the spirit and confidence of black southerners. The real frustration of Reconstruction congealed with the sellout of 1877. When a black militia company was massacred at Hamburg, South Carolina, in July 1876, it marked the end of Republican rule in the state and the return to power of Wade Hampton and his allies the "red shirts." The militia had been arrested for interfering with traffic during a parade. Their trial was postponed and they refused to apologize for their actions. Heavier arms and munitions were then summoned by whites, and gunfire broke out between the two groups. Outnumbered and facing superior firepower, the blacks were vanquished. The subsequent withdrawal of federal troops by President Rutherford B. Hayes merely ratified a result that had already transpired.

President Hayes's act was part of a back-room deal completed at a hotel in Washington, D.C., owned by James Wormley, a wealthy black businessman. Hayes, to secure a disputed election, promised to remove the 5,000 federal troops stationed in the South to protect the former slaves. There was something farcical about the deployment of troops to begin with, believing 5,000 of them could safeguard the rights of blacks throughout the South. It would be equivalent to twenty cops patrolling New York City.

In short, the power of southern landowners soon joined with certain northern captains of industry to speed along the process to disenfranchise blacks, denying them access to free land and capital, thereby paving the way to the reinstitution of black codes and the heinous caste system that would stand for the next century or so as a barrier stifling black economic, social, and political progress. Within a tumultuous decade, the expectations of blacks, which had soared so optimistically high at the close of the Civil War, now plummeted to a new low. For most of the emergent black sharecroppers, there was no mule, no land, and huge debt at the end of the year.

Still, a good number of them held on, determined to make a go of it. One source of encouragement came from the ideas promoted by radical agrarian organizations. Unable to join the all-white Southern Farmers' Alliance, black farmers formed the Colored Farmers' National Alliance and Cooperative Union in 1886. Within five years it boasted more than a million members in twelve state organizations. An attempt to merge the two alliances failed after black farmers called for a general strike of black cotton pickers. White farmers opposed the action, arguing that blacks were trying to improve their conditions at the expense of whites.

The populist impulse would flounder in a similar manner, and for similar reasons, despite a brief period in North Carolina when black power was ascendant. Populism of today should not be confused with the populism of the 1890s, which referred essentially to a third-party movement. It was the egalitarian aspects of the movement that most enticed blacks. An outspoken leader of this reform movement was Tom Watson of Georgia, who initially supported the enfranchisement of blacks but later reversed his position when it seemed he would alienate his Democratic constituents. Watson's reversal was a harbinger and soon disenfranchisement was sweeping across the South like a prairie fire.

Populism was never really that popular with blacks. That it had any appeal at all stemmed mainly from the possibility of an alliance that was torpedoed by that old devil called racism. There remained a few alternatives to the backlash of the defeated white southerners. Blacks could stay in the South and fight the Klan and other night riders; they could head North (not that labor unions there invited black workers with open arms); they could follow other "exodusters" to the West; or they could get out of the country altogether.

A large segment of the black population in the South—broke, busted, and disgusted, and still fuming over the land that never was—were personally insulted when the government reneged on what they believed to be a solid promise. To them this was just another affront in a long history of neglect and disrespect, so the idea of leaving the country was again a compelling topic of discussion. For several years the "back to Africa" motif, popularized by emigrationists, was relegated to the back burner while black America listened to the advice of Frederick Douglass, who as early as 1840 was the most influential black leader in the nation. All during the pre–Civil War years Douglass argued against those unwilling to give America another chance, seeking relief in some Never-Never land.

SOUNDBITE

"Any man that says I am [for colonization or going back to Africa] behind my back is an assassin and a coward; any man that says it to my face is a liar, and I stamp the infamous charge upon his forehead!"

—HENRY HIGHLAND GARNET,
MINISTER AND ABOLITIONIST[19]

BACK TO AFRICA
—

"ALL THIS NATIVE land talk is nonsense," Douglass said. "The native land of the American Negro is America. His bones, his muscles, his sinews, are all American. His ancestors for two hundred and seventy years have lived, and labored, and died on American soil, and millions of his posterity have inherited Caucasian blood."

One of his chief adversaries was a former colleague, Martin

Delany. Ultimately Delany would temporarily set aside his emigrationist zeal and become a ranking officer in the Union army during the Civil War, a position achieved by not more than one hundred blacks (excluding chaplains). But by the early 1870s he, too, had turned his back on Reconstruction, which, in his opinion, had ruined race relations and divided blacks among themselves. The "Father of Black Nationalism" was ready to renew his membership card in the "back to Africa" club. A restless man, Delany even had a short flirtation with the white Democrats of Charleston, but as they more and more consolidated their position at black expense, the deception became clear. Delany's last stab at colonization or emigrationist ideas occurred in 1877, when the West African nation Liberia was the hot topic.

Delany accepted a position with the Liberian Exodus Joint-Stock Steamship Company, joining their board of directors. His chief duty was to negotiate with the Liberian government for land grants for African-American settlers. In a fiasco reminiscent of Chief Sam, who bilked hundreds of people out of thousands of dollars, the company hastily bought a ship in order to meet its commitment to take two hundred immigrants back to Africa. The trip was grueling and plagued with delays, deaths, and added expenses. Delany was the chairman of the financial committee; it was his task to straighten out the mess and get the steamship company back on an even keel. Eventually, unable to raise the money needed to pay the debts, the company was forced to sell the ship. It was Delany's last hurrah.

Within a couple of years Bishop Henry McNeal Turner, no stranger to emigrationism, would pick up where Delany left off. Dismayed by the Supreme Court ruling of 1883 that declared the 1875 Civil Rights Act unconstitutional, Turner called the Constitution "a dirty rag, a cheat, a libel, and ought to be spit upon by every Negro in the land." As a nationalist, Turner had worked vigorously for black identity and total emancipation; he had also made four trips to Africa, and given the fervor of his pronouncements, another trip appeared imminent.

Turner was a forceful orator and he authored a passel of biting articles. A good example of his rage and conviction appeared in an editorial he wrote for the *Voice of Missions.*

Entitled "Negro, Get Guns," the editorial was a response to the intensifying attacks of whites against defenseless blacks: "Let every Negro in this country who has a spark of manhood in him supply his house with one, two, or three guns . . . and when your domicile is invaded by the bloody lynchers or any mob . . . turn loose your missiles of death and blow the fiendish wretches into a thousand giblets . . ."[20]

Through the pages of his publication the *Voice of the People,* Turner kept the flame of emigrationism burning, but by the turn of the century the flame was a mere flicker. Turner's last breaths were reserved to castigate America and its symbols: "I used to love what I thought was the grand old flag, and sing with ecstasy about the Stars and Stripes, but to the Negro in this country the American flag is a dirty and contemptible rag. Not a star in it can the colored man claim, for it is no longer the symbol of our manhood rights and liberty . . . Without multiplying words, I wish to say that hell is an improvement on the United States where the Negro is concerned."[21]

Turner died April 8, 1915, seven months before Booker T. Washington succumbed to a stroke, and a year before Marcus Garvey arrived in the United States to refresh and to resurrect the "back to Africa" theme. One of Turner's final displays of outrage occurred when the United States declared war against Spain. His support for people of color caused as much reaction as his earlier assertion that "God is a Negro." His good wishes were extended to the Cubans and the Filipinos, who he hoped would wipe the invaders "from the face of the earth."

A ROUGH TIME WITH
THE ROUGH RIDERS
—

HAD COLONEL TEDDY Roosevelt heard this comment, he might have violated his axiom to "speak softly and carry a big stick," which he popularized in 1901 upon entering the White House. On the other hand, the general response from the black community was one of "here we go again," though many were very upset about the sinking of the battleship *Maine* in which 266 persons perished, including 22 blacks. The *Maine* had been sent to Havana to look after American interests imperiled by the struggle between Cuban rebels and their Spanish rulers. What caused the explosion on the *Maine* remains a mystery, sealed up in Davy Jones's locker, though recent studies seem to indicate there was an accidental explosion on board, and not a Spanish mine planted beneath the keel.

E. E. Cooper, editor of the Washington *Colored American*, championed the entry of blacks into the war, commenting that to join in this common cause would contribute to "an era of good feeling the country over and cement the races into a more compact brotherhood through perfect unity of purpose and patriotic affinity."[22] Cooper's conclusions must have sounded familiar to most blacks, but were met with revulsion by the small, feisty coterie of black anti-imperialists. In any event, black regular army units, brought up to wartime strength by hurriedly recruiting volunteers who could neither read nor write, were rushed to deployment points.

Two of the four black regiments called up for the war were the 9th and 10th Cavalry, with veterans who only months before were fighting on the plains, "pacifying" the Sioux, Lakotas, and other Native Americans. Some of them had been called "buffalo soldiers" by the natives because their hair resembled the kinky hide of the buffalo. In song and dance the exploits of the buffalo soldiers are often viewed with pride by those who fail to see how black troops were used in the extermination of the indigenous people. The task before them in Cuba was no less ignoble and dishonorable.

It made sense that the 9th and 10th Cavalry were deployed, along with the 1st Volunteer Cavalry, the famed "Rough Riders," organized by Teddy Roosevelt and commanded by Colonel Leonard Wood, as part of one brigade under "Fighting Joe" Wheeler. Rather odd, though, the black cavalry was without horses. Space on the transport ships being limited, they had to leave their steeds in Florida. They had no other choice but to fight on foot, like their black comrades in the 24th and 25th Infantry.

Eager for the fight, black troops wasted no time in distinguishing themselves. They were with the 1st Cavalry when it swept over San Juan Hill. What is often neglected in the story of this battle is that Roosevelt and his Rough Riders might have been demolished had it not been for the arrival of "Black Jack" Pershing and his 10th Cavalry. Much of what happened at San Juan Hill, Kettle Hill, and Las Guasimas remains muddled. Was Roosevelt forced to draw his pistol to get black troops to fight? What were his true feelings about the blacks who fought alongside him? To some extent, this last question was answered when Roosevelt, at the end of the war, admitted that blacks had fought gallantly—"no better man beside me in battle than these colored troops," he stated.

Roosevelt promised to tell the full story at a later date. But when that story was finally published, Roosevelt and his Rough Riders were the heroes; the black troops were nonexistent when they were not being criticized. If the black troops accomplished anything, it was due to the leadership of their white officers, Roosevelt claimed. He wrote of black soldiers "drifting away from the battlefield" and who at pistol point were returned to the front lines. It was a disparaging report, and several black troops who were members of the cavalry units voiced their objections. Sergeant Preston or Presley Holliday of the 10th Cavalry clarified a few of the issues in the *New York Age,* May 11, 1899. He said the blacks were going to the rear because they had been ordered by an officer to bring up rations and entrenching tools, and to carry the wounded to safety. Holliday said that the officer in charge had explained this to Roosevelt at the time, and on the following day Roosevelt admitted he had misunderstood the actions of the black soldiers. That Roosevelt chose to revise the story may have been a decision based on political expediency. Seeking the presidential bid in 1900, Roosevelt was probably sensitive to how his praise of blacks would play in Dixie. He may have won supporters in the South, but his name was mud in the black community. With social Darwinism all the rage,

Roosevelt's views could be easily assigned to that school of thought.

More than fifteen regiments of black volunteers were raised for the Spanish-American War, but the war was over so fast—it lasted ten weeks—that the majority of them never got a chance to show their mettle. The black community expressed only limited resentment to participating in the liberation of Cuba; there was a strong identification with the island and its inhabitants. But sending the boys to the Philippines was another thing. President McKinley, according to some black newspapers, was trying to civilize and Christianize a people at gunpoint. Whatever the mission, black troops, especially the infantry units, served with distinction. However, had it been Booker T. Washington's call, the troops would have stayed home. "Until our nation has settled the Indian and Negro problems, I do not think we have a right to assume more social problems," Washington declared.[23]

BETCHA DIDN'T KNOW

At the outbreak of World War I, Major Charles Young (1864-1922), who had distinguished himself during military campaigns with the 10th Cavalry, was declared unfit for service. To prove that he was fit, Major Young, then fifty-two, rode five hundred miles on horseback from Wilberforce, Ohio, to Washington, D.C., in sixteen days, but the decision was not reversed.

BOOKER T. AND W. E. B.
—

AND IF ANYONE could speak with authority about social problems, it was Booker Taliaferro Washington. At the turn of the century he was the most prominent black man in America. His highly respected critic W. E. B. Du Bois, writing in his classic *The Souls of Black Folk*, summarized the leader's status: "Easily the most striking thing in the history of the American Negro since 1876 is the ascendance of Mr. Booker T. Washington."[24] Washington's "ascendance" is partly attributable to the hard-work ethic he adopted, and prescribed for others, and his shrewd manipulation of people and events. He gained national attention in 1895 at the Cotton States Exposition in Atlanta when, to a mixed audience of blacks and whites, he delivered his famous "Atlanta Compromise" speech.

In this speech Washington compressed the whole of his philosophy, most of which was distilled from his early training at Hampton Institute under the school's head, Samuel Armstrong, and the rest a patchwork of commonsense homilies an ex-slave might acquire from that other school of hard knocks. It would be remiss, though, to discount the influence of certain white philanthropists—Andrew Carnegie, Julius Rosenwald, and John D. Rockefeller. Each of them had found in Washington a worthy beneficiary, and their charitable donations were instrumental in the founding of Tuskegee Institute. Surely these individuals and events were on Washington's mind that day in Atlanta when he said that "in all things that are purely social we can be as separate as the five fingers, yet one as the hand in all things essential to mutual progress."

In his autobiography *Up From Slavery*, Washington recalled his anxiety in preparation for this historic moment:

> While I cannot recall in detail what I said, I remember that I tried to impress upon the [Exposition] committee, with all the earnestness and plainness of any language that I could command, that if Congress wanted to do something which would

58

assist in ridding the South of the race question and making friends between the two races, is should, in every proper way, encourage the material and intellectual growth of both races. I said that the Atlanta Exposition would present an opportunity for both races to show what advance they had made since freedom, and would at the same time afford encouragement to them to make still greater progress ... I spoke for fifteen or twenty minutes, and was surprised at the close of my address to receive the hearty congratulations of the Georgia committee and of the members of Congress who were present.[25]

Washington's assessment of his speech is perhaps a trifle disingenuous since by the time he wrote his autobiography, he must have seen accounts of it. Nevertheless, he had not only properly placated the movers and shakers of the South, his bit of wizardry had also beguiled the blacks in attendance. As Du Bois saw it, "The radicals received it as a complete surrender of the demand for civil and political equality; the conservatives, as a generously conceived working basis for mutual understanding."[26] Washington's gift of rhetoric, his ability to appease differing outlooks at the same time, was a special knack, and it would serve him well as he developed his powerful "Tuskegee Machine" and arbitrated the major issues of his day. The speech was timely, too, since it occurred in September, eight months after the death of the great Frederick Douglass. Washington was the new king of the hill, the emperor of black social and political thought.

But as William Edward Burghardt Du Bois and his cohorts decided, the emperor had no clothes, and they risked telling him. The first significant volley from Washington's detractors, in fact, was Du Bois's moving essay, published in 1903. If Washington had his "Atlanta Compromise" to launch him, Du Bois had his *The Souls of Black Folk*. And the book was an immediate success and a veritable bible for young black intellectuals opposed to Washington's fawning and "Uncle Tomism." Du Bois's book was much more than a critique of Washington, however. To a large extent, it was the culmination of Du Bois's variety of pursuits and interests, his grasp and analysis of black history, his emotional response to elements of black culture, particularly the "sorrow songs," and, most pertinently, his philosophy, which stressed an uncompromising demand for equal rights.

Like Washington, Du Bois was not an overnight success. The two had in common, as well, a mulatto ancestry, both were relatively young (Washington was forty-four, Du Bois ten years younger), and they were equally blessed with a strong sense of purpose. Otherwise, they were miles apart. And these differences help to explain their contrasting views on social and political issues. Washington was born a slave in West Virginia. Du Bois was born free in Great Barrington, Massachusetts. Du Bois's educational background epitomized the best in the Western world, with study at the University of Berlin and a Ph.D. from Harvard. Washington was the product of Hampton, where manual arts and industrial training were the objectives. And except for their ideological distinctions, the unique way they looked at education is probably the most graphic example of their differences.

A summary of Washington's approach to education can be gleaned from this anecdote, which appears in his autobiography: "One of the saddest things I saw during the month of travel . . . was a young man, who had attended some high school, sitting down in a one-room cabin, with grease on his clothing, filth all around him, and weeds in the yard and garden, engaging in studying French grammar."[27] It was silly to pursue the classics before you take care of some basic things, Washington seemed to suggest. And then there was the practical aspect. What good is it to know Greek and Latin, for example, if you can't take care of yourself? Seek ye first the kingdom of practicality and self-help, Washington implied, and all else will follow.

Du Bois's love for the classics is fairly obvious, and his retort to Washington's anecdote appears early in his book of essays: "And so thoroughly did he learn the speech and thought of triumphant commercialism, and the ideals of material prosperity, that the picture of a lone black boy poring over a French grammar amid weeds and dirt of neglected home soon seemed to him the acme of absurdities. One wonders what Socrates and St. Francis of Assisi would say to this."[28]

Socrates and St. Francis would probably say what Du Bois said, as he denounced Washington's narrow prism on things most dear to blacks' self-respect and dignity. He excoriated Washington for his disavowal of the struggle for political power, civil rights, and higher education. Blamed the Tuskegee administrator for the widespread "disenfranchisement of the Negro, the legal creation of a distinct status of civil inferiority for the Negro, and the steady withdrawal of aid from institutions for the higher training of the Negro."[29] Uppermost on Du Bois's mind was the speech in Atlanta, which, as he saw it, led directly to *Plessy v. Ferguson* and the legal implementation of separate-but-equal laws.

Clearly Du Bois had no patience with Washington's accommodationist strategy, which, given his circumstances, left him with few options. Washington was an empire builder, a developer of institutions, and he knew that to advocate certain political objectives would jeopardize the flow of cash from his benefactors. Only later, long after Washington was dead and gone, did we learn of his secret donations to such initiatives as the antilynching campaign. Even a so-called Uncle Tom is not entirely useless. But Washington has more than this to commend him. Tuskegee Institute continues to be among the leading black schools in the nation, and while the emphasis remains on applied learning, you can get your French grammar together there, too.

One can also leave behind a legacy of struggle, and this was Du Bois's niche. He can claim the NAACP, Pan-African thought, the perfection of sociology, and black studies as part of his contribution to the shaping of American culture. It is not a cop-out to say that both Washington and Du Bois were equally wrong and equally right about what they deemed as important from an educational and political standpoint. Washington's obsession with a manual arts curriculum, making your own bricks and what have you, was misplaced, and his ideas along this line were almost outmoded at their very inception. He had a blind spot when it came to understanding the connection between industrial education and the exigencies of the industrial revolution. His penchant for an aggressive policy of economics left him little time or interest to deal with civil rights. On this particular point almost the reverse can be said of Du Bois. Moreover, Du Bois's vision was somewhat impaired by a skein of inconsistencies and an often stultifying ambivalence. Taken together, though they never were, they were the twin towers of black power at the dawn of the twentieth century, but it is a good bet they would not agree on this.

Booker T. and W.E.B.

"It seems to me," said Booker T.,
"It shows a mighty lot of cheek
To study Chemistry and Greek
When Mister Charles needs a hand
To hoe the cotton on his land,
And when Miss Ann looks for a cook
Why stick your nose inside a book?"

"I don't agree," said W.E.B.
"If I should have the drive to seek
Knowledge of Chemistry or Greek,
I'll do it. Charles and Miss can look
Another place for hand or cook.
Some men rejoice in skill of hand,
And some in cultivating land,
But there are others who maintain,
The right to cultivate the brain."

"It seems to me," said Booker T.,
"That all you folks have missed the boat
Who shout about the right to vote,
And spend vain days and sleepless nights
In uproar over civil rights.
Just keep your mouths shut, do not grouse,
But work, and save, and buy a house."

"I don't agree," said W.E.B.
'For what can property avail
If dignity and justice fail.
Unless you help to make the laws,
They'll steal your house with trumped up clause.
A rope's as tight, a fire as hot,
No matter how much cash you've got.
Speak soft, and try your little plan
But as for me, I'll be a man."

—DUDLEY RANDALL

TO GIVE A TINKER'S DAMN

BLACK SCIENTISTS, DOCTORS, inventors, and tinkers were among those breeds who absorbed the spirit of the Du Bois and Washington ethic. To bring their ideas to fruition, they needed imagination, creativity, and practicality. There was no either/or situation with them, but a both/and. No long introduction is necessary to see how their contributions were vital to progress and modernity.

George Washington Carver (1864–1943). He was best known as the "Peanut Man" because of his research on industrial uses of the peanut. A popular saying in the black community was that Carver could do more with a peanut than a monkey could, and that was true—he developed more than three hundred products from a peanut. Born near Diamond Grove, Missouri, Carver, along with his mother, was kidnapped and sold as a slave. His owner secured his return by trading him for a horse; his mother was never seen again. Carver's list of achievements is as long as his life was eventful. He was the first black to graduate from Iowa State College—at the top of his class. By 1896, Booker T. Washington had enticed him to take a position at Tuskegee Institute, where he was soon the director of agricultural research. With the division of disease survey and mycology (a branch of botany dealing with fungi), he was a collaborator, and over the years he collected some 20,000 fungi. Carver never attempted to patent any of his developments, but his discoveries helped to improve the agrarian industry in the South—and around the world.

Elijah McCoy (1843–1929). They called him "the Real McCoy," and for good reason. If the machine age was cranking and clanking onto the historical stage, then it would need a superb lubricator. McCoy was awarded over fifty-seven patents, mostly for various kinds of steam cylinder lubricators.

The "drip cup," which eliminated the need to stop and shut down large machinery in order to apply the vital lubrication, was McCoy's basic invention in 1873. He was born in Canada. His parents had been slaves in Kentucky who fled from their master. After the Civil War McCoy came to the United States and settled near Ypsilanti, Michigan, where he worked in a machine shop. He taught himself the intricacies of moving machine parts and then spent two years perfecting a device to apply oil while machines were running. Eventually he set up his own company in Detroit and continued to find ways to keep the machine age humming.

Halle Tanner Dillon (1864–1901). Sister of the famed painter Henry Ossawa Tanner, Halle was an artist in her own right, but with the stethoscope and the application of medicine. After completing a three-year medical course at Women's Medical College in Philadelphia, Halle was invited to Tuskegee Institute by Booker T. Washington to become the resident physician. Meanwhile, she had to prepare for the state's rigorous exams. She passed the difficult exams with flying colors and became the first black woman ever admitted on examination to practice medicine in Alabama. From 1891 to 1894 Halle was the resident physician at Tuskegee Institute. During her tenure, Dr. Dillon established the Lafayette Dispensary and Nurses' Training School. In 1894 she married the Reverend John Quincy Johnson, and they eventually moved to Nashville. She bore three sons and died in childbirth in 1901.

Norbert Rillieux (1806–1894). If anyone deserves the honor of being called the pioneer black inventor, then Norbert Rillieux is the one. Born in slavery, Rillieux was recognized at an early age as a genius, and his master sent him to Paris to study. His progress was remarkable, and by the time he was twenty-three, he was an instructor at L'Ecole Centrale. While there, he published several papers on the steam engine and steam economy. Subsequently he returned to Louisiana and became the state's most celebrated engineer. His major contribution occurred in sugar manufacture: In 1846 he developed the vacuum chamber to enclose condensing coils to evaporate the liquid portion of sugarcane juice. His process was immediately hailed by sugar manufacturers and adopted all over the world. In 1854 Rillieux left Louisiana and returned to France, where for many years he was a researcher with the Champollions deciphering Egyptian hieroglyphics.

Jan Ernst Matzeliger (1852–1889). Take a look at your shoes. See how the upper portion of the shoe fits over the last and attaches itself to the bottom? Well, what looks so simple now was not in the 1870s when Matzeliger began experimenting with ways to do this by machine, speeding up the slow lasting process done by hand. Finally, six years after he arrived in Lynn, Massachusetts, from Surinam, speaking no English, Matzeliger perfected the machine to solve the problem. When he applied for a patent and sent his diagrams to Washington, they were too complex for the patent reviewers to decipher. An expert was sent to Lynn to see the machine itself. Several weeks later Matzeliger received the coveted patent, and soon the machine was marketed nationally, vastly improving the production and quality of shoes.

Granville T. Woods (1856–1910). Subway and streetcar passengers are perhaps most grateful to the innovative mind of Granville Woods. It was he who conceived various ways to speed the cars from one point to another. The subway's "third rail" is among Woods's thirty-five patents, which range from a steam boiler furnace (1884), and an incubator (1900), to the automatic air brake (1902). Like many inventors, Woods, a native of Columbus, Ohio, spent his early years around a machine shop. To this foundation he added experience working on a railroad and study at an eastern college. While he patented more than a dozen inventions for electric railways and many for electrical control and distribution, his major achievement in the area was the "induction telegraph," a system for communicating to and from moving trains. He was contested by Edison and Phelps Company, which was working on a similar device, but won the patent. Many of his electrical inventions were sold to the American Bell Telephone company and the General Electric Company. His air brake patent was acquired by Westinghouse.

Biddy Mason (1818–1891). Biddy Mason was not exactly a scientist or an inventor, but she saw to it that a lot of them made it into the world. As a skilled midwife and nurse, Mason was without equal west of the Mississippi. She came to southern California as a slave, walking behind her master's three-hundred-wagon caravan from Mississippi. Using skills that depended on the precise application of herbs and roots, enhanced by exercise and diet, Mason was always in demand, and her services were utilized by all people, including Anglo immigrants, Native Americans, and the wealthy. Through her work and thrift, this former slave eventually achieved economic independence and purchased her dream home. This house became a homestead and a base for her generous charitable and philanthropic work with the poor. Mason was not only there to ensure a birth, but she also provided the succor and sustenance when a refuge was needed. In 1872 she founded the Los Angeles branch of the First African Methodist Episcopal Church. Mason was just one among many black women, such as Annie Neal, Mary Fields, Clara Brown, Elvira Conley, and Mary Ellen "Mama" Pleasant, who helped open the gates to the West in the nineteenth century.

Lewis H. Latimer (1848–1928). When we think of the light bulb, Thomas Edison comes to mind, but without the help and insight of Lewis Latimer, we would still be somewhat in the dark. Latimer, a native of Chelsea, Massachusetts, and a Civil War veteran, made numerous important applications of the principles of electricity. On the basis of Edison's work, he invented and patented the first incandescent electric light bulb with a carbon filament in 1881. As an employee of the Edison company, he supervised the installation of electric lights in Philadelphia, New York City, Canada, and England. Latimer authored the first book on the Edison electric system. Earlier it was his drawings that accompanied the patent application for the telephone of Alexander Graham Bell.

Charles Drew (1904–1950). Before Charles Drew put his gifted mind to the problem, there was no efficient way to store large quantities of blood plasma for use during emergencies or for wartime use when blood transfusions were vital. At Columbia University, where he was awarded a scholarship, and later at Montreal General Hospital, Drew began his research that would eventually lead to ways to preserve blood for transfusions. In 1940 he published *Banked Blood: A Study in Blood Preservation,* and at the request of the Royal College of Surgeons, Drew started the "Blood for Britain" project, which consisted of collecting and drying blood plasma. In April 1950 he was killed in an auto accident in North Carolina, a tragedy sharpened by the irony of its circumstances. Drew was traveling by car to avoid the segregated public accommodations when he crashed and was taken to a segregated hospital, which had no blood plasma available that might have saved his life.

Garrett A. Morgan (1875–1963). At the International Museum of African American History in Detroit there is a replica of the automatic stop sign invented by Garrett Morgan in 1923. A model of Morgan's stop light in Motown seems quite appropriate, but the actual device itself was sold to General Electric for forty thousand dollars. Morgan was born in Paris, Tennessee, where he developed his first invention, a belt fastener for sewing machines in 1901. Thirteen years later he won the First Grand Prize gold medal at the Second International Exposition of Sanitation and Safety for his breathing helmet and smoke protector. It was the precursor to the later development of the gas mask.

Elizabeth Keckley (c. 1824–1907). For those interested in seeing some of Elizabeth Keckley's gorgeous gowns, they can be found in Harlem at Lois Alexander's Black Doll Museum. At the center of the collection is the gown she made for Mary Todd Lincoln for her husband, Abe's, first inaugural ball. Born a slave in Dinwiddie, Virginia, Keckley at an early age demonstrated a prowess with needle and thread, and the sewing machine. After several frustrating years in St. Louis seeking freedom for herself and her son, Keckley finally received a financial loan from a friend, and she and her son became citizens. Keckley was a bright, industrious woman, and was soon the proprietor of a bustling sewing business. The clientele frequenting her Baltimore shop included some of the nation's most prominent women—Mrs. Jefferson Davis, Mrs. E. M. Stanton, and Mrs. Stephen Douglas. One of four seamstresses and dress designers interviewed to make Mrs. Lincoln's inauguration reception gown, Keckley, because of her bearing and possibly her connections, to say nothing of her talent, was an easy choice for Mrs. Lincoln. (In 1961 black seamstress and designer Ann Lowe would perform a similar task in making Jackie Kennedy's inaugural gown.) During the following years, Keckley would become a close companion to Mrs. Lincoln, providing moral and physical support during the series of tragedies that struck the family.

Dr. Daniel Hale Williams (1856–1931), a surgeon who pioneered open-heart surgery in 1893, **Dr. Ernest E. Just** (1883–1941), a biologist who paved the way for research in cellular reproduction, and **Dr. Percy Julian** (1899–1975), who extracted an ingredient from the soybean to ease inflammatory arthritis, are only the most notable black doctors and scientific researchers whose work at and around the turn of the twentieth century was so crucial for American growth and transition. While they were extending the frontiers of science within the body, others were broadening our geographical and artistic horizons, particularly in literature, dance, theater, and music.

THE RAG MAN

ONE MUSICAL INNOVATION that had extensive impact was ragtime. A corruption of the term "ragged time," used to describe the idiomatic syncopation characteristic of a style of popular music, ragtime rivaled the blues in appeal at the turn of the nineteenth century. In effect, the music was an imposition of African polyrhythms on the rather staid piano music of the period. As conceived by black itinerant pianists from the Southwest and Midwest, the music was melodically inventive and rhythmically lively. At its most exemplary, ragtime consisted of a bright, steady double beat in the bass line with fully expressed tonal progressions in the melody. It was mainly a written genre, although its tunes and performances played a decisive role in shaping the solo and ensemble improvisation of early jazz.

Who was the inventor of ragtime? That is impossible to determine, but it can be said without too much argument that Scott Joplin (1868–1917) was its greatest exponent. Unlike the audacious Jelly Roll Morton, who claimed he invented jazz, Joplin with his laid-back demeanor was incapable of such bold assertions. Joplin, born in Texarkana, Texas, was the product of a musical family. His father was a competent violinist and his mother played the banjo and sang. Joplin's musical aptitude emerged at an early age, and he expressed his love for the piano at the house where his mother worked as a domestic. His parents encouraged this aspiration, scraping together enough money to buy an old-fashioned piano. Then came a succession of music teachers who exposed him to the rudiments of musical theory and introduced him to the contemporary romantic music of Europe. There was no need to worry about the absorption of traditional African musical forms; they were unavoidable in his environment.

Joplin was a good performer, but his potential as composer pointed toward greatness, although his first compositions were primarily in the mode of sentimental Victorian tunes. When the ragtime music began to appear with increasing frequency, Joplin was among the first adherents. By 1899 he had compiled quite a trove of tunes, including "Original Rags" and "Maple Leaf Rag," a perennial best-seller. But it was not until he met John Stark, a white music-sheet salesman, that Joplin's career really shifted to high gear. For ten years Stark was Joplin's publisher, promoting his music to their mutual ends, and offering solace during the dry spells. "Maple Leaf Rag" was such a smashing success that Stark was able to move his company from Sedalia, Missouri, to St. Louis to be closer to Joplin.

While Stark sold and distributed the composer's fifty-some ragtime compositions, Joplin worked like a man possessed on his opera *Treemonisha*, which, because of a lack of funds, was given only one preview. It failed to impress potential backers. Joplin took this rejection very hard, and in the fall of 1916 he was taken to the Manhattan State Hospital on Ward's Island in the East River. Several months later he died. Joplin was given a send-off like a dignitary, as thousands marched behind the funeral possession that snaked its way through Harlem.

Joplin's death was only incidental to the fading popularity of ragtime; its appeal had begun to decline several years before, mostly from overexposure, and the ascendance of jazz and the blues. Ragtime and Joplin did experience a momentary revival in the 1940s, and later from the motion picture *The Sting,* which featured Joplin's music. In 1981 another film, *Ragtime,* starred Howard Rollins, Jr., as Coalhouse Walker, a ragtime pianist. Rollins was convincing in his role and was nominated for an Oscar.

SOUNDBITE

"I started it all; I was the cause of it all."

—BENJAMIN "PAP" SINGLETON,
IN RESPONSE TO A CONGRESSIONAL COMMITTEE
INVESTIGATING THE CAUSES OF THE GREAT EXODUS
OF 1879 WHEN THOUSANDS OF BLACKS MOVED
NORTHWARD FROM TENNESSEE, TEXAS,
SOUTH CAROLINA, MISSISSIPPI, AND LOUISIANA[30]

EXODUSTERS

A SIZABLE PORTION of black folks' trek to the West had been under way ever since Estevanico tramped all over the Southwest, and York escorted Lewis and Clark over hills and through the wilderness at the turn of the eighteenth century. In fact, many blacks first appeared in Indian Territory in the

1830s as slaves, owned by members of the so-called Five Civilized Tribes—Choctaw, Creek, Cherokee, Chickasaw, and Seminole—who had picked up the practice while living among white southerners, adopting the harsh slave codes to control and subjugate their captives. Morris Sheppard, a former slave owned by a Cherokee master, recalled his days in bondage: "Us Cherokee slaves seen lots of green corn shootings and de like of dat, but we never had no games of our own. We was too tired when we come in to play any games. We had to have a pass to go any place to have singing or praying, and den they was always a bunch of patrollers around to watch everything we done. Dey would come up in a bunch of about nine men on horses, and look at all of our passes, and if a Negro didn't have no pass, dey wore him out good and made him go home. Dey didn't let us have much enjoyment."[31]

After the Civil War most of the Indian slaveholders freed their captives, and blacks were allowed to set up their own farms and households. "Among Creeks, Seminoles, and Cherokees," William Loren Katz explained, "black people made economic strides they could rarely duplicate in U.S. society. African-Cherokees owned barbershops, blacksmith shops, general stores, and restaurants. Some had become printers, ferryboat operators, cotton gin managers, teachers, and postmasters."[32]

By the 1870s when Bass Reeves, a black marshal, was rounding up varmints and desperadoes in the Indian Territory, blacks had settled in a number of small towns and represented nearly ten percent of the total population of 68,000. This number would increase considerably within a decade or two following the arrival of the "exodusters" led by Benjamin "Pap" Singleton. The exodusters had mainly migrated to Kansas after leaving parts of the South, but their white neighbors proved a bit too cantankerous, and thousands of blacks departed for the Oklahoma Territory, which was opened for settlement in 1889.

If left to the Hollywood writers and producers, blacks were not on the Chisholm Trail, had nothing to with the herding of cattle along the Red River; even the idea of a black cowboy was seldom entertained, though the term "cowboy" itself, if Mario Van Peebles is right, was a way of ridiculing the black men who rode on the trail and punched cattle. To ignore the riding feats of Bulldogger Bill Pickett, the bronze bronc buster, Nat "Deadwood Dick" Love, and Cherokee Bill is to brush aside some of the most tantalizing tales west of the Pecos. And when there was a black westerner like Jim Beckwourth, whose contributions were too large to avoid, Hollywood just made him white—without burnt cork.

A BLACK MAN IN GREENLAND

IN THE MONTHS before Henry Ford introduced his Model T Ford to the world and Orville Wright crashed his plane, Matthew Henson was braving subzero weather a few yards from the precise point of the North Pole. This was Henson's fourth and, as he told Admiral Robert E. Peary, the expedition's leader, final trip in what many thought was a futile search for the magical north point. Henson (1867–1955) was a valuable companion who got along well with the Eskimos—they believed him to be somehow related to them because of his brown skin—knew how to handle the huskies, and was generally knowledgeable about the climate and terrain.

On this day, April 7, 1909, an exhausted Peary called a halt to the expedition, and took a reading on his sextant. By his calculation they were only a few yards from the actual center point of the North Pole. Peary asked Henson to take the flag and walk the last perilous yards. When Peary, peering through his sextant, commanded him to stop, Henson placed the flag precisely on the spot Peary designated. At last they (or at least Henson) had reached ninety degrees latitude—the North Pole.

After the historic expedition, Henson experienced, from a social standpoint, days much chillier than any he had ever encountered in the Arctic. He was a forgotten man, and to make ends meet he secured employment as a parking lot attendant. Later he worked as a clerk and finally retired at seventy. In 1937 he was made a member of the Explorers Club, but the federal pension he sought was tied to a bill and stalled in Congress. President Harry S Truman paid tribute to Henson in a celebration at the Pentagon in 1950, and President Dwight D. Eisenhower honored him four years later. A bronze plaque was erected in his name at the state house of Maryland in 1961. Before he died in 1955, Henson's autobiography, *A Negro Explorer at the North Pole,* written in 1912, was republished.

FALL OF THE GREAT WHITE HOPE
●

WHITE AMERICA MAY have dispatched a meek, humble Henson to the margins of society with relative ease, but Jack Johnson was a whole other thing. Sure, there had been black fighters of renown before Johnson strutted around the ring—the refined and masterful Peter Jackson, heavyweight contender Tom Molineaux who fought two bloody matches with champion Tom Crib or Cribb in 1810 and 1811, George Dixon (world's featherweight champion 1892–1900), Joe Wolcott (world's welterweight champ 1901–04), and Joe Gans (world's lightweight champ 1901–08)—but Johnson's clout reached well beyond the arena into state legislatures, the Congress, and even the British Parliament. This giant of a man cast a shadow of doubt over any who would dare assert the idea of white supremacy.

Johnson's first piece of notoriety was not of his own making. The first act opened the day after Christmas 1908 in Sydney, New South Wales, about the same time Matthew Henson was rounding up a team of huskies and some Eskimo assistants for the dash to the pole. Johnson knocked out Tommy Burns in the fourteenth round and was crowned the heavyweight champion of the world. A stunned white America had but one recourse, find a "White Hope" to put the uppity black in his place. James Jeffries, the undefeated champ who had held the crown since the summer of 1899, was coaxed out of retirement.

One hundred years after Crib beat Molineaux into submission, Johnson exacted a semblance of revenge, taunting and punishing Jeffries for fifteen rounds. Newspaperman and novelist-to-be Jack London was at ringside and offered this account: "Once again has Johnson sent down to defeat the chosen representative of the white race, and this time the greatest of them all ... Johnson played as usual ... With his opponent not so strong in attack, Johnson, blocking in masterly fashion, could afford to play. And he played and fought a white man, in a white man's country before a white man's audience. The greatest battle of the century was a monologue delivered to 20,000 spectators by a smiling Negro ..."[33] More succinctly, and far more memorable, are the words Johnson's mother used to sum up the fight. "He said he'd *bring home the bacon*, and the honey boy has gone and done it." No earlier citation is known for this expression.

The last words on this lopsided affair belong to Jeffries: "I would rather have been beaten three times over by a man of my own race ... It was to tear Johnson away from his honor that I consented to fight ... The color line should be drawn outside the ring. It cannot be done inside the ropes."[34] Like Jeffries, white supremacy had taken a devastating, unforgettable blow, and Jeffries was prescient as to where to draw the racial line. And the fighter was certainly not aware how closely his remark resembled Du Bois's prophecy that "the problem of the twentieth century is the problem of the color line."

Damage control was effected immediately. A number of state legislatures barred the showing of the fight films, claiming that the picture of a white man flat on his back with a smiling black man standing over him would be against public policy. It would be sending the wrong message, they contended. Johnson dined with Booker T. Washington, wasting no time rubbing the defeat in the face of white America.

But as Johnson would soon learn, it is not nice to fool Mother Nature or to thumb your nose at white America. A few weeks before Johnson had made mincemeat out of Jeffries and "brought home the bacon," the Mann Act was passed by Congress. This law was popularly known as the "white slave traffic act," which prohibited interstate or international transport of women for "immoral purposes." While the act grew out of public concern over "white slavery," with its oxymoronic overtones, particularly the importation of European girls to work in American brothels, it seemed designed specifically for the rambunctious Johnson. When Johnson was finally snared, it made no difference that the white woman with him was there of her own free will (he would eventually marry her)—they had the "black braggart" where they wanted him. He had crossed that line outside the ring. Ironically, the judge at his indictment was Kennesaw Mountain Landis, who later, as baseball commissioner, would be singularly responsible for keeping blacks out of the major leagues.

Now that he'd been convicted of a morals charge and hounded by law enforcement officials, Johnson's career took a nosedive. His fights were canceled, he was barred from hotels and public places, and the "cash cow" he could count on from appearances at various functions dried up. Johnson was persona non grata, and conveniently "blacklisted." Desperate for income, he agreed on a match with another "White Hope," big Jess Willard. Only the controversy after the fight exceeded the hype before it took place. Did Johnson take a dive in order to escape going to prison and to end the unceasing harassment? Or was he beaten fairly by a younger man of superior ability? The fight occurred at an outdoor arena in Havana, Cuba, and the film footage suggests that Johnson took the easy way out. If he was indeed knocked out, why did he appear to be shading his eyes from the sun? Johnson's body language may have gotten the last word.

Whatever the case, Johnson surrendered his belt, donned prison garb (he did eight months in Leavenworth), and slowly slid from the spotlight. A master of defense in the ring, Johnson was helpless against the tide of reaction outside of it. Having rid itself of a major nemesis, the boxing world took every precaution against the emergence of another "unruly contender." The color bar was fixed rigidly in place and such great fighters as Sam Langford, Harry Wills, and Joe Jeannette never got a shot at the crown.

Johnson's prowess in the ring was exemplary of the budding dominance of blacks in other sports. Other than boxing and horse racing (and black jockeys such as Isaac Murphy and Jimmie Lee were on the verge of extinction), black athletes were confined to an amateur status, unless they participated in segregated leagues and arenas. Fritz Pollard of Brown University and Paul Robeson of Rutgers both earned all-American honors in football in the first quarter of the twentieth century. By 1920 Rube Foster, who at one time stood in for Jack Johnson so he could evade the law, had founded the Negro National League, which by the 1930s would feature such stellar attractions as Josh Gibson, Leroy "Satchel" Paige, and Cool Papa Bell. Foster himself was an outstanding player who is said to have taught the great New York Giants pitcher Christy Mathewson how to throw the fadeaway pitch. Among some of the older players who plied their skills for Foster's league were Moses Walker and his brother Welday. "Fats" Jenkins and "Tarzan" Cooper were basketball standouts with the Harlem Rens a decade before Abe Saperstein founded the Harlem Globetrotters in Pinckney, Illinois, in 1927. In track and field John B. Taylor of the University of Pennsylvania was the intercollegiate champion in the 440-yard-dash and later a member of the U.S. Olympic team in 1908. Howard Drew of UCLA held the AAU championship title in the hundred-yard dash for 1912 and 1913. A score of years before Jesse Owens would be considered the world's fastest human, Drew laid claim to the title.

Along with the disappearance of black jockeys was the fading presence of black bicyclists, though the impressive skills of Marshall "Major" Taylor of Indianapolis would provide the sport a final glow of luster. In 1899 and 1900 Taylor was the undisputed world champion, and soon after won two world titles in Montreal. The cyclist's first European tour in 1901 was extremely successful, both competitively (he won forty-two of fifty-seven races) and socially, as overflow crowds turned out to see him. His color was more a novelty than an issue. Taylor's popularity was in sharp contrast to Jack Johnson's, and while in France, he signed several lucrative contracts. Four years after his conquest of Europe, Taylor collapsed from fatigue and canceled his next European tour. Ensuing lawsuits necessitated that Taylor take a three-year hiatus from racing, an absence that contributed to an unsuccessful tour in 1908.

BETCHA DIDN'T KNOW

By 1896 plans were completed to unite the National Federation of Afro-American Women with the National League of Colored Women. The new organization was named the National Association of Colored Women (NACW). Mary Church Terrell and Margaret Murray Washington were among the leaders of the NACW.

CLOSE RANKS

IF TAYLOR HAD returned to Indianapolis by the winter of 1909, he could have enjoyed a magnificent Henry O. Tanner art exhibit at the John Herron Art Institute. Tanner (1859–1937), like Taylor, knew firsthand about European hospitality, having lived in France since 1891. By the time of the Herron exhibit, Tanner had completed some of his most recognized paintings, including *The Last Moments of John Brown, The Banjo Lesson, The Young Sabot Maker,* and *The Annunciation.* He had also completed many years before his famous *The Thankful Poor,* which is now a cherished piece in Bill and Camille Cosby's priceless collection of art.

When Tanner decided to leave the United States to study in Europe, it had less to do with the prevalence of racism—though his father, Bishop Benjamin Tanner of the A.M.E. Church,

could cite chapter and verse on the incidents he encountered—
than the lure of the academies. Studying at the Pennsylvania
Academy of the Fine Arts under Thomas Eakins, Tanner concluded, was sufficient enough, and on January 4, 1891, he set
sail for Rome, via Liverpool and Paris. His artistic aim, he stated,
was to concentrate on sober, sympathetic depictions of African-
American life to offset a history of one-sided comic representa-
tions. And in this regard the task before him was herculean.

Tanner's reputation in Europe was adequate, but it was to
buyers in America he looked to sell his paintings. Not until the
mid-1920s would success truly come his way. Meanwhile, his
home and studio in Paris were always open to passing artists
such as sculptor Meta Vaux Warick Fuller and painters William
Johnson, Laura Wheeler Waring, Hale Woodruff, and Aaron
Douglas. And his influence on African-American artists was far
more extensive than even he realized, especially on sculptors
Augusta Savage and Selma Burke, whose portrait of Franklin
D. Roosevelt appears on the dime. Sculptors Savage and Burke
continued a tradition blazed by Edmonia Lewis (1845–?), the half-
black and half-Chippewa artist whose *Forever Free* sculpture, celebrating the emancipation of the slaves, is a classic. But, according
to black printmaker Albert Smith (1896–1940), Tanner's work was
probably even more respected by white American artists.

Despite his permanent residence in France, Tanner was a
lifetime member of the NAACP, and even during those difficult, lean years his contribution never waned, and he seemed
to have been in rather constant contact with James Weldon
Johnson and Du Bois.

DAWN OF THE NAACP
—●—

IN A 1901 article in the *Dial*, Du Bois cited Tanner as one of
a vital group of black leaders who "seek . . . that self-develop-
ment and self-realization in all lines of human endeavor
which they believe will eventually place the Negro beside

other races."[35] Du Bois took time out to write this during a
period of intense political activity prior to his emergence on
the national scene as the leading antagonist of Booker T.
Washington and his involvement with the Niagara Movement,
which would provide the springboard to the NAACP. Twenty-
nine members of the so-called Talented Tenth, a concept
coined by Du Bois to represent the percentage of the black
community needed for leadership, participated in the meeting.
Professor Kelly Miller of Howard University, and Archibald
Grimke, a longtime abolitionist, were two of the twenty-nine
delegates. (Later, the meetings would be infiltrated by spies
from Booker T. Washington's camp. Richard Greener, a Howard University instructor, and Charles Anderson, a New York
collector of Internal Revenue, would be among those most
responsible for getting information about the proceedings
back to Washington.)

When the Niagara Movement met for the first time in 1905
at Niagara Falls, Canada, they had a list of troubling issues to
consider. High on the agenda for the two most notable orga-
nizers, Du Bois and William Monroe Trotter—whose father,
James Monroe Trotter, was a member and leader of the 54th
Regiment of Massachusetts during the Civil War, who stacked
their rifles and refused to drill until they received equal pay—
was a plan of action to deal with the rise of racial hatred and
terrorism across the country, and to move more aggressively
in the quest of full citizenship for black Americans.

"We believe in manhood suffrage," the Movement's declaration of principles asserted. "We believe that no man is so
good, intelligent, or wealthy as to be entrusted wholly with
the welfare of his neighbor."[36] From this initial meeting to
annual sessions in Harpers Ferry, Boston, to the last gathering
at Oberlin, the all-black organization was imbued with a singular purpose of securing the basic principles of brotherhood. Being imbued with integrity is fine, but much more is
needed to sustain a political organization. Depending on
whose account is believed, either nineteen or fifty people
showed up at Oberlin. "The sun do move," John Jasper, a
Baptist minister, used to preach, but the Niagara Movement
was practically dead. A significant part of its demise can be

blamed on the weaknesses of the local branches or their inability to "take care of business." Plus, the movement was fighting a futile ideological war with Washington's Tuskegee juggernaut. Its main contribution rested on the defiant stand it made for legal redress and its relentless spirit of protest, and as a bridge to the next political development, for which its importance should not be minimized.

In 1909, with the nation still holding its collective breath following the atrocities that marked the Springfield race riot, the Niagara militants were invited to a conference to be held in New York City. Most of them accepted, but conspicuous by his absence was Trotter, who had difficulty sitting down talking political and racial strategy with white people. There were some, too, who had pointed to his "egoism" as being a key factor in undermining the goals of the Niagara Movement. That point is debatable, given the increasingly moribund status of the organization.

The roll call at the initial confab of the organization that would be called the National Association for the Advancement of Colored People reads like a who's who of the noted and distinguished—Du Bois, social activist Jane Addams of Hull House, New York City social worker Mary Ovington White, author William English Walling, whose stirring report on the Springfield riot had helped inspire such a meeting, educator and theorist John Dewey, author William Dean Howells, who had written so authoritatively on the poetry of Paul Laurence Dunbar, Dr. Henry Moskowitz, a Socialist and social worker, and Oswald Garrison Villard, the grandson of William Lloyd Garrison, the prominent abolitionist, were among those who signed the call. Two influential black women also attended: Ida Bell Wells Barnett, the fiery activist and journalist, and Mary Church Terrell, founder of the National Association of Colored Women and a former acolyte of Booker T. Washington. Terrell, always a bit ambivalent about Washington's policies, finally severed ties with him after he threatened to jeopardize her husband's reappointment to a judicial post.

By the spring of 1910 the organization was officially sanctioned, with Moorfield Storey, a Boston lawyer, as the first national president. The director of publicity and research was

Du Bois, the group's only black officer. With Du Bois at the center of things, it should come as no surprise that equality of educational opportunities, complete suffrage, and civil rights were the foremost issues to be tackled. The essence of their early platform would reach around the world and into South Africa, touching the African National Congress, who, a year later, based its Freedom Charter on the NAACP's constitution. The NAACP had also promised to mount a strong antilynching campaign, which must have warmed the cockles of Ms. Barnett's heart since she was one of the most vocal opponents of the violent practice. Her original enthusiasm for the NAACP soon cooled after the organization bungled its handling of the lawsuit in Chicago to ban the movie *Birth of a Nation* in 1915. Further distance from the organization followed when disagreements arose over her reports and an NAACP field representative's accounts of lynchings and mob violence in East St. Louis and Helena, Arkansas, which the representative insisted Ms. Barnett overstated. One thing Barnett stressed repeatedly was that the NAACP should have its own publication to express the views of the organization.

The Crisis was what Barnett had in mind, and it was launched in 1910 with Du Bois as editor. Du Bois's style and militancy characterized the premiere issue's stated policy: ". . . Its editorial page will stand for the rights of men, irrespective of color or race, for the highest ideals of American democracy, and for reasonable but earnest and persistent attempts to gain these rights and realize these ideals. The magazine will be the organ of no clique or party and will avoid personal rancor of all sorts. In the absence of proof to the contrary it will assume honesty of purpose on the part of all men, North and South, white and black."[37]

One problem that plagued the magazine right from the start was the separation of two warring ideals, to paraphrase Du Bois; that is, how would the editor's policy and opinion steer clear of the organization's philosophy? Fortunately—and the tenor of the times is partly the reason—the ideas of Du Bois and the NAACP converged without too much consternation. But then, how much disagreement was possible during the first decade or so when lynching occupied so many pages in the publication? Something may have been said about the gory details and the graphic descriptions of lynchings; if so, it was a criticism of no mean import since things continued without alteration.

In July 1918 the magazine published one of its strongest and most widely read editorials. There was clearly no chasm between Du Bois and the organization on this "close ranks" position:

This is the crisis of the world. For all the long years to come men will point to the year of 1918 as the great Day of Decision, the day when the world decided whether it would submit to military despotism and an endless armed peace—if peace it could be called—or whether they would put down the menace of German militarism and inaugurate the United States of the World.

We of the colored race have no ordinary interest in the outcome. That which the German power represents today spells death to the aspirations of Negroes and all darker races for equality, freedom and democracy. Let us not hesitate. Let us, while this war lasts, forget our special grievance and close ranks shoulder to shoulder with our own white fellow citizens and the allied nations that are fighting for democracy. We make no ordinary sacrifice, but we make it gladly and willingly with our eyes to the hills.[38]

There was nothing remarkably strange about such an assertion coming from the NAACP, but to hear a militant like Du Bois, who had earned his spurs excoriating a country so consistently remiss in democratic practice, asking for a shoulder-to-shoulder camaraderie, and "to forget our special grievance," must have knocked a few black militants for a loop. Du Bois's rhetoric, like the sound of Irving Berlin's bugle boy, was so keening that more than one black man and woman was ready to go to war. And they could be forgiven if they found the word "democracy" so irresistibly appealing.

BETCHA DIDN'T KNOW

The first black graduate of West Point was Henry O. Flipper. He received his commission in 1879. After five years of service, Flipper was charged with making false statements during an embezzlement investigation and was dismissed from the service. Ninety-five years later, he was posthumously vindicated when the Army Board held that the punishment was too severe. He was granted an honorable discharge.

THE HELL FIGHTERS

THIS WAR, BLACK America thought, would be different. Now there was a common enemy, an ogre upon which all Americans could channel their hatred and frustration. This war was not against the Native Americans, it was not against the mother country, nor was America fighting against itself. No, it was time to make the world safe for democracy. There was a flaw in all this, however. How could America ensure something that she herself had never practiced? The thought crossed more than a few black American minds. But Du Bois had set out the line of march, and we would put our complaints on ice until this campaign was over; there was a larger threat on the horizon.

A few weeks after America formally entered World War I, the Selective Service Act was passed. Every able-bodied American between twenty-one and thirty-one was eligible for the draft.

Within a month more than 700,000 black Americans had signed the dotted line. Meanwhile, as enthusiasm for the war reached a fever pitch, some 10,000 blacks and others were not so caught up in the excitement that they forgot to deal with some pressing problems on the home front. To demonstrate their outrage against the East St. Louis riots and other acts of violence, in which blacks had been set upon by unruly white mobs, they marched silently down New York City's Fifth Avenue, stepping slowly and deliberately to the muffled sound of drums. If the march had a drum major, it was Du Bois, striding along in a straw hat and swinging his cane.

Hundreds of miles from these determined protestors were other marchers, but these black men wore uniforms and were at boot camps across the South, which presented a host of new problems for the blacks and the army. Black soldiers were hardly through the first weeks of basic training when a combat mission arose. Members of the highly decorated 24th Infantry, a unit that had served with distinction during the Spanish-American War, were accosted by whites in Houston, Texas, and a riot ensued. In training to meet a new enemy, the black troops were forced to deal with an old one. Believing the black soldiers would use their guns to defend themselves, white army officers made an attempt to disarm them. But to no avail, and during a skirmish seventeen whites were killed.

After a sham of a trial, thirteen blacks were hanged for murder and mutiny, forty-one imprisoned for life, and forty others were held pending further investigation. It was difficult not to think of the Brownsville incident, which had occurred eleven years earlier in 1906 and had similar results after black soldiers defended themselves against a white mob. President Theodore Roosevelt, on the basis of a report by a single investigator, dismissed the entire black battalion without honor and disqualified its members from participating in either the military or civil service. At another training facility in Spartanburg, South Carolina, the 15th Infantry out of New York only narrowly averted a shootout with white civilians. Noble Sissle, whom we will meet again as songwriting partner to pianist and composer Eubie Blake, the drum major for the unit's band, entered a hotel to purchase a newspaper and was cursed by the owner when he failed to remove his cap. As Sissle stopped to explain, the man knocked his hat from his head and commenced to strike him, and then kicked him out of the hotel. An enraged Sissle hurried back to the barracks and told the other soldiers what had happened. The armed soldiers were on their way to shoot up the town when they were met by the band director, Lieutenant James Reese Europe, who convinced them to return to the barracks. Later they would try again, only to be dissuaded by the commanding officer, Colonel William Hayward.

Secretary of War Newton Baker dispatched Emmett Scott, formerly Booker T. Washington's aide, to investigate the situation. At last, the War Department decided that the best way to avoid another Houston was to deploy the entire regiment to France immediately. Major Arthur Little, a white officer, recalled the reaction to the event: "Our movement was secret, and our destination unknown; but as we swung long through the camps of the 12th, 71st, and 7th Regiments, in the course of our hike, thousands of brave New York lads of the 27th Division lined the sides of the roadway, and sang us through to the tune of 'Over There.' "[39]

And "over there" was soon where the 15th Regiment, newly christened the 369th Regiment, landed as the first contingent of black combat troops to arrive on the battle front. The 369th hardly had time to recover from seasickness before it was given an awesome assignment in mid-April 1918 to hold a four-and-a-half-kilometer sector. Oddly, the 369th, which represented only 1 percent of American troops in France, held 20 percent of all territory then assigned to the American army. Within a few weeks the 369th would enter the war annals of memorable battles, and set the stage for the first Americans to win the croix de guerre. One night Sergeant Henry Johnson and Private Needham Roberts were stationed at an observation post in a "no-man's land" when they heard suspicious noises. A German raiding party had cut through the barbed-wire entanglement and were preparing to attack. Johnson and Roberts took on the Germans single-handedly, and even after being severely wounded, continued to lob hand grenades, fire their rifles, and even engage in hand-to-hand combat, repelling the invading Germans. They killed four Germans and wounded thirty-two. Most of the affliction on the Germans had been delivered by Johnson since Roberts's wounds limited his participation. For their heroism, Sergeant Johnson and Private Roberts were awarded France's highest honor, the croix de guerre.

Indeed, the valorous 369th and its brave troops showcased black heroism and sacrifice during the war, but for the most part, the full potential of the black soldiers was never realized, despite their numerous successes. Racism, false charges of cowardice, and secret memoranda were some of the impediments that hampered the black troops. In addition, many promotions were denied, and battlefield commissions for black soldiers were rare. Of the more than 371,710 blacks who served during the war, there were only 1,353 officers. Blacks in the armed forces had helped to make the world safe for democracy, but there was little semblance of it in their own ranks. The one good thing about all this was that the war was over, and shorn of their innocence and illusion, the black soldiers took their two months' discharge bonuses (about sixty dollars for enlisted men). While many of them proudly displayed their Distinguished Service Crosses, the majority of them possessed the "colored man's medal," as one newspaper called it—the "double cross."

For many of the 191 unbroken days in the trenches where the 369th was under blistering fire in France, it was without that invigorating morale supplied by its band, under the baton of James Reese Europe. There was a brief reunion at the harbor in Brest while awaiting departure, which was not without its racism as blacks were among the last to leave, but this meeting was a comparatively tame one for the band—if they kicked up too much of a fanfare, it might further delay their departure. When they arrived in New York City and assembled to march up Fifth Avenue, Lieutenant Europe and his charges were back in America, and the band was ready to let it all hang out.

David Levering Lewis captured this moment of homecoming and epiphany in his book *When Harlem Was in Vogue:*

The tide of khaki and black turned west on 110th Street to Lenox Avenue, then north again into the heart of Harlem. At 125th Street, the coiled, white rattlesnake insignia of the regiment hissed from thousands of lapels, bonnets, and windows. A field of pennants, flags, banners, and scarves thrashed about the soldiers like elephant grass in a gale, threatening to engulf them. In front of the unofficial reviewing stand at 130th Street, Europe's sixty-piece band broke into "Here Comes My Daddy" to the extravagant delight of the crowd. At this second platform, Harlem notables and returning heroes beheld each other with almost palpable elation and pride. No longer now in the dense, rapid-stepping formation learned from the French, ranks opened, gait loosened. "For the final mile or more of our parade," Major Arthur Little recalled, "about every fourth soldier of the ranks had a girl upon his arm— and we marched through Harlem singing and laughing."

Colonel Hayward shouted a command: the march halted. The Hell Fighters were home. They had come, as thousands of other returning Afro-American soldiers came, with a music, a lifestyle, and a dignity new to the nation—and soon to pervade it.[40]

Sadly, though, this dignity and courage, which served these Men of Bronze so well at Meuse-Argonne, Champagne, and Belleau Wood, meant nothing to the hateful mobs of whites in Mississippi, Alabama, and Georgia. At least ten of the lynchings in 1919 were black veterans, some of them still in uniform. In Pine Bluff, Arkansas, a black veteran refused to get off the sidewalk when commanded by a white woman; it was a free country, he told her, and he would walk where he wanted. A mob took him from town, lashed him to a tree with tire chains, and shot him forty or fifty times. When Private William Little, who had only recently been mustered out of the army, arrived at the railroad station in Blakely, Georgia, he encountered a band of whites. They ordered him to doff his army uniform and walk home in his underwear. Little was rescued from the mob by several other whites and he was allowed to walk home unmolested. Later, still wearing his uniform, because he had no other clothing, Little received notes demanding he stop wearing his uniform or leave town. He ignored the threats. Several days later Private Little was found dead on the outskirts of town, apparently beaten by a mob. He was still dressed in his army uniform.

But these violent acts were not confined to soldiers or to black men. Black women were also the target of race hatred and lynch mobs. One grisly and repulsive example will suffice: the lynching of Mary Turner in Valdosta, Georgia. Turner was pregnant when she was hanged from a tree, doused with gasoline and motor oil, and burned. As she dangled from the rope, a man with a pocketknife approached her and slit open her stomach. Her premature baby, Walter White reported, tumbled to the ground. "Two feeble cries it gave," he said, "and received for answer the heel of a stalwart man, as life was ground out of the tiny form."

Billie Holiday's version of "Strange Fruit" is a testament to the widespread atrocities:

> Southern trees
> bear a strange fruit
> Blood on the leaves
> and blood at the root.
> Black bodies swinging
> in the southern breeze
> Strange fruit hanging
> from the poplar trees.
> Pastoral scenes
> of the gallant South
> Bulging eyes
> and the twisted mouth
> Scent of magnolia
> sweet and fresh
> Then the sudden smell
> of burning flesh.
> Here is a fruit for the crows to pluck
> for the rain to gather, for the wind to suck
> For the sun to rot
> for the trees to drop.
> Here is a strange and bitter crop.

Holiday's interpretation of Lewis Allen's evocative lyrics

tones down the underlying protest of the song, but there is no denying the gripping imagery of the menace blacks faced in the "pastoral" South. Claude McKay, grappling with the same social injustice, gave it a more defiant spin:

> If we must die, let it not be like hogs
> Hunted and penned in an inglorious spot,
> While round us bark the mad and hungry dogs,
> Making their mock at our accursed lot.
> If we must die, O let us nobly die,
> So that our precious blood may not be shed
> In vain; then even the monsters we defy
> Shall be constrained to honor us though dead!
> O kinsmen! we must meet the common foe!
> Though far outnumbered let us show brave,
> And for their thousand blows deal one deathblow!
> What though before us lies the open grave?
> Like men we'll face the murderous, cowardly pack
> Pressed to the wall, dying but fighting back!

And the fighting back by blacks was expressed in a number of ways; some of the response was elegant and poetic, and some of it was just as violent and deadly as that which they received. Race riots were one form of retribution, and in 1919, the year of the Red Summer (because of the rivers of human blood spilled—mostly from blacks), there were approximately twenty-five race riots, primarily in major cities like Chicago.

Harry Haywood, who later would be a major figure in the Communist Party, U.S.A, and the ranking black theorist, mustered out of the army in 1919 and began working on the Michigan Central Railroad, making the Wolverine run through Michigan. He finished a run one day and stepped off the train right into the middle of the Chicago race riot. When the word hit the grapevine that a young black boy had drowned at a Lake Michigan beach, the black community was up in arms. The crosscurrent of rumors then drifted all over town, with black and white mobs gathering on street corners waiting for the other shoe to fall.

Haywood recalled going to the Regimental Armory to find

some of his buddies from the army regiment. "I knew they would be planning an armed defense, and I wanted to get in on the action. I found them and they told me of their plans. It was rumored that Irishmen from west of the Wentworth Avenue dividing line were planning to invade the ghetto that night, coming across the tracks by way of Fifty-first Street. We planned a defensive action to meet them."[41]

It was a terrible clash of emotions, and when the police finally restored order, 38 people were dead and 537 wounded. Hundreds of citizens, black and white, were left homeless.

Two years later in Tulsa, Oklahoma, another social tinder-box exploded. In this blood feud nine whites and twenty-one blacks were killed. It all stemmed from the charge that a young white woman had been assaulted by a black man. The black community, alerted to the arrest of the man, went to the jail to protect him from a lynch mob. Fights broke out at the jail and spread rapidly all over town. To quell the riot, four companies of National Guardsmen were summoned, with an air unit dropping bombs on the city. It was the first time the United States had been bombed from the air. Property damage from the altercations totaled $1 million.

SOUNDBITE

". . . The African Blood Brotherhood is essentially a secret organization, though at present engaged in open recruiting in the northern states (U.S.). We are organized for immediate protection purposes and eventual revolutionary liberation in Africa and other countries where Negroes constitute a majority of the population."

—CYRIL BRIGGS, 1921, THE CRUSADER[42]

UP, YOU MIGHTY RACE!

AMERICA WAS ABOUT to be hit by another bomb, only this one did not fall from the sky. This explosive device came in a human package, and was, as Du Bois described him, "a little, fat black man, ugly, but with intelligent eyes and a big head." Du Bois's disdain was obvious, but the description, which would be the source of bitter enmity between the two men, stopped short of capturing what Marcus Mosiah Garvey (1887–1940) meant to millions of blacks who were sick and tired of being sick and tired. Many of the destitute were recent migrants from the West Indies and the South, who had fled the periodic floods, the night riders, and the menace of the boll weevil and its devastation of the cotton, and they would take relief wherever they found it.

In the pages of the *Negro World*, Garvey's paper, he replied to Du Bois's character assassination: "Now what does Du Bois mean by ugly? . . . How he arrives at his conclusion that Marcus Garvey is ugly, being a Negro, is impossible to determine, in that if there is any ugliness in the Negro race it would be reflected more through Du Bois than Marcus Garvey, in that he himself tells that he is a little Dutch, a little French, and a little Negro. Why, in fact, the man is a monstrosity." Cheek to jowl, the two men were poised for a fight, and it got uglier before it got better.

By the time of the Tulsa riot, Garvey and his organization, the Universal Negro Improvement Association, was at its peak, and while it may not have had the two million membership it claimed, it was nonetheless a powerful and formidable assembly of reaction to American racism and intransigence.

Garvey, who came to the United States in 1916 with the intention of meeting Booker T. Washington, was a year late and a few dollars short. He had read Washington's autobiography *Up From Slavery* and was inspired by his ideas on self-help and the building of institutions. Tuskegee might have been sufficient for a Washington, but Garvey's dream was to build a nation, a vast empire populated with black princes and princesses, Dukes of the Nile, and other notions of frippery and outrageous royalty. Race pride was his response to the denigration he observed when he arrived from Jamaica and toured the country. "Where is the black man's government?" Garvey asked rhetorically. "Where is his king and kingdom? Where is his president, his country, his ambassador, his army, his navy, his men of big affairs?"[43] They could not be found, Garvey concluded, and thus it was his responsibility to bring them into existence.

The symbols of power and majesty were far easier to attain than the actual substance. And it's easier, also, to summarize Garvey's quest with a series of slogans—"Up, you mighty race! You can accomplish what you will!" "Africa for the Africans, at home and abroad," and "One Aim, One God, One Destiny!" Slogans, however, cannot measure the extent of Garvey's influence, his dynamic magnetism, his audacity and flamboyance, the fascinating charisma that comes maybe once in a century to bedazzle, bamboozle, and at last, exasperate the hopes of a people. Garvey anointed himself the Provisional President of Africa—a land he would never see—but he had trouble taking care of his various enterprises in Harlem. Bad investments, pitiful advice, a cabal of powerful black detractors, and Garvey's grandiose schemes all served to undermine his dream of empire. Accused of using the mail to defraud, Garvey was railroaded off to prison, though, with typical arrogance, he facilitated his own conviction. "Look for me in the whirlwind," he told a small band of supporters crowded on a New Orleans dock. The bravado was still intact, although the jig was up and he boarded a ship headed back to Jamaica, after serving two years of a sentence in Atlanta Penitentiary, and then being pardoned by President Coolidge. At last Garvey's goal of separation was realized, but the "venerable trickster," as Robert Hill called him, had not planned it that way. The trick was on him.

I JUMP JIM CROW

NOBLE SISSLE, THE drum major for James Reese Europe's "Hell Fighters" band, the man who had been slapped around at the hotel in Spartanburg, South Carolina, was still exhilarated over the success of his new musical *Chocolate Dandies* when Garvey was busted in 1925. Sissle (1889–1975) originally had studied for the ministry at Butler University in his native Indiana. Highly susceptible to the bite of the music bug, Sissle toured with the Thomas Hann Jubilee Singers from 1911 to 1913 and with Joe Porter's Serenaders until 1915. During this same year he began collaborating with pianist and composer Eubie Blake. He resumed writing with Blake after the war, and in 1921 the two, known as "Dixie Duo," produced their first show, *Shuffle Along*. This show is often credited with igniting the Harlem Renaissance.

Other than a novelty show with a luscious score by Sissle and Blake, and several talented performers and dancers, there was nothing unique about *Shuffle Along*. Only the budget was thinner than the plot, which was basically about two grocery store owners (and black actors Aubrey Lyles and Flournoy Miller each had a layer of burnt cork applied to their faces) who run for mayor against Harry Walton. Sissle and Blake's tune "I'm Just Wild About Harry," which Harry S Truman would later use during his presidential campaign, was the overwhelming hit from the show. In a series of pratfalls and sight gags, the two steal funds from their stores, and hire the same detective to spy on each other. When one of them wins, he appoints the other as chief of police. Eventually Harry runs both of them out of town.

Florence Mills, who replaced Gertrude Saunders in the lead role, sang the other hit tune from the show, "Love Will Find A Way." Chanteuse Josephine Baker, later a smash in Paris, would also be featured in the chorus line. Paul Robeson ap-

93

peared briefly as one of the Four Harmony Kings. The show premiered at the Howard Theatre in Washington, D.C., and then had a successful run at the Dunbar Theatre in Philadelphia. Though the reviews were only lukewarm, the performance had an extensive run and was strongly supported by white patrons. If the show had any consistent problem, it was finding girls for the chorus line. Baker's stint lasted only long enough for her to bolster her resume and then she was off to international acclaim with a banana skirt and the top spot at La Revue Negre. "White critics of the theater have all refused to admit the impact of *Shuffle Along* on the evolution of the American musical comedy form," Harold Cruse stressed in *The Crisis of the Negro Intellectual*.[44]

Nor have the critics given much thought or attention to the role of minstrelsy in the development of American music and culture. *Shuffle Along,* particularly with the stars Miller and Lyles cavorting around stage in blackface, was directly linked to the minstrel tradition. The minstrel show had a convoluted evolution. It originated from black entertainers perfecting the act of a white man imitating a black man who was making fun of a happy slave. In effect, knowing how cunning a slave could be, the whole thing, right from the start, was possibly a farce perpetrated by slaves. Nonetheless, if one man can be said to have set the ball rolling, it was Thomas D. Rice. The "D" was for Dartmouth, but everybody called him "Daddy" Rice. The story goes that Rice was passing by a plantation in Louisville, Kentucky, when he observed a slave doing a song-and-dance routine: "Wheel about, turn about, do jus' so/and ebery time I wheel about, I jump Jim Crow."

Amused fascination was followed by immediate expropriation, and Daddy Rice was on his way to fame—and the bank. He took his little jig on a national tour, wheeling and spinning "jus' so" until he was deemed the creator of the style. No great amount of deconstruction is needed to see the pro-slavery advocacy of minstrelsy, but that cannot obfuscate the African retentions or survivals—the looseness, the unrestrained rhythm and dance movements. On its surface minstrelsy, particularly when performed by whites in blackface, conveyed the image of the "contented slave"; black performers like Miller and Lyles were often clever enough to extract the positive musical components without perpetuating the negative images of Jim Crow or an Uncle Tom. To be sure, it was a fine line, and only the skillful entertainers such as Bert Williams and his partner George Walker could execute this fandango or tomfoolery without falling on their "burnt cork" faces.

The minstrel show or "Ethiopian Opera" remained America's most popular form of entertainment until it was absorbed in or eclipsed by vaudeville and the film industry. Al Jolson and Eddie Cantor were instrumental in extending the minstrel tradition into vaudeville and film. Ironically, it was a black architect, Paul Williams, who designed the Al Jolson Memorial Shrine. While there is a definite overlap between minstrelsy and vaudeville, the same cannot be said of the "darky melodies" and "coon" songs. The darky melodies tended to be largely sentimental, and the coon songs much more risqué and bawdy. In the vernacular of white southerners, however, very little distinction was drawn between the two concepts. Both darky and coon were derogatory, connoting a chicken-stealing, watermelon-loving clown.

SOUNDBITE

"If I had known I was going to live to be a hundred, I would have taken better care of myself."

—EUBIE BLAKE (1883–1983),
PIANIST/COMPOSER WHO,
WITH LYRICIST NOBLE SISSLE,
WROTE THE MUSIC FOR SHUFFLE ALONG[45]

THE HARLEM RENAISSANCE
—

IF *SHUFFLE ALONG* possessed a trace of denigration, it escaped the critics of the day, and certainly those "New Negroes" who congregated around Alain Locke and Langston Hughes would have bellowed if something was askance of being "politically correct." And these brash Young Turks, comprising maverick intellectuals, scholars, writers, poets, actors, painters, dancers, and a slew of professionals, were not afraid to speak their mind. They were a new breed, and they did not hesitate to let you know. Hughes, a leader of this 1920s black pack, or what Zora Neale Hurston termed the "niggerati," sounded their manifesto:

> We younger Negro artists who create now intend to express our individual dark-skinned selves without fear or shame. If white people are pleased we are glad. If they are not, it doesn't matter. We know we are beautiful. And ugly too. The tom-tom cries and the tom-tom laughs. If colored people are pleased we are glad. If they are not, their displeasure doesn't matter either. We build our temples for tomorrow, strong as we know how, and we stand on top of the mountain, free within ourselves.[46]

With this clarion call the Harlem or Negro Renaissance was officially launched, gathering its footing from productions like *Shuffle Along,* the blues of the Smith girls, Bessie, Mamie, Clara, and Trixie, from the blistering tempos of Joe "King" Oliver and his protégé Satchmo Armstrong, and from the defiance of a Jack Johnson, while shedding the mold of the past artistic wave personified by Paul Laurence Dunbar, Frank Webb, Charles Chesnutt, and Du Bois. And Du Bois and the old guard would snap back at the upstarts, but it was all bark and bravado, no bite. In Hughes the movement had a versatile wordsmith and restless wanderer, who was seemingly everywhere during this dynamic historic era. Hughes sounded the alarm and tended the fire, but Alain Locke was the real architect, the inventive thinker and anthologist who kept the books, and deployed the troops. It should be remembered that while the term *New Negro* has been largely attributed to Locke, he was by no means the first to use it. Hubert Harrison, the socialist orator and Garveyite, and James Weldon Johnson had used the expression in titles of newspapers and poetry anthologies, respectively.

Locke, like Hughes, was pretty good with words, and he summed up who and what the New Negro was all about: "He now becomes a conscious contributor and lays aside the status of beneficiary and ward for that of a collaborator and participant in American civilization," Locke said of black people and artists in his essay "Enter the New Negro," written in 1925.

> The great social gain in this is the releasing of our talented group from the arid fields of controversy and debate to the productive fields of creative expression. The especially cultural recognition they win should in turn prove the key to that revaluation of the Negro which must precede or accompany any considerable further betterment of race relationships. But whatever the general effect, the present generation will have added motives of self-expression and spiritual development to the old and still unfinished task of making material headway and progress . . . And certainly, if in our lifetime the Negro should not be able to celebrate his full initiation into American democracy, he can be at least, on the warrant satisfying new phase of group development, and with it a spiritual Coming of Age.[47]

The Harlem Renaissance artists were a varied lot, coming from all over the country and the world, representing a hodgepodge of political tendencies, from assimilationist to separatist to the otherworldly. For the sake of simplicity, if there indeed was aesthetic consensus, it vaguely resembled an inchoate Afrocentricity. That is, black folklore, jazz, the blues, and African themes popped up in plays, song titles, novels, and, above all, the poems. Countee Cullen's "Heritage" is symbolic of this identity with Africa, despite its questioning tone:

> *What is Africa to:*
> *Copper sun or scarlet sea,*
> *Jungle star or jungle track,*
> *Strong bronzed men, or regal black*
> *Women from whose loins I sprang*
> *When the birds of Eden sang?*
> *One three centuries removed*
> *From the scenes his fathers loved,*
> *Spicy grove, cinnamon tree,*
> *What is Africa to me?*

Many of Cullen's detractors had some questions as well about the poet's stance on color, Africa, and if he viewed himself as a black poet. But Cullen was not the only artist under interrogation about his or her aesthetics; in fact, most of the writers and artists of the period were more or less conflicted, haunted by some color, class, sexual, religious, philosophical, or identity dilemma.

Langston Hughes (1902–1967). Hughes was like a colossus whose genius and creativity were as boundless as the horizons he pursued. Considering the magnitude of his literary production, only Du Bois matches Hughes, and no writer possessed his versatility. He was born in Joplin, Missouri, and at an early age his writing talent was evident. Rarely on good terms with his father, who lived in Mexico City, Hughes moved out after a temporary residence with him and returned to the States, soon enrolling at Columbia University. But college could not compete with the allure of nearby Harlem, especially for a young published poet. There were brief encounters with Alain Locke, Du Bois, and other emerging Harlem artists, but the ever restless and curious Hughes was soon on a ship bound for Africa. Traveling through Europe, Hughes met Locke in Paris, who requested some of his poems for publication.

Hughes was working as a waiter at the Wardman Park Hotel in 1925 when he slipped some of his poems under Vachel

Lindsay's plate. Within months, thanks to Lindsay, a noted white poet, Hughes was being sought by major publishing companies, and in 1926 Hughes came out with his first book of poetry, *The Weary Blues*, and followed this success with another collection of poetry, *Fine Clothes of the Jew*.

In 1929 he received his B.A. degree from Lincoln University and began touring the country reading his poetry. Hughes's brief collaboration with Zora Neale Hurston on "Mule Bone" ended with each writer blaming the other for the rift. In the 1940s, after assuming a "fellow traveler" status with Communists, he launched his social satire and biting commentary through his character Jesse B. Semple, who revived Hughes's career. As a lyricist and librettist, he teamed with Kurt Weill, and he recorded a number of albums wherein he recited his poetry or lectured on black history and culture. During his lifetime Hughes worked with, assisted, or influenced nearly every major black artist in America. His essay "The Negro Artist and the Racial Mountain" and his poem "The Negro Speaks of Rivers" are enough to ensure his immortality.

Claude McKay (1889–1948). Much like his colleague Hughes, Jamaican-born McKay was a recognized poet while still in his teens, and at the age of twenty-three, he received a medal from the Jamaica Institute of Arts and Science. There was a brief flirtation with higher education at Tuskegee Institute (1912) and Kansas State University (1913), which only delayed his arrival in Harlem in 1914. He burst on the national scene with his poem "If We Must Die," his furious reaction to the Chicago riot in 1919. Again like Hughes, McKay was not about to rest on his laurels or to rest at all, as he was soon off to Europe and then to Russia, where he would spend six months. Always eager to mix his art with politics, McKay schmoozed with the socialists in London and with Trotsky, Zinoviev, and Bukharin in Russia, where he was invited to address the Fourth Congress of the Third Communist International. A party or two with Russian Communism and the affair was over.

When his itinerary resumed, he settled for longer stays in Berlin, France, and North Africa. From 1922 to 1934 McKay lived abroad, from where he watched his literary fame grow in America. His books included *Harlem Shadows* (1922), a volume of poetry; *Home to Harlem* (1928), the first best-selling novel by a black author; *Banjo* (1929); and while living in Tangiers, he completed *Gingertown* (1932) and *Banana Bottom* (1933), which critics consider his best work.

Thus, during much of the legendary heyday of the Harlem Renaissance, McKay was not around, not that anyone would have cared, especially Garvey, who McKay thought was "a curious blend of bourgeois obsolescence and utopian fantasy," although he confessed an envy of Garvey's mass appeal. Of the Renaissance writers, only the acerbic, neoconservative George Schuyler or the superbly talented but neurotic Wallace Thurman could rival McKay's "signifyin' " and tart impressions of others. Alain Locke, the doyen of the movement, was in McKay's estimation a "remarkable chocolate soufflé of art and politics."[48] And this, according to one gadfly of the period, could have been for McKay a self-assessment, as well.

Four years before his death, McKay was baptized a Roman Catholic. It seemed a fitting end for a young man who had come of age in Clarendon Parish.

Jessie Fauset (1882–1961). Fauset's impeccable work as an editor and novelist was indicative of her background. Born in Camden County, New Jersey, of a father who was a minister in the A.M.E. Church, Fauset knew firsthand about discipline and piety. When she entered Philadelphia's prestigious High School for Girls, she was the only black student. Always an excellent student, she graduated Phi Beta Kappa from Cornell in 1905. Increasingly upwardly mobile, she next did a summer stint at the Sorbonne, and then on to the University of Pennsylvania, where she earned her M.A. in Latin and French in 1919. Her first job was with *The Crisis*, and as literary editor, she nurtured such writers as Langston Hughes, particularly his famous "The Negro Speaks of Rivers," Jean Toomer, George Schuyler, Countee Cullen, and Claude McKay. She honed and polished the Renaissance's "diamonds in the rough." Meanwhile, she was busy crafting her own essays and novels—*There is Confusion* (1924); *Plum Bun* (1929); and *The Chinaberry Tree* (1931). Fauset also devoted a number of years to teaching, and taught French at De Witt Clinton High School in New York City from 1927 to 1944. In 1949 she taught a class at Hampton Institute in Virginia.

Edward Kennedy "Duke" Ellington (1899–1974). Given his sartorial splendor and immaculate taste in the fineries of life, Duke was the perfect nickname for this musical maestro. Product of a solid middle-class family, Duke started piano lessons at six. Thirteen years later he had organized his own ensemble. In 1920 Duke was living in New York City and playing with Barron Wilkins. By 1927 he was once more in charge, leading his band at the Kentucky Club. Soon he was swept up in the contagious rhythm swing of the Harlem Renaissance and a long stay at the famed Cotton Club. But despite his overwhelming popularity at the club, the color barrier remained intact, with only an occasional lapse. With the Depression a fox at the door, and the partying all but over in Harlem, Duke hit the road in 1933. For the next thirty years or more, his reputation would increase beyond category. The Duke Ellington Orchestra epitomized the best of American music; it was a veritable institution, universally loved and always in demand. His band was both a bane and a boon; while it tended to obscure his phenomenal gifts as a pianist, it was also of great importance for the composer and arranger, who had at his disposal an instant playback of his creations. And what creations: "Take the 'A' Train," "Sophisticated Lady," "Mood Indigo," "Caravan," and "Daydream," to mention but a few of his compositions that have become standards.

Gladys Bentley (1907–1960). Bentley arrived in Harlem in 1923 after a childhood of turmoil in Pennsylvania. Though never a major artist, Bentley was nevertheless a very popular entertainer with a rollicking piano style to accompany her lusty voice. Unwilling to camouflage her masculine features, she chose rather to enhance them with stiff-collared shirts, bow ties, and Eton jackets. An evening with her at a cabaret was such a memorable event that more than one author developed characters based on her captivating persona. Having won over her audiences, Bentley felt secure enough finally to step all the way out of the closet, often flaunting her lesbianism. In the late 1920s she secured a recording contract with Okeh Records, and subsequently owned and performed in Barbara's Exclusive Club. Her bizarre appearance and hilarious sense of humor made her one of the Renaissance's most unforgettable personalities.

Jean Toomer (1894–1967). Like so many of the Renaissance's literary lions, Toomer could point to a fairly privileged childhood. Born and raised in Washington, D.C., Toomer was surrounded by accomplishment and prestige; his grandfather was P. B. S. Pinchback, a former lieutenant governor of Louisiana and a wealthy investor. He attended Dunbar High School and then took classes at a number of colleges, without completing any of them. By 1921 his wanderings terminated in Sparta, Georgia, and an administrative job at a small industrial academy. This experience in the rural South was grist for his mill. His articles and essays in major journals soon brought him a gaggle of enthusiastic supporters, among whom were writer Waldo Frank and photographer Alfred Stieglitz. As the southern exposure seeped deeper into Toomer's consciousness, he began to think of putting his impressions into a book. *Cane* (1923) was the remarkable result, although sales were abysmally low. With acclaim came new associations and Toomer gradually drifted away from the Harlem crowd into séances and mystical meetings with such mediums as P. D. Ouspensky, who converted him. In 1924 he spent the summer at Institute for the Harmonious Development of Man under the guidance of Georgi Gurdjieff, a Russian mystic. From this moment on, his obsession for the occult increased. At least this was the general conclusion until after his death when a trunk of his manuscripts were found. The collection is now housed at Fisk University. During the last twenty-seven years of his life, Toomer was a member of the Society of Friends in Doylestown, Pennsylvania.

Joel Augustus Rogers (1880–1966). In Ben Sidran's book *Black Talk* the author mistakenly asserts that J. A. Rogers, who had written an essay entitled "Jazz at Home" in 1925, was a white jazz critic. It was a honest mistake, perhaps based on the assumption that there was no such thing as a black jazz critic in the 1920s. Rogers was not only sufficiently knowledgeable about jazz, he was a journalist, historian, anthropologist, and world traveler with a vast amount of facts at his fingertips about African and African-American history. A native of Jamaica, Rogers arrived in the United States in 1906, and being of light complexion, he learned right away something Marcus Garvey took years to comprehend, if ever—that in America discrimination against blacks extends to all shades. Incensed by the repeated charge that blacks had no history and had made no contribution to the world's culture, Rogers set on a lifetime crusade to correct such misconceptions. He wrongly believed that racial prejudice would subside if whites were aware of what blacks had done to make the world a better place to live. *From "Superman" to Man* (1917), a fictional account of sharp exchanges between a young educated porter and a southern legislator, was Rogers's first book. In rapid succession, at his own expense, came: *As Nature Leads* (1919), *The Maroons of the West Indies and South America* (1921), and *The Ku Klux Spirit* (1923). But his most popular books were the series of volumes on *Sex and Race, The World's Great Men of Color,* and *Africa's Gift to America.* Rogers's facts were often the source of dispute, particularly his mostly unfounded assertions about the possible black ancestry of such historical figures as Beethoven, Warren G. Harding, and Alexander Hamilton. True or false, these charges did nothing to improve Rogers's standing among white historians and some blacks, not that he cared one iota. His major contribution was the sense of race he instilled in a beleaguered people who were sick of hearing they were inconsequential members of the human family.

Zora Neale Hurston (1891–1960). Thanks to the yeoman efforts of author Alice Walker, the world knows a lot more today about the fascinating career and significant accomplishments of Zora Neale Hurston. Hurston's independent spirit was probably directly connected with her having lost her mother at nine. As a student at Howard University, she had her first contact with a member of the soon-to-be Harlem Renaissance—Alain Locke was one of her professors. Her writing career would also began at Howard when she contributed an essay to a student publication called the *Stylus.* By 1925, having authored several notable essays, short stories, and a play, "Color Struck," Hurston took up residence in New York City and began taking classes at Barnard College. She quickly made her mark in anthropology, and was asked by Franz Boas, the nation's preeminent anthropologist, to assist him in a research project. Later, he would recommend her to the Association for the Study of Negro Life and History for a fellowship to gather folklore, jokes, songs, and dances in the South. An ensuing trip to Louisiana for research on voodoo was sponsored by Charlotte Mason, one of the Renaissance's leading patrons of the arts.

This experience led to a series of widely circulated essays and sketches. The Renaissance was practically a memory when her most acclaimed books were published: *Jonah's Gourd Vine* (1934); *Their Eyes Were Watching God* (1937); and *Moses, Man of the Mountain* (1939). Hurston's activities among the denizens of the Renaissance may have been sporadic, but in several ways they were deeply intimate. She was also affiliated with a few white intellectuals such as Fannie Hurst and Carl Van Vechten.

In 1942 she wrote an autobiography, which many pundits suggest is unreliable. But that would not be inconsistent for a complex woman like Hurston who was often making it up as she went. Even towards the end of her life, Hurston, briefly involved with right-wing politics, was still leaving folks guessing. She died in virtual obscurity in her home state of Florida.

A'lelia Walker (1885–1931). An heiress to her mother's empire built from treating black women's hair, A'lelia Walker was spared the poverty her mother experienced. If Harlem was somewhat short of the rumored luster when she arrived in 1914 to manage the headquarters of her mother's beauty empire, in a few years she had restored the gloss. After her mother's death in 1919, Walker took her sizable inheritance—her mother, Madame C. J. Walker, was reputed to be America's first black millionaire—and threw some of the most lavish parties Harlem had ever seen. At any one bash painters, poets, dancers, entertainers, actors, royalty, and racketeers all caroused at either her "Dark Tower" on 136th Street and Lenox, at her apartment on Edgecomb Avenue, or at her magnificent half-million-dollar Villa Lewaro mansion at Irvington-on-the-Hudson.

At six feet tall and rich enough to buy whatever pleased her, Walker was a sight to behold. When she wasn't partying, she was gambling or dancing at Connie's Inn, her favorite nightclub. Like her life, her funeral was a spectacle in which Reverend Adam Clayton Powell, Sr., read the eulogy, Langston Hughes recited a poem in her honor, Mary McLeod Bethune offered a few words, and the singing quartet the Bon Bons sang Noel Coward's "I'll See You Again." She went out in a swinging fashion, Hughes recalled in his book *The Big Sea*, "as she might have liked it."

Charles Johnson (1893–1956). Normally Charles Johnson is thought of as a renowned sociologist and the author of the phenomenal study *The Negro in Chicago* (1922) and *Shadow of the Plantation* (1934). But the astute, erudite scholar also played a decisive role in stimulating the Harlem Renaissance. Johnson was born in Virginia and learned Greek, Hebrew, and Latin from his Baptist minister father, who had learned them from his slave master. Johnson was a graduate of Virginia Union and then completed graduate school work at the University of Chicago.

His research on the Chicago riot of 1919 led to a book he coauthored with Graham Taylor, a white social scientist. Two years later, Johnson was executive director of research and publicity at the Chicago branch of the National Urban League. In 1923 he founded *The Opportunity* and began organizing literary contests, insisting that harmony between the races could be found through literature. By 1928 Johnson was on his way south again, where he assumed the presidency of Fisk University. He is best remembered as one who discovered, nurtured, and supported black writers, to say nothing of his own monumental research in race relations.

BETCHA DIDN'T KNOW

Black Swan Record Company was founded in 1921 by Harry Pace and the Handy music publishing company. Its first hit was Ethel Waters singing "Down Home Blues" and "Oh Daddy." In 1924 the company was sold to Paramount.

BLUES DIVAS

IT'S NOT THAT Bessie Smith (1894–1937) would have felt out of place among the aesthetes—"hokum," as termed by George Schuyler, or the "niggerati," in Zora Neale Hurston's words—who kicked up their heels at one of A'lelia Walker's all-night soirees; she would have been too busy getting ready to take her act on the road. And the road was where Bessie had been since she was a little girl in Chattanooga traveling around with her father, who was a part-time preacher. After she was booted out of a chorus line for being too black, Bessie teamed with Buzzin' Barton in Park's Big Revue in 1914, and then toured with her mentor Ma Rainey (1886–1939) in Fat Chappelle's Rabbit Foot Minstrel Show.

In those days Ma Rainey was the reigning diva of the blues, with pianist/composer Thomas Dorsey as her accompanist; he would later gain fame as the premier gospel composer, penning the often requested "Precious Lord." By the early twenties Bessie had hit her stride and her name was as big as any in the South. Up North, however, she had to take a backseat to Mamie Smith (1883–1946). In 1920 Mamie, along with pianist/composer Perry Bradford, recorded "Crazy Blues" and "It's Right Here for You (If You Don't Get It . . . 'Taint No Fault of Mine)" for Okeh Records. Okeh originally wanted white vocalist Sophie Tucker for the date, but she was busy; oddly, Bessie Smith was rejected in favor of Mamie. These recordings by Mamie were the first solos by a black artist, and a "race record" outstripped Black Swan, the black recording company established by Harry Pace and John Nail. Three weeks after "Crazy Blues" hit the streets, Bradford received a check for ten thousand dollars, which, even in these inflationary times, is a considerable sum, but especially then with many companies leery of a music they dismissed as subversive.

What Mamie Smith and Bradford did was to promote that segment of the blues arranged for recording and the stage, which opened the door for those rougher forms of the music played by itinerant troubadours on the back roads or in the Delta of Mississippi. Nobody can say for certain when the blues began, although many contend that the first time a slaver put his hands on Africans and forced them into the holds of ships, those moans, those wails, announced the arrival of the blues.

W. C. Handy's "Memphis Blues" is often cited as the first published blues, but what about the thousands of unpublished field hollers and shouts, vendors' cries, calls, work songs, and African musical reditions that form the foundation of the music? And to what degree does the "primitive blues" borrow on existing American folk forms and sacred music? What can be said with some degree of certainty is that the popularity of the blues did not occur until the dawn of the twentieth century. At that juncture the musical form took on a new dynamic, becoming extremely personalized with the musician engaging in song with himself or herself, through the African element of call and response.

Sure, the music was increasingly characterized by the solo performance, but paradoxically, it retained that basic spirit of the commune, receiving affirmation from a collective ethos that in turn emphasized the performer's singularity. If one definition will suffice, then here is Ralph Ellison's solo:

The blues is an impulse to keep the painful details and episodes of a brutal experience alive in one's aching consciousness, to finger its jagged grain, and to transcend it, not by consolation of philosophy but by squeezing from it a near-tragic, near-comic lyricism.[49]

If this fails to bring the matter to an elegant head, then there is only one thing left, and that is to find you some Leadbelly, Charley Patton, Blind Lemon Jefferson, Robert Johnson, Son House, Lightin' Hopkins, Mississippi John Hurt, Koko Taylor, Buddy Guy, Muddy Waters, Etta James, Howlin' Wolf, or B. B. King and put them on the box and listen. In all of these performers, and for "numerous of others," as John Lee Hooker used to say, the line between the sacred and the profane, between the angelic voice and the "devil's music," becomes blurred. The singer is at once preacher, shaman, and "Doctor Feel Good," and with the Depression right around the corner, the old blues singer had a number of patients pleading for whatever succor and relief he or she could provide.

WHEN BLACKS WERE RED
—

WHEN THE GREAT Depression arrived in 1929, according to some calendars, many black people did not know the difference. There was nothing new about chronic unemployment, poor housing, and relentless poverty. Of course, consideration must be made for the relative impact of that "Black Tuesday." Its appearance in the South may have been even less noticeable. Maya Angelou offers this informative vignette from those days when she was coming of age in Stamps, Arkansas. "The Depression must have hit the white section of Stamps with cyclonic impact," she writes in *I Know Why the Caged Bird Sings*, "but it seeped into the black area slowly, like a thief with misgivings. The country had been in the throes of the Depression for two years before the Negroes in

Stamps knew it. I think that everyone thought that the Depression, like everything else, was for white folks, so it had nothing to do with them. Our people had lived off the land and counted on cotton-picking and hoeing and chopping seasons to bring in the cash needed to buy shoes, clothes, books and light farm equipment. It was when the owners of cotton fields dropped the payment of ten cents for a pound of cotton to eight, seven and finally five that the Negro community realized that the Depression, at least, did not discriminate."[50]

If there was any relief in sight from the plummeting misery index, it came from the government, and by 1935 one out of every four, or two million blacks, were on the dole. In some urban centers blacks on relief was as high as 40 percent, a figure three or four times as high as the number of whites on relief. Money for rent, a decent place to live, and enough food to eat were increasingly scarce. And with no visible signs of a decrease in discrimination, there was a growing conviction among blacks that no part of their meager budgets should be spent where they could not work. In the mid-thirties "Don't Buy Where You Can't Work!" campaigns occurred mostly in northern cities. At its inception, the campaign in Harlem, with Sufi Hamid wailing from the corners, did not have the best spokesperson. Hamid, arrayed in Nazi riding boots, colorful turbans, with silk scarves flowing from his neck, assailed Harlem store owners for not hiring blacks. Hamid soon earned the sobriquet "Black Hitler" for his anti-Semitic assertions aimed at Jewish store owners. Having accomplished some success, Hamid could not control his excessive denunciations and was arrested for inciting a riot. Hamid's ultimate disappearance was as mysterious as his arrival from Chicago at the start of the Depression. The Jewish community shed no tears over his sudden departure.

Nor did Adam Clayton Powell, Jr., minister at Harlem's most famous Baptist church. Powell believed Hamid and Father Divine, whose missions fed thousands of hungry Harlemites during the Depression, were charlatans who were only interested in using the miserable conditions to promote themselves. While he scorned their efforts, he stepped up his own, joining the picket lines boycotting the stores. From the pulpit and from his newspaper column at the *New York Post*, where he had been asked to write a series of articles on the Harlem riot of 1935, Powell named the companies and public utilities that discriminated against blacks. His rhetoric sounded too much like the Communists to suit some of his detractors, who charged that he was in cahoots with the local Reds. The government-inspired "Red baiting," however, was still a few years away.

Choosing to tar Powell with the Communist brush was purely selective since there were a number of issues—rent strikes, mass marches for the Scottsboro Boys, who had been falsely accused of raping two white women on a train in Alabama in 1932, sits-ins, and unionization drives, rallies against cuts in WPA funds—and other noted demonstrators supporting these causes. There was no use wasting time Red-baiting Benjamin Davis (1903–1964), though; he was an admitted Communist from the day he arrived in Harlem in 1933.

Davis was the product of a privileged black family in Atlanta, and he later attended Amherst College and Harvard Law School. His first big case as an attorney was his defense of Angelo Herndon, a black Communist accused of agitating and "inciting an insurrection" among the unemployed of Atlanta. He lost the case and Herndon was sent to prison; Davis joined the Communist party and moved to New York City after his life was threatened. Among his first duties as a party member was to edit the *Harlem Liberator* and the *Daily Worker*. As a key member of the National Negro Congress, a group independent of the Communist party but friendly, and in various campaigns against racial discrimination, Davis was soon one of Harlem's most visible activists.

In 1942 Davis became the first black Communist to be elected a New York City council member. Davis had been tapped by Powell to succeed him in this position following his bid for Congress. Davis won the election and was reelected in 1945. Like other blacks on the left, Davis was a victim of Cold War tensions, and in 1948 he was indicted under the Smith Act (subversive activity), convicted, and sentenced to prison. The Smith Act was largely a strategy to destroy the Communist party, which had gained a foothold in a number of labor organizations and civic groups. "And ancillary to this insidious move," said Howard "Stretch" Johnson, a party member and a defense witness for the Communists placed on trial, "was the Taft-Hartley Act and the McCarran Act, which effectively put an end to the trade union movement and the Communist party."[51] After his release, Davis returned to Harlem, but the old Red had lost much of the vigor that made him such a formidable opponent of oppression.

During his heyday Davis had done much to revive the Communist zeal that surfaced for a moment when the African Blood Brotherhood and its cadre—Cyril Briggs, Richard B. Moore, Otto Huiswood, Otto Hall, Claudia Jones, and Harry Haywood—were "boring within the Garvey movement," and organizing clandestinely in Harlem. Haywood (1898–1985) would by the late 1920s be one of the chief formulators of the "black nation thesis," the idea that certain states in the South constituted a "Negro nation." As a theoretical construct it was apparently meaningless since the blacks who lived in the so-called "black belt" had no conception of themselves as a nation, even if the other Stalinist definitions of a nation apply.

While it is fair to say that the Communist party had a profound effect on the black community in the early stages of the Depression—its assistance of blacks evicted from their homes, its mobilization of thousands of blacks through the trade unions, legal defense organizations, and cultural groups—it fell short of grabbing its big moment in American history. With the tattered backsides of democracy fully exposed, the Communist party launched impressive campaigns against racism, discrimination, lynchings, Jim Crowism, and many unpopular causes, but just when Uncle Sam was ripe for plucking, they blew it. One of the party's main failures was its inability to overcome the racism among its rank-and-file members. Publicly trying a member for racist behavior—which they did—was no more than a showcase, which did not get at the root causes. Further, the party tended to dominate leadership positions without consideration for developing a black cadre, and this was true even for organizations such as the League of Struggle for Negro Rights, in which blacks were the majority. And these contradictions were exacerbated in the late 1930s when the party set aside its concern for the "Negro question." The party's focus on the problems of black people slowly dissipated and was completely liquidated by the 1950s.

Another prominent factor in the political or ideological race to win the hearts and minds of black people occurred with the election of Franklin Delano Roosevelt to the White House. Roosevelt's first move was to set in motion a program of national welfare, which, though it made no special provisions for blacks, seemed to offer some relief to the pressing social conditions. The hope in the black community was that the newly devised New Deal would not be the same "old raw deal." And the food allowances, clothing allotments, and distribution of surplus commodities was a form of direct relief, and a gift horse accepted without reservation.

INSIDE ROOSEVELT'S CABINET
—

ROOSEVELT'S PUBLIC WORKS Administration helped to reduce the congested living conditions for black families in major urban centers. Black youths flocked to the Civilian Conservation Corps and the Works Progress Administration, where thousands of them gained at least part-time employment. Moreover, there was the National Youth Administration, with the resourceful educator Mary McLeod Bethune, founder of Bethune-Cookman College, at the helm. Through her close association with Eleanor Roosevelt, the president's wife, Bethune had access to the Oval Office and to federal purse strings like no other member of the "Black Cabinet." Many believed that it was with Bethune's encouragement that Mrs. Roosevelt withdrew her membership from the Daughters of the American Revolution in 1939 when the organization denied the use of Constitution Hall for opera singer Marian Anderson. (In light of recent research, it now appears this historic snub is a very complicated incident. The DAR contends Anderson was rejected because the hall was already booked for that Easter Sunday by the National Symphony Orchestra, although this does not obviate the fact that the group had a "white artists only" restriction.)

Perhaps the Roosevelt administration's most effective stroke was the creation of the Black Cabinet, which should be attributed more to such aides as Harold Ickes, secretary of the interior, than to the president himself. It all began when Ickes received permission to bring in a special advisor on black affairs. Peculiarly, the man hired was Clark Foreman, a white liberal from Georgia. The black community was incensed, and when protestations reached a breaking point, Ickes brought Robert Weaver, a black economist, on board as an aide to Foreman. This appointment was followed by several appointments, including Bethune's to the National Youth Association. William Hastie, who held several key positions, was installed as a judge of the Virgin Islands; Editor Robert L. Vann of the *Pittsburgh Courier* was special assistant to the attorney general; and Writer Frank S. Horne served primarily with the federal housing programs. With these notable appointments, Roosevelt's Black Cabinet received its finishing touches.

Overall there were more than a dozen blacks working at the upper echelons of government. Blacks in high places were obviously no guarantee that all was well at the bottom. In fact, trouble was brewing in several agencies, particularly with the recovery programs. Blacks working in industry took exception to the idea that a special low wage might be instituted to ensure their employment. Persuaded by the National Urban League, officials at the National Recovery Act dumped this move, insisting that blacks should demand equal wages even at the risk of being fired. Blacks also faced some disadvantages in agriculture. The Agricultural Adjustment Act of 1933 authorized a decrease in the amount of land used to cultivate tobacco and cotton. Farmers who agreed to restrict crops were to receive payment from the government. This was the theory, but the practice left thousands of workers at the mercy of eviction and without land to till. Soon the dispossessed tenant farmers and sharecroppers, often denied their pay-

ments from the planters, organized the Southern Tenant
Farmers' Union.

SOUNDBITE

"Our principal cash crop was cotton. My father was
able to produce 100 to 150 bales every year, which
provided us with the other necessities of life: clothes,
shoes, medicine, and contributions to church. But
there were no frills. With twelve children to support,
he made certain that nothing was spent on frivolity
and nothing wasted."

—REVEREND RALPH ABERNATHY,
CIVIL RIGHTS ACTIVIST[52]

WITHOUT REGARD
TO RACE OR COLOR

THE SOUTHERN TENANT Farmers' Union, an interracial protest
movement, was located mainly in eastern Arkansas. In the
struggle to win its share of crop reduction payments from the
federal government, the Union was assisted by the Socialist
party. By 1936 the Union claimed more than 25,000 members
in five southern states. But a couple of things were festering
to undermine the organization. Internally there was dissension between the Communists and the Socialists; externally
there were assaults by terrorists that minimized field operations. The relative gains of the Union are best measured in
the cooperation between black and white sharecroppers, how-

ever short-lived. Within a decade all farmers, large, small, or tenant, would feel the impact of the rise of industrial labor.

The history of blacks in industrial labor unions is one of great expectation followed by painful disappointment. From the outset, with the Knights of Labor, formed in 1869, black workers experienced the first setback. "Without regard to race or color" was the union's motto, and to a large degree this call was honored. However, the Knights collapsed before they could make any meaningful change in the relations between labor and management. Replacing the Knights was the American Federation of Labor, founded in 1881. That it was ostensibly a craft union did not auger well for black workers. In the end, its focus, almost solely on the welfare of skilled laborers to the exclusion of the unskilled, left black workers yearning for representation again.

Several Socialist organizations rushed to fill the void, and a few members of these groups, such as Albert Parsons, were formerly affiliated with the Knights of Labor. Parsons, an anarchist and labor organizer, arrived in Chicago in 1873 with his wife, Lucy Parsons (1853–1942)—a former slave of black and Mexican Indian descent—from Texas after his anti-Klan newspaper collapsed. On May 1, 1886, he helped organize the world's first May Day celebration, an event staged ostensibly to win an eight-hour workday. A few days after the affair, a bomb exploded at a rally at Haymarket Square, killing one person and injuring seventy. Shortly thereafter, six policemen died from wounds suffered at the Square, albeit many of the wounds were inflicted by fellow officers who fired indiscriminately into a crowd of unarmed workers.

Hundreds were arrested, but only thirty-one were indicted, from which eight, including Parsons, were selected for prosecution. A biased jury and a prejudiced judge assured the men's conviction, and Parsons was among the four men who were hanged. Lucy, who had been campaigning for the martyrs' freedom during the trial, continued to work in behalf of the oppressed, speaking from state to state on the rights of blacks, workers, and women. For many years she was a tireless organizer for the Socialist Labor party and the Chicago Working Women's Union. She was a founder of the IWW (Industrial Workers of the World), and one of the first women to join the union.

Unlike the AF of L, the IWW, or the "Wobblies," proposed a different line. In its founding charter it stated that "the working class and the employing class have nothing in common." It was to be a racial labor union big enough to embrace all of the unorganized no matter what color, creed, or sex. The Wobblies never wavered from their commitment, but their integrity was powerless against the machinations of government repression, and by 1923 the dream of one "big union" had faded.

A. Philip Randolph (1889–1979) tried to capture what remained of the Wobblies' spirit when he organized his Brotherhood of Sleeping Car Porters in 1924. An exponent of Du Bois's "Talented Tenth," Randolph arrived in Harlem in 1911 already imbued with Socialist ideas. While he defined himself as a "racial radical" and was opposed to the accommodationist philosophy of Booker T. Washington, Randolph espoused a separatist approach to equal rights. In the 1920s after brief alliances with Marcus Garvey and opposition to blacks serving in World War I, Randolph sought political office running for the state comptroller on the Socialist ticket. He received 200,000 votes. But in a few years he was disenchanted with the Socialists, quit the party, and devoted himself to organizing sleeping car porters.

In 1926, after Randolph and the Brotherhood failed to carry out a threatened strike, the organization suffered a loss in membership. Eleven years later, defying rumors of its demise, the Brotherhood signed its first union contract. Working hours were reduced from 400 to 240 a month, and union membership jumped to nearly 15,000. Meanwhile, Randolph waged running battles with the AF of L, challenging its racist exclusionary policy. Randolph's prominence would soar even higher by 1941 when he threatened a march on Washington, protesting segregation in the defense industries. Roosevelt acceded immediately to Randolph's demand and signed Executive Order 8802, prohibiting segregation in the defense industries.

SOUNDBITE

"I consider my life story as part of the worldwide struggle for freedom. As a black man from the South U.S.A. and a black auto production worker in Detroit, my experience has proved to me that history is the record of the fight of all oppressed people . . . to get human freedom in this world."

—CHARLES DENBY,
AUTO WORKER AND AUTHOR OF
THE INDIGNANT HEART[53]

DOUBLE V CAMPAIGN

ON DECEMBER 7, 1941, almost six months after Roosevelt ended segregation in the defense industries, Pearl Harbor was attacked. It was a day, Roosevelt had intoned, "that would live in infamy." It was a day, too, in which a courageous black sailor, Dorie Miller, shot down four Japanese planes. Miller, of Waco, Texas, a messman aboard the battleship USS *Arizona*, had come topside to remove a wounded captain. After a gunner was shot, Miller took his place behind the machine gun and brought down four enemy planes before the sinking battleship had to be abandoned. For his "distinguished devotion to duty, extreme courage, and disregard of his personal safety during attack," Miller was awarded the Navy Cross. His heroism helped to influence the navy to end its discriminatory policy that restricted black enlistees to the messman branch. Still, it would not be until late 1942 that Bernard Robinson was sworn in as the first black officer in the navy.

And if black sailors were up to their bell-bottom trousers in trouble overseas, the situation was just as intolerable at bases in the States. In the fall of 1944, fifty black seamen stood accused of mutiny. The attorney sent by the NAACP to defend them was Thurgood Marshall. These sailors on trial were the survivors of the worst domestic disaster of the war: the explosion at Port Chicago, California, that claimed 320 lives, including 202 black men. After the explosion, which had a number of causes, including the rushed handling of loaded munitions, white seamen who survived received leaves to recuperate; blacks were ordered to return to work. Over 200 black men refused to march to the still dangerous docks. Fifty of them were singled out for court-martial and charged with mutiny.

The trial took six weeks, but the jury reached a verdict in eighty minutes. All fifty black seamen were found guilty of mutiny. Sentences ranged from a minimum of five years to the maximum of fifteen years. Dishonorable discharges awaited them after they served their time. Appeals were filed immediately, and even Eleanor Roosevelt got involved in the case. Not until the war was over did the men have their sentences reduced. Eventually forty-seven of the men were released from prison but not from the navy. There was a "probationary period" they had to endure before returning to civilian life.

Conditions were no better for black women who wished to join the armed forces. The WAVES, the navy's women's reserve, did not allow black women to enlist until 1944, almost two years after it was officially organized. And the situation was the same in the SPARS, the women's coast guard reserve, which also did not allow black women in until the war was almost over. The other branches of the armed forces never made an attempt to enlist black women.

As Langston Hughes would later confirm, the merchant marines was always open for black seamen, although there is no way to say for certain since it did not keep files by color or race. There were fourteen Liberty ships, some of them possessing names of the historically black colleges or figures. Among the fleet's captains, four of them were black, including Hugh Mulzac, who daringly piloted his ship, the SS *Booker T. Washington*, across the submarine-infested Atlantic Ocean seven times. Mulzac had gained much of his experience working as a captain for Marcus Garvey's ill-fated Black Star Line.

Though there were a number of folk tales about blacks who could fly, the U.S. Army Air Force was unconvinced, whether blacks had wings or not. Dale White and Chauncey Spencer did not have the wings of angels, but they knew how to handle a plane, and they flew from Chicago to Washington to demonstrate that blacks could learn to fly. But this was a fact as early as 1922 when Bessie Coleman astonished Europe—since no aviation school in America would let her in—with her gravity-defying aerial feats. And there was Willa Brown, who operated a flying school in Chicago. It would be remiss to ignore Hubert Julian, who was dubbed the "Black Eagle." The flamboyant Julian went to Ethiopia in 1935 and offered his services to the emperor Haile Selassie during the war against the Italian invaders. When he returned to the States, he frequently lectured on his exploits, but he was not accepted for flight duty in the United States Army Air Force during World War II.

White and Spencer ultimately achieved their purpose and a program of civilian pilot training for blacks was established. Not too long after the raid on Pearl Harbor, the army air forces began training a few black cadets at Tuskegee Institute. These cadets were in the air forces but were prohibited from enjoying the full status of the position. As it had done with the training of black officers at Fort Des Moines during World War I, the army had no serious intention of using the pilots once they qualified; it had acted out of political expediency, and it was hoped the training alone would end the protest.

Despite the indifference from commanding officers, the black airmen of the 99th Fighter Squadron gradually earned their wings. When Captain Benjamin O. Davis, Jr., a graduate of West Point, took over the unit, he instilled a military discipline commensurate with his temperament as a veteran commissioned officer. He even learned to fly, though the instructors complained that he banked his plane with the kind of square turn more appropriate on the parade grounds at the Academy. Segregation remained intact at the base in Tuskegee, with only a few airmen given an opportunity to serve in nonsegregated units at other bases. A plan to send some of the airmen to Liberia fell through because the Liberian government did not want the high salaries they would command to impact on the nation's fragile economy.

North Africa was the next designation, and the airmen were only slightly better prepared than the Hell Fighters when they landed in France in 1918. Unfortunately, the airmen were assigned to the 33rd Fighter Group, with 40 percent of its white pilots from the South. It was a case of flyboys and just plain "boys." Although the black airmen were insulted and disrespected, they never lost sight of their military objective: They came to fly and to engage in combat. Which they finally did in the summer of 1942, flying missions over the island of Pantelleria in the Mediterranean. Within a month First Lieutenant Charles Hall scored the unit's first verifiable hit. It was the first African American hit since Eugene Bullard had downed a German plane during World War I.

Then came the charges: The black airmen lacked the aptitude to fly combat missions, they were not aggressive enough, their reflexes were too slow, and they lacked stamina. Army command failed to consider that the squadron was never up to full strength, having ten fewer pilots than the white squadrons. If the unit was going to meet its quota of hours in the sky, each black airman would have to log more than his required hours, and this led to physical fatigue. It was another no-win situation. After Captain Davis was transferred from the unit, Spanky Roberts, an excellent black pilot and inspirational leader, shaped up the unit. By the time the war in Europe was over in the spring of 1945, the black 332nd—made up of the 99th, 100th, 310th, and 302nd Squadrons—was escorting bombers deep into Germany. And they lost nary a bomber under their escort, even though the enemy was using newly developed jet-propelled planes. First Lieutenant Roscoe Browne, flying a P-51D, downed one of the jets. The black airmen scored a number of decisive hits, but they went unrecognized, and only years after the war was over did they receive the honor they deserved.

More than one million black men and women served in

several branches of the armed services during World War II, and half of them saw action overseas. Many of them took part in the celebrated invasion of Normandy, though the media and history books provide scant word of their heroic performance. One black veteran, Charles Gates of the 761st Tank Battalion, recounts his experience during the great invasion: "In '44, General [George] Patton requested the best separate battalion they had left in the United States. He wanted 'em for the Third Army. We weren't in a division. Patton had made a statement that Negroes were incapable of being tankers. The equipment was too technical. And who should General Patton see when he went into the armored field? Us. Here we come, the best they had left in the United States."

The "Double V Campaign" symbolized a determination by blacks to fight against the enemy at home and abroad. And on both fronts the attacks were fierce, but black Americans were equally ferocious and resolved not "to back up one iota," Paul Robeson once asserted. Heavy influxes of black migrants from the South overwhelmed the segregated urban enclaves. Added to the housing shortage and the lack of public services, blacks were surrounded by race-baiters and hate-mongers, and the law enforcement officials were impotent and unable to check the rage that erupted between the groups. During the war Harlem and Detroit experienced their worst race riots in history. Faced with fighting on two fronts, it was amazing that black Americans were able to contribute as well as they did in the plants and the various "arsenals of democracy."

Black women, in particular, stepped into the grueling foundry and factory jobs when black men were drafted into the army. Yes, some of the Rosie the Riveters and Tillie the Toilers were black women. But their jobs were often the "dirtiest and most taxing jobs," Paula Giddings writes in her study *When and Where I Enter*. "In the steel mills they were assigned to the sintering plants as grinders; in the defense industries they were more often than not in custodial positions."[54] By the end of the war black women represented a sizable portion of the workforce in every war industry. In the auto plants of Detroit, many converted to produce war machinery, black women were on the assembly line, in the pits, and tending the smelters. The bulk of them had managed the transition from mostly domestic work to factory jobs without a hitch. As the war wound down, they knew their days were numbered at the plant and the lucky ones would be able to return to housework; the rest were destined for the unemployment lines, along with a host of black veterans.

BETCHA DIDN'T KNOW

In 1993 Brigadier General Clara Adams-Ender, commanding general of Fort Belvoir, Virginia, and deputy commanding general of the Military District of Washington, was the highest-ranking woman on active duty in the army. During her thirty-three-year career in the service, she has been chief of nursing for Walter Reed Medical Center, chief of the Army Nurse Corps during the Persian Gulf crisis, and director of personnel for the army surgeon general. She is also the recipient of the Distinguished Service Medal.

SOUNDBITE

"I heard it was in the Clef Club [in Minneapolis] that the beautiful and democratic singer Peggy Lee convinced Benny Goodman to hire Lionel Hampton as the first black musician in a major white big band."

—NELSON PEERY,
AUTHOR AND ACTIVIST[55]

BIGGER, BIRD, AND THE MAN
FROM CAT ISLAND
—

IN SEVERAL WAYS World War II, like the previous war, expanded the horizons of black Americans, many of whom had never ventured beyond the small towns and urban jungles. The restriction to farms and ghettoes not only narrowed their global dimensions, it also imposed limitations on the imagination. Blacks in the armed forces were among the first to break the bounds, but the artists were right behind them. Richard Wright, James Baldwin, Ralph Ellison, Ann Petry, Chester Himes, Gwendolyn Brooks, William Attaway, Willard Motley, and Dorothy West were a few post–World War II writers who refused to allow white America to choose their subjects or to define their art. And they were joined by rebels from the musical realm, especially those iconoclastic jazz innovators such as Charlie "Yardbird" Parker, Dizzy Gillespie, Thelonious Monk, Kenny Clarke, Bud Powell, Charlie Mingus, and Max Roach, who would shake the very foundations of swing music with a revolutionary sound. Vocalists, too, would feel the pulse of this new urgency and pair their lyrical inventions with the lengthy, well-known solos. The song form Satchmo Armstrong had virtually invented by accident during a recording session in the 1920s when his music fell from the stand and he had to improvise the words was perfected by Eddie Jefferson and King Pleasure many years later and properly titled "jazz vocalese." They both had popular versions of James Moody's extended solo on "I'm in the Mood for Love," which every hipster committed to memory:

(Boy)
There I go, there I go, there I go, there I go . . .
Pretty baby you are the soul who snaps my control
Such a funny thing but every time you're near me

I never can behave
You give me a smile and then
I'm wrapped up in your magic
There's music all around me, crazy music
Music that keeps calling me so very close to you
Turns me your slave
Come and do with me any little thing you want to
Anything baby just let me get next to you
Am I insane or do I really see heaven in your eyes
Bright as stars that shine up above you
In the clear blue skies
How I worry 'bout you
Just can't live my life without you
Baby come here and have no fear
Oh, is there wonder why I'm really feeling
In the mood for love
So tell me why stop to think about this weather my dear
Each little dream might fade away
There I go a talkin' out of my head again
Won't you come and put our two hearts together
That would make me strong and brave
Oh, when we're one I'm not afraid, I'm not afraid,
If there's a cloud up above us go on and let it rain
I'm sure our love together will endure a hurricane
Oh, my baby won't you let me love you
Give me some relief from this awful misery

(Girl)

What is all this talk bout loving me my sweet
I am not afraid, not anymore, not like before
Don't you understand me
Now baby please pull yourself together do it soon
My soul's on fire
Come and take me I'll be what you make me, my darling
My dear

(Boy)

Oh, baby
You make me feel so good

Let me take you by the hand
Come let us visit out there in that
new promise land
Maybe there we can find
A good place to use a loving state of mind
I'm so tired of being without
And never knowing what love's about
James Moody, you can come and blow now, if you want to
We're through.

There were a number of black nonconformist painters, dancers, sculptors, actors, critics, and intellectuals who had traveled widely and been exposed to a variety of modern themes and techniques. Experiences in Paris, Rome, London, Stockholm, Copenhagen, even in Moscow had enlarged and sharpened their perspectives, and they knew now that there was more to life and possibility than the outskirts of Peoria and East St. Louis. With this improved focus, blacks, and certainly black thinkers, began to see through deception and trickery, to improvise on the shoddy hands fate had dealt them, to understand better their overall mission, both from an individual and a collective standpoint. Whether in Hollywood, on Broadway, Madison Avenue, Tin Pan Alley, or Main Street, blacks were poised for a change, and this time they were not going for the okeydoke, so they said.

BETCHA DIDN'T KNOW

Harry Belafonte's *Calypso* (1955) was the first album to sell a million copies.

Richard Wright (1908–1960). At the center of Richard Wright's artistic truth was the idea that black people were America's metaphor. His first and last impulse, through sev-

eral novels, poems, short stories, and essays, was to distill his
art from his own turbulent life and experiences. The opening
salvo *Uncle Tom's Children* (1938), a collection of four short
stories, provided a startling glimpse into the sharecropper existence from which he sprang. Like the protagonist in a
"Long Blacksong," one of the short stories in *Uncle Tom's
Children*, Wright cannot escape his past, a past, quite paradoxically, that feeds his imagination and from which he draws
inspiration. For this book he won a literary prize from *Story*
magazine.

In 1940 Wright rocked the literary world with *Native Son,* a
searing portrait of a conflicted black youth searching for self-
identity and struggling to overcome a hostile environment.
Bigger Thomas is the troubled black boy at the center of this
best-seller—it sold more than a quarter of a million copies in
one month—and when he is not an aggressive brute, he's
quaking in fear. His behavior may be unpredictable, but his
fate is not. Given the sordid circumstances of his life and his
psychopathic reaction to them, death at an early age is assured. Bigger is a doomed cretin who only feels alive when
he kills. After he accidentally kills Mary Dalton, a blind white
woman, Bigger panics and he flees in fear. When he next
bludgeons his girlfriend to death, there is no turning back;
there are no more refuges, no constructive gain from his
mindless rebellion.

In 1942 Wright broke with the Communist party after being
a member for twelve years. Three years later he completed
his next blockbuster, *Black Boy,* a detailed account of his
youth. By 1946 Wright, his wife, and daughter left for Paris,
France, where he would reside for the rest of his life. He
wrote four more novels, a book of short stories, and several
nonfiction works, including the provocative *White Man, Listen!*
(1957). *Black Power* (1954), and *Pagan Spain* (1957) were also
well received. During his final years Wright returned to writing poetry, particularly haikus, a Japanese poem form of three
lines and seventeen syllables. He was also finishing the editing
on a collection of short stories that was posthumously issued
as *Eight Men.*

Ann Petry (1911–). A native of Saybrook, Connecticut,

Petry, until a few years ago, lingered in the shadows of Wright, Ralph Ellison, and other noted literary peers. But with the reissue of her remarkable novel *The Street* (1946), her popularity has increased. Petry, a graduate of the University of Connecticut with a degree in pharmacy—a family tradition—did not begin her writing career until she was in her thirties. Her short stories first appeared in *Phylon* and *The Crisis* in 1943. Within a couple of years she had begun a novel whose earlier chapters were enough to win her a fellowship. For a while she worked as a reporter for the *Amsterdam News,* an experience that provided her insight on the naturalistic effects of her novel.

Despite the success of this novel, Petry remained rather obscure, and by 1948 she had left New York City and returned to her hometown. Her novel *Country Place* (1947) is in sharp contrast to the urban naturalism that pervades *The Street.* The change in environment induced a change in characters, plot, and style. The most noticeable change is that all the characters in *Country Place* are white.

In her novel *The Narrows* Petry splits the difference, and the protagonist Link Williams is black, while his wife, Camilo, is white. Her rich, deep prose won her new supporters, despite the novel's complexity and the intricately woven subplots. The next shift aroused very little attention as Petry immersed herself in the writing of children's books. *Harriet Tubman: Conductor of the Underground Railroad* (1955) garnered praise, especially from schoolteachers and librarians. *Miss Muriel and Other Stories* (1971), coming as it did amid the wave of black nationalism, did not bring the recognition many critics deemed it warranted.

Since the mid-1970s she has continued to write, with teaching stints at the University of Hawaii.

James Baldwin (1924–1987). It is still debated in literary circles whether Baldwin was a better novelist than a essayist. That it has been a debate at all should be enough to recommend his brilliance no matter what idiom Baldwin chose. Before Baldwin packed his typewriter and Bessie Smith albums and left for Paris in the late 1940s, he was considered the quintessential Harlemite. Born and raised in Harlem, Baldwin spent his youth evading a vituperative stepfather and consuming every book in the Countee Cullen Public Library. As a member of a Pentecostal church, young Baldwin was soon in the pulpit himself, but by the time he was seventeen, he renounced the church and moved out of his father's house.

A voracious reader, Baldwin fell under the influence of Richard Wright after reading *Uncle Tom's Children* and *Native Son*. During Baldwin's first years in Paris, Wright was a resourceful companion, helping him to win a scholarship to complete his first novel *Go Tell It on the Mountain* (1953). Meanwhile, he had already written several powerful essays criticizing Wright's novels that would sever his relationship with his mentor. It was necessary, some authorities contend, in order for Baldwin to establish his own literary voice and place.

Though his first novel did not hit with the impact of his "literary" father's, it did not go unnoticed. At the core of the riveting novel is the Grimes family, with its hellfire-and-brimstone patriarch. That this is an artistic rendering of Baldwin's tormented childhood is irrefutable. And his other novels would also capture episodes of his life, particularly his doubts about his identity and sexuality. *Giovanni's Room* (1956) and *Another Country* (1962) are both entangled with racial, sexual, and cultural issues.

Over the succeeding years, especially during the civil rights movement, Baldwin spent more time in America, and his popularity reached its peak. And his intimate association with the movement and such notable leaders as Dr. Martin Luther King, Jr., affected him greatly. *Tell Me How Long the Train's Been Gone* (1968) and *If Beale Street Could Talk* (1974) were direct products of this period. *Just Above My Head* (1979) found Baldwin back on the familiar turf of religion and sexuality.

Along with his novels came the volumes of essays, plays, screenplays—*One Day, When I Was Lost* (1972) was Baldwin's script on the life of Malcolm X on which Spike Lee based his version—and *Evidence of Things Not Seen* (1985), his last nonfiction piece, about the Atlanta child murders.

At the time of his death he was working on a play and a biography of Martin Luther King, Jr.

Charlie Parker (1920–1955). "Bird," as Parker was known

to intimates and eventually to the world, soared only a brief while over the jazz firmament, but his flight was majestic and unequaled. Parker was thirteen when he began studying the alto saxophone, and within two years he was already playing among the top musicians in the hotly competitive Kansas City area. In 1939 Parker made his first visit to New York City; he stayed for a year and began experimenting with different changes, playing, as he said, "on the higher intervals of the chord as a melody line."

From 1940 to 1942 he traveled with Jay McShann and took part in his first recording session in 1941 in Dallas. After serving a fruitful apprenticeship with McShann, Parker joined Earl "Fatha" Hines's band and then went on to Billy Eckstine's famed bebop band, which included Dizzy Gillespie, Gene Ammons, Sonny Stitt, Sarah Vaughan, Art Blakey, King Kolax, Linton Garner (Errol's brother), Miles Davis, and Fats Navarro. When Eckstine's band was in the New York City area, Parker and his cohorts would venture up to Harlem, where they polished their skills, and further experimented, at jam sessions held at Minton's Playhouse and Monroe's Uptown House.

The jam sessions, nights on the road, and relentless practicing made Parker the most talented and innovative of the emerging bebop giants. It was at this juncture that he and Gillespie began to front ensembles under their leadership. In 1945 Parker and Gillespie bopped Hollywood with a scintillating sound, but this success was soon overshadowed by Parker's nervous breakdown and addiction to alcohol and heroin. Bird was on the horse, so to speak, and it would be a torturous, endless ride, and considering the torment and horrendous side effects, it is simply amazing he left such a wealth of music behind.

By 1947 Parker had formed one of his most prolific bands, featuring Miles Davis (trumpet), Duke Jordan (piano), Tommy Potter (bass), and Max Roach (drums). Parker kept this band intact for about four years, recording such jazz standards as "Scrapple from the Apple," "Ornithology," "Round Midnight," "Donna Lee," "Parker's Mood," and "Yardbird Suite."

Parker was stripped of his New York cabaret license in 1951, and for two years his employment was hampered. Back in action in 1953, Parker was in poor physical and mental health. After two suicide attempts he was admitted to Bellevue Hospital in New York City. On March 5, 1955, Bird flew for the final time at Birdland, a club named in his honor. He died seven days later in the apartment of Baroness Pannonica de Koenigswarter at the Hotel Stanhope in New York City.

Dorothy Dandridge (1922–1965). To the fallow, colorless fifties the emergence of Dorothy Dandridge on the Hollywood scene brought a spark of glamorous relief. Following in her mother, Ruby's, footsteps (Ruby had a number of minor roles in films, but it was her portrayal of Oriole on the "Beulah" radio show that brought her the most popularity), Dorothy began singing and dancing with her sister Vivian at an early age. During the Depression the Wonder Girls, as they were called, had few opportunities to show their stuff, although if you pay close attention to the Marx Brothers movie *A Day at the Races* (1937), they can be seen briefly performing with vocalist Ivie Anderson, once a singer with Duke Ellington's Orchestra.

The girls made one more film appearance with Louis Armstrong and Maxine Sullivan in *Going Places* (1939). By the early 1940s Dorothy was a solo act and featured in several musical shorts, including *Paper Doll* with the Mills Brothers. Her appearance in *Sun Valley Serenade* is memorable because of her performance with her soon-to-be first husband, dancer Harold Nicholas of the Nicholas Brothers. The marriage did not last long, and Dorothy returned to her career with vigor.

Now she could pursue her dream of getting more than cameo parts, to eclipse the impact made by Nina Mae McKinney, Fredi Washington, and Lena Horne. There was a modicum of success in such forgettable films as *Tarzan's Peril* (1951), *The Harlem Globetrotters* (1951), and *Bright Road* (1953). Her most sizzling and realized performance came in 1954 when she starred in *Carmen Jones*. For her sultry portrayal Dandridge received an Oscar nomination, the first by a black woman in a leading role.

In 1957 she broke a long-standing taboo in Hollywood: She played a romantic lead opposite white actor John Justin in *Island in the Sun*. The film was the source of much attention, but Dorothy's quest for stardom was still not fulfilled. Nor would she do any better as Bess in *Porgy and Bess* (1959).

Then would come a succession of miserable B flicks with Dorothy the only attraction, but the silver screen was fading to black for the bronze beauty. In her final days there was a momentary fling in the intimidating nightclubs, and a flicker of renewal, but for Dorothy there was no second act, if she really ever had the first. A few weeks after signing a movie contract she was found dead in Los Angeles from an overdose of an antidepressant.

Sidney Poitier (1927–). At one time it was almost possible to tell the nature of American race relations by Sidney Poitier's next film. This is an obvious exaggeration; however, it does indicate how closely aligned his career has been to the changing dynamics of Hollywood and how it has dealt with black images. When Poitier arrived in New York City from Cat Island in the Bahamas, he was still a teenager with empty pockets. To survive he plucked chickens, washed dishes, worked on the docks, and held an assortment of menial jobs. After answering an ad in New York's *Amsterdam News* from the American Negro Theatre (ANT), Poitier auditioned and was told by Frederick O'Neal, the theater's director, to scram and seek his fortune doing something else. "You're no actor," O'Neal told the dejected Poitier.

Poitier believed it was his accent that blocked his chances on the stage. For six months he worked hard on his speech, returned to the ANT, and was accepted as a member of a repertory group that included Ossie Davis, Ruby Dee (who later became Davis's wife), Earle Hyman, Harry Belafonte, and Lloyd Richards, now a noted director. He had gathered a small amount of experience when, as if blessed by the gods, he won a role in *No Way Out* (1950). It was a solid part, one that would have excited his Hollywood predecessors, James Edwards, Clarence Muse, and Paul Robeson. Clearly this was no Mantan Moreland, Eddie "Rochester" Anderson, Willie Best, or Stepin Fetchit buffoonery. And the list of serious parts would continue through the 1950s with *Cry the Beloved Country* (1952), *Red Ball Express* (1952), and *Blackboard Jungle* (1955), among several others.

In this early phase of his career Poitier's roles were practically devoid of politics. As the civil rights movement roared into the national picture, his parts took on a bolder tone—*Edge of the*

City (1957) and *The Defiant Ones* (1958). In the early 1960s he finally hit his stride with *A Raisin in the Sun* (1961), and there was talk about an Oscar, but that would have to wait until *Lilies of the Field* (1963). His Oscar for *Lilies* was the first for a black actor since Hattie McDaniel won one for supporting actress in *Gone With the Wind* in 1939. Then, as if to offer a flip side of the defiant, militant posture, Poitier took a series of roles wherein his characters assert no strong black racial identity, and this perturbed his fans: *A Patch of Blue* (1965), *To Sir With Love* (1967), and *Guess Who's Coming to Dinner?* (1967).

In the 1970s Poitier was the odd man out, as Melvin Van Peebles and Ron O'Neal set a new course with their fashionable antiheroes, signaling the arrival of "blaxploitation films." But the ever resilient Poitier was back on top again in 1972 with the totally engrossing *Buck and the Preacher,* which he directed and starred in with Harry Belafonte. His confidence as a director went up a notch after a batch of hilarious comedies with Bill Cosby, including *Uptown Saturday Night* (1974) and *Let's Do It Again* (1975).

Throughout the 1980s Poitier devoted much of his attention to directing, with an occasional role, if one came along, to his liking. Most recently his role in *Sneakers* (1993), though respectable, did not place him among the top box office attractions.

SOUNDBITE

"It's much better to play a maid than to be one. The only choice permitted me is either to be a servant at seven dollars a week or portray one for seven hundred dollars a week."

—HATTIE MCDANIEL (1895-1952),
ACTRESS, SINGER[56]

TO SECURE THESE RIGHTS
—

SIDNEY POITIER WAS still trying to lighten the *a*'s and remove the singsong pattern from his speech when President Harry S Truman issued an order calling for equal opportunity throughout the armed services in 1948. He had already appointed a blue-ribbon committee of prominent black and white Americans to inquire into the condition of civil rights and to make recommendations for improvement. This was the *To Secure These Rights* report. Truman's new armed services policy further increased enlistments among blacks, which were already moving along at a record pace since, for the first time in history, blacks had been formally invited to join the peacetime military.

Perhaps President Truman had taken his cue from the Brooklyn Dodgers, who a year earlier had signed Jackie Robinson to be the first black player in major league baseball. Robinson's breakthrough was good news for civil rights but bad news for the old Negro Leagues, where "only the ball was white" and where such all-time greats as Josh Gibson, Ray Dandridge, Oscar Charleston, and Judy Johnson toiled in obscurity. And there was Cool Papa Bell, who was so fast, they say, he could cut off the light and be in bed before the room got dark, and also the inimitable Leroy "Satchel" Paige, whose folky aphorisms—"Don't look back, something might be gaining on you"—were just as poignant as his fastball and hesitation pitch were unhittable.

As a few domestic walls were being toppled, the United States began to chip away at its isolationist policy, those international barriers. A new world order was in order, particularly with such a lethal arsenal stockpiled, making total annihilation a real possibility. To offset this danger the United Nations Organization was established in San Francisco in 1945. It was too big an endeavor to escape the notice of black America.

Walter White, Mary McLeod Bethune, W. E. B. Du Bois, were all invited to the UN as observers. Of deeper significance was the presence of Ralph Bunche (1904–1971), the State Department's acting chief of the Division of Dependent Territories. A native Detroiter, Bunche won distinction as an athlete and scholar, graduating with honors from the University of California in 1927. Seven years later he earned his Ph.D. in political science from Harvard. During World War II he worked with the Office of Strategic Services, and later contributed to Gunnar Myrdal's classic study *An American Dilemma*.

At the UN Bunche helped to draw up the charter for all trusteeships and territories. From 1948 to 1954 he served as director of the Department of Trusteeship and Non-Self-Governing Territories, and in the interim was awarded the Nobel Peace Prize in 1950 for mediating the Arab-Israeli crisis. From 1957 to 1967 he was the undersecretary of Special Political Affairs. In 1968 as undersecretary general, Bunche held the highest rank of any American at the UN.

Having a notable black at the UN may have provided some extra stimulus to the NAACP in 1947 when it presented a 155-page document to the body's Office of Social Affairs. The demand was for a redress of grievances on human rights, which the document declared were denied African-Americans. There would be other grievances presented to the UN by the National Negro Congress, a coalition founded in 1936 by trade unionists, civil rights activists, church groups, and fraternities, and one filed by the Civil Rights Congress in 1951 in which the authors, principally attorney William Patterson and Paul Robeson, charged the United States with genocide.

ROBESON AND ROBINSON

THAT PAUL ROBESON was in a position to assist Patterson was remarkable, given the intense condemnation and the relentless attacks from the State Department. Two years earlier, in April 1949, Robeson, never one to concede a principle, had made statements in Paris at a World Peace Congress that the press effectively misconstrued. The wealth of America, Robeson said, had been built "on the backs of millions of blacks ... And we are resolved to share it equally among our children. And we shall not put up with any hysterical raving that urges us to make war on anyone. Our will to fight for peace is strong. We shall not make war on anyone. We shall not make war on the Soviet Union."

Purporting to quote from Robeson's speech, the Associated Press released a statement that was picked up across the United States: "It is unthinkable that American Negroes would go to war on behalf of those who have oppressed us for generations against a country [the Soviet Union] which in one generation has raised our people to the full dignity of mankind ..."[57]

With this distortion Robeson found himself between cries of traitor from white America and denial from blacks, who rushed to insist that he did not speak for them. In an atmosphere in which the Cold War, the ideological conflict between the United States and the Soviet Union, was in its initial stages, when the Smith Act, which made it unlawful for anyone to advocate the overthrow of the United States, was in effect, when the Trenton Six (condemned to death for allegedly murdering a white man, they were spared execution, but all received life imprisonment) and Willie McGee (convicted and later executed for allegedly raping a white woman in Mississippi) were being railroaded, and when the House Un-American Activities Committee (HUAC) was revving up its repressive machinery and beginning to serve subpoenas, Robeson's best bet was to seek sanctuary out of the country, although that, too, would soon be a problem when his passport was lifted by the State Department.

Robeson's remarks were made to order for HUAC, not that they needed any incentive. It was time for a loyalty check among black Americans. Two hundred years of dedication and fighting heroically in every war, yet there was still some doubt about the loyalty of black Americans. Such a charge was preposterous to most black and white citizens, but the die was cast and HUAC was determined to smoke out the "pinkos," those Communists waiting to strike at the heart of democracy.

Among the most celebrated to hear the question "Are you now and have you ever been a member of the Communist party?" was Jackie Robinson. And his appearance before the HUAC committee was all the more baffling and ironic since he was there expressly to denounce Robeson, a man who had worked so tirelessly to break the color bar in the major leagues. Assessing his remarks before the committee, it was not so much Robinson versus Robeson as the ballplayer's patriotic zeal on display, a zeal that may have been prompted in part by information disclosing Robinson's membership in the Young Communist League while a student at UCLA. "I can't speak for any fifteen million people any more than any other person can," Robinson said toward the end of his testimony. "But I know that I've got too much invested for my wife and child and myself in the future of this country, and I and other Americans of many races and faiths have too much invested in our country's welfare, for any of us to throw it away because of a siren song sung in bass."[58]

Robinson had done a little singing of his own, and when the testifying was over he would go on to win Most Valuable Player in the National League; he didn't exactly strike out before HUAC, either. If 1949 was a banner year for Robinson, it was a bummer for Robeson. In 1948 he had thrown his support wholeheartedly behind the presidential candidacy of the Progressive Party nominee, Henry Wallace, who ran a poor fourth behind even Strom Thurmond. Now the towering singer/activist had been denounced by the people's choice, Jackie Robinson. What next? he might have asked. Peekskill.

The quiet dignity, courage, and uncompromising integrity that defined Paul Robeson (1898–1976) was fully tested at Peekskill, New York, in 1949. After the first Peekskill concert in August ended in a melee (Robeson never made it to the picnic grounds on this occasion), members of the Civil Rights Congress planned another one in September. More than 20,000 people were in attendance, and Robeson, surrounded by a phalanx of trade unionists, was in splendid form. When the concert ended, the riot began. For several miles along the roads leading from the grounds, concertgoers were forced to run a gauntlet of brutal thugs and vigilantes, many of them members of the American Legion, who pelted them with rocks and hurled large stones through the windshields of their cars and buses. At least 140 persons were injured and a number of cars were damaged.

Outraged by the attack on innocent people, hundreds of people took their complaint to Governor Thomas Dewey, but he rebuked them, blaming the "Communist groups" for provoking the incident. Robeson and others filed a suit against Westchester County and two veterans' groups. It was a waste of time; three years later the federal court dismissed the case and all charges against the defendants. "The Peekskill affair accelerated many events that were already in progress and made many others possible that seemed only probable before," was how Dr. Charles Wright, a Detroit gynecologist and longtime Robeson scholar, summarized the event. "Republican Senator Joseph R. McCarthy of Wisconsin was already testing the anti-Communism line with which he would strangle the nation with brief and terrifying success."

BETCHA DIDN'T KNOW

The 24th Infantry Regiment, an all-black unit, won the first battle in the Korean War at Yech'on on July 22, 1950.

CHRONOLOGY
—

1950

Dr. Carter G. Woodson, the esteemed historian, founder of the Association for the Study of Negro Life and History, and creator of Negro History Week, died in Washington, D.C., April 3.

Gwendolyn Brooks, author of a collection of poetry, *Annie Allen,* was awarded the Pulitzer Prize for poetry, May 1.

The Supreme Court ruled in *Sweatt v. Painter* that equality in education involved more than identical physical facilities. The plaintiff, Herman Sweatt, was allowed admission to the University of Texas, but Sweatt never attended. On this same day the Court ruled in *McLaurin v. Oklahoma* that once a black student is admitted to a previously all-white school, no distinction can be made on the basis of race. McLaurin had been segregated within the University of Oklahoma, June 5.

Ezzard Charles successfully defended the world heavyweight title against Freddie Beshore (August 15), Joe Louis (September 27), and Nick Barone (December 5).

1951

Prima ballerina Janet Collins, performing in *Aida,* was the first black artist to dance on the stage of the Metropolitan Opera House in New York City. She had earlier won the Donaldson Award for the best dancer on Broadway.

Oscar DePriest of Chicago, who was the first black elected to Congress since George White in 1901, died, May 12.

Private First Class William Thompson of Brooklyn, New York, was awarded the Congressional Medal of Honor (the first by a black soldier since the Spanish-American War) posthumously for heroism in Korea, June 21.

NAACP formally launched an attack on segregation and discrimination at elementary and high school levels, June.

The South Carolina court held that segregation was not discrimination, June 23.

Jersey Joe Wolcott knocked out Ezzard Charles in the seventh round to win the world heavyweight championship in Pittsburgh, Pennsylvania. At thirty-seven, Wolcott was the oldest person to gain the title, July 18.

The 24th Infantry Regiment, last of the all-black units authorized by Congress in 1866, was deactivated in Korea, October 21.

1952

The University of Tennessee admitted its first black student, January 12.

Actor Canada Lee, remembered for his strong portrayal of character roles, particularly his riveting performance in Alfred Hitchcock's *Lifeboat* in 1944, died in New York City, May 9.

Mel Whitfield won the 800-meter race and Harrison "Bones" Dillard won the 110-meter hurdles race at the Summer Olympics at Helsinki.

Author Ralph Ellison published his *Invisible Man* and enjoyed immediate critical and financial success.

Fletcher Henderson, noted pianist and bandleader, whose arrangements were important in the careers of many musicians, including Benny Goodman, died in New York City, December 29.

1953

The movement of black families into previously all-white Trumbull Park housing project in Chicago triggered a continuous three-day riot that took more than one thousand policemen to quell, August 4.

Take a Giant Step, a dramatic play written by Louis Peterson and starring Louis Gossett, Jr., opened on Broadway, September 24.

Hulan Jack was sworn in as borough president of Manhattan, December 31.

Go Tell It on the Mountain, James Baldwin's first novel, was published.

The Outsider, Richard Wright's second novel, was published.

1954

The Supreme Court ruled in the historic *Brown v. Board of Education of Topeka* case that racial segregation in public schools was unconstitutional, May 17.

Mary Church Terrell, a charter member of the National Association of Colored Women and its first president, died in Washington, D.C., July 24.

Benjamin O. Davis, Jr., whose father was a general in the army, became the first black general in the air force, October 27.

Charles C. Diggs, Jr., a licensed mortician, was elected Michigan's first black congressman, November 2.

1955

Emmett Till, a fourteen-year-old from the South Side of Chicago, was lynched near Money, Mississippi, August 28. The incident began when Till, while leaving a store, told a white woman, " 'Bye, baby.'' Three days later the woman's husband, Roy Bryant, and his brother-in-law were told that Mose Wright's nephew was the one who had spoken to his wife.

They drove over to Wright's cabin, and despite his pleading, abducted Till. Three days later Till's body was found with a barbed wire holding a cotton gin fan around his neck, a bullet through his skull, an eye gouged out, and his head crushed on one side. The nation would gaze on Till's battered face in the pages of *Jet* magazine. Bryant and Milam, to everybody's surprise, were quickly indicted for kidnapping. If there was to be a case against the two white men, somebody would have to testify. Till's cousin, Curtis Jones, who witnessed the abduction, was back in Chicago, and his mother forbade him to return to Mississippi for the trial, fearing for his safety. That left only sixty-four-year-old Mose Wright. Wright had not returned to his home since the kidnapping, and though obviously fearful, courageously decided to testify.

On the witness stand Wright stood and pointed to Milam as one of the men who took his nephew away, saying, "Thar he." Next he pointed to Bryant as the other abductor. It was the first time a black man had ever stood in a Mississippi court and accused a white man of killing a black person. Wright's testimony emboldened other blacks to come forward and testify at the trial, and after doing so, all of them, including Wright, were spirited out of the state.

The jury wasted no time reaching a verdict—"Not guilty," said the foreman. Nationwide, the black community took to the streets, protesting another miscarriage of justice. Three months later Rosa Parks, aware of Mose Wright's stance, was ready to take hers.

I AIN'T NO WAYS TIRED!

"WHEN I GOT off from work that evening of December 1, 1955, I went to Court Square as usual to catch the Cleveland Avenue bus home. I didn't look to see who was driving when I got on, and by the time I recognized him, I had already paid my fare. It was the same driver who had put me off the bus back in 1943, twelve years earlier," Rosa Parks recalled. ". . . I saw a vacant seat in the middle section of the bus and took it . . . The next stop was Empire Theater, and some whites got on. They filled up the white seats, and one man was left standing. The driver looked and noticed the man standing. Then he looked back at [the four of] us. He said, 'Let me have those front seats,' because they were the front seats of the black section. Didn't anybody move . . . The man in the window seat next to me stood up, and I moved to let him pass by me, and then I looked across the aisle and saw that the two women were also standing. I moved over to the window seat. I could not see how standing up was going to 'make it light' for me. The more we gave in and complied, the worse they treated us.

". . . The driver of the bus saw me still sitting there, and he asked was I going to stand up. I said, 'No.' He said, 'Well, I'm going to have you arrested.' Then I said, 'You may do that.' . . . Eventually two policemen came. They got on the bus, and one of them asked me why I didn't stand up. I asked him, 'Why do you all push us around?' He said to me, and I quote him exactly, 'I don't know, but the law is the law and you're under arrest.' "

With this defiant act, the civil rights movement was launched. The impression many have of Rosa Parks is that she was just an ordinary seamstress who was too tired to move to the back of the bus that day. Seamstress, yes, but she was by no means tired. "People always say that I didn't give up my seat because I was tired," she explained in her autobiography, "but that isn't true. I was not tired physically, or no more tired than I usually was at the end of a working day. I was not old, although some people have the image of me as being old then. I was forty-two. No, the only tired I was, was tired of giving in."

Parks was not tired. She was a seamstress, but that was an avocation; she made her living as the secretary for the Montgomery NAACP. It must be remembered, too, that she had attended workshops at Highlander Folk School in Monteagle, Tennessee, where she saw it was possible for people of differing races and backgrounds to work together in peace and harmony. And in her autobiography she also dispelled the notion that her act was planned in advance. "People have asked me if it occurred to me then that I could be the test case the NAACP had been looking for. I did not think about that at all. In fact, if I had let myself think too deeply about what might happen to me, I might have gotten off the bus. But I chose to remain."[59]

Parks spent a few hours in jail, was released, and E. D. Nixon, the former head of the Montgomery branch of the NAACP, asked Parks if she would be willing to make her incident a test case against segregation. She agreed, and within days the Montgomery Improvement Association (MIA) was formed, with Dr. Martin Luther King, Jr., then the pastor of Dexter Avenue Baptist, as its president. For the next thirteen months the MIA, along with the Woman's Political Council, led the Montgomery Bus Boycott. During the boycott, Dr. King and E. D. Nixon's homes were bombed. On February 21, 1956, eighty-nine blacks were indicted by the grand jury for conspiring to boycott, including Dr. King, who was later found guilty and sentenced to 386 days of hard labor or a five-hundred-dollar fine and court costs. The boycott received national attention.

The boycott then got tangled in court proceedings with segregationists challenging the ruling of the Supreme Court, which had upheld a lower court's decision outlawing segregation on buses. Finally a written mandate from the Supreme Court arrived in Montgomery on December 20, and the next day blacks boarded Montgomery City Line buses.

But for members of the White Citizens' Council and violent segregationists, the issue was not settled. The home of Reverend Ralph David Abernathy, minister of First Avenue Baptist Church, was bombed, as were four other black churches and the homes of two pastors, and snipers fired at buses, wounding a pregnant woman.

As things gradually simmered down in Montgomery, other cities in the South experienced boycotts. And out of the informal network of southern churches arose the Southern Christian Leadership Conference (SCLC), with Dr. King as its elected president. It was a promising culmination of the Montgomery boycott, Dr. King recalled: "The story of Montgomery is the story of 50,000 Negroes who were willing to substitute tired feet for tired souls and walk the streets of Montgomery until the walls of segregation were finally battered by the forces of justice."[60]

The civil rights soldiers had won the Battle of Montgomery, but the war against racism and discrimination still loomed before them. And these soldiers, these civil rights workers and volunteers, came from every walk of life. They were black and white, Christians and Jews, and they were joined for one purpose: to tear down the walls of discrimination and segregation, to tear the sheet from the face of the Klan, to rip down the signs that set the races apart, to demonstrate, legislate, and agitate old Jim Crow right out of existence.

> *I know one thing we did right*
> *Was the day we started to fight*
> *Keep your eyes on the prize*
> *Hold on, hold on.*
> —A TRADITIONAL CIVIL RIGHTS MOVEMENT SONG

SOUNDBITE

"What the world needs now is more love and less paperwork."

—PEARL BAILEY (1918–1990),
ACTRESS, SINGER, COMEDIENNE, AUTHOR[61]

BIRMINGHAM BOUND

DR. MARTIN LUTHER KING, JR., is hailed as the father of the civil rights movement and the leading advocate of nonviolent protest, but he was by no means the first to propose such a tactic. Historically that honor can be claimed by the moderate abolitionists who believed in "moral suasion," and even more recently by the Fellowship of Reconciliation (FOR).

The FOR began preaching nonviolence in the early part of the twentieth century. It was founded in 1914 by an English Quaker and a pacifist chaplain, and opened its first American chapter in 1915. In 1947 the organization sponsored the first "Freedom Ride," which was called "The Journey of Reconciliation." This project sent an interracial group of thirteen on a bus ride through the upper South to test the Supreme Court decision that segregated seating on interstate buses and trains was unconstitutional. They also played a significant role in the Montgomery bus boycott by sending two of its leaders— Reverend Glenn Smiley, its national field secretary, and Bayard Rustin, its race relations secretary—to serve as consultants.

The FOR was joined in the first Freedom Ride by CORE (Congress of Racial Equality), a group founded in Chicago in 1942. One of CORE's charter members and later its national director, James Farmer, was originally with FOR. He was largely responsible for convincing FOR to authorize the establishment of CORE. Farmer also helped design the Freedom Ride strategy in which whites in the group would sit in the back of the bus. Blacks would sit in the front and refuse to move when ordered. At every rest stop, blacks would go into the whites-only waiting rooms and try to use all the facilities. "We felt we could count on the racists of the South to create a crisis so that the federal government would be compelled to enforce the law," Farmer explained.[62]

In 1961 CORE initiated a Freedom Ride similar to the one by FOR. James Peck, a white CORE member, was the only Freedom Rider who had experienced the ride in 1947. They departed from Washington, D.C., in May to travel through Virginia, North Carolina, and South Carolina. The ultimate destination was New Orleans, and they wanted to arrive there by May 17 to commemorate the anniversary of the 1954 *Brown v. Board of Education* decision. In Atlanta the group divided into two. Bound for Birmingham, the Greyhound carrying the first group was stoned, had its tires slashed, and was attacked by an angry mob of two hundred white people. Later it was attacked again six miles down the road, and a firebomb tossed through the rear door. The passengers got out just as the bus burst into flames.

The other half of the group in the Trailways bus fared no better. When it arrived in Birmingham the welcoming committee was a mob of whites and no police officers. The riders were viciously assaulted, and one of them, William Barbee, was paralyzed for life. Jim Peck also suffered extensive head wounds. The attack was not only national news, it was now being dispatched all over the world. President John Kennedy, faced with racial disorders for the first time and on the eve of a major summit with Nikita Krushchev, the Soviet premier, met with his brother, Attorney General Robert Kennedy, to see what could be done to quiet things down.

Meanwhile, the Freedom Riders, undaunted, continued their perilous odyssey, joined by students from Nashville, Tennessee. Fisk University student Diane Nash, fresh from the sit-in battles in Nashville, helped coordinate the volunteers for the ride from Birmingham to Montgomery. Once more the Freedom Riders were beaten unmercifully by a white mob when they arrived in Montgomery. The shirts and suits of John Lewis and Jim Zwerg were bloody red. Angry disputes and encounters continued, with the Justice Department debating Alabama state officials on how to bring about a peaceful resolution.

Protected by a contingent of federal marshals, Dr. King convened a mass meeting at Reverend Abernathy's First Avenue Baptist Church in support of the Freedom Riders. By nightfall the church was surrounded by thousands of angry whites threatening the blacks inside. Federal marshals were attacked and several cars were torched. Finally, under pressure from the White House, and after further confrontations between the mob and federal marshals, Governor John Patterson declared martial law in the state, ordering the state police and the national guard to disperse the crowd of whites. The blacks inside the church were escorted to safety. Now the Freedom Riders were ready to embark for Mississippi, the state that had four i's but could not "see" its way to racial justice.

In Jackson, Mississippi, the Freedom Riders were greeted by a mob, but a deal had been made between President Kennedy and Mississippi's United States Senator James O. Eastland, and instead of violence, all the Freedom Riders were arrested for violating state laws. They were but the first of hundreds of Freedom Riders who invaded the South, chipping away at America's long-standing apartheid.

STUDENT NONVIOLENT COORDINATING COMMITTEE

—

THE STUDENT NONVIOLENT Coordinating Committee (SNCC, pronounced "snick"), founded April 15, 1960, evolved from conferences sponsored for students of the sit-in movement by SCLC and hosted first by Septima Clark (1898–1987), and then by Ella Baker (1903–1986). Baker cajoled Dr. Martin Luther King, Jr., to donate eight hundred dollars from the Southern Christian Leadership Conference's meager budget to defray expenses.

The conference at Shaw University in Raleigh, North Carolina, was actually the second gathering of the students, and James Lawson, who had led the Nashville workshops on nonviolence, was invited to deliver the keynote address. Lawson's speech, which stressed that "love is the central motif of nonviolence," was very effective; so effective that the students, including John Lewis, Diane Nash, and white northerner Tom Hayden, took his message of nonviolence and incorporated it into the name of their new organization. Marion Barry, later the mayor of Washington, D.C., was elected the first president of SNCC.

Though the group had unanimously adopted Dr. King's strategy of nonviolence, it was Ella Baker's gentle wisdom that guided them in the formative stages. Baker, then fifty-seven, was a seasoned organizer with a long association with the NAACP and was a founding member of SCLC. In the 1930s she was an ally of author George Schuyler in the Young Negro Cooperative League, whose main objective was to establish consumer cooperatives.

"I had no difficulty relating to the young people," said Baker, whose grandfather was a rebellious slave minister. "I spoke their language in terms of the meaning of what they had to say. I didn't change my speech pattern, and they didn't have to change their speech pattern. But we were able to communicate."[63]

She would play a prime role in developing SNCC's massive voter registration drives and its opposition to the war in Vietnam. So ardent was her demand that SNCC retain its independence from SCLC that her ties with the parent body were severed. In 1964 she would help to establish the Mississippi Freedom Democratic Party (MFDP), and gave the keynote speech at its founding convention.

By the summer of 1961 the fledgling organization was ready for its real baptism when they invaded Albany, Georgia, to help organize against segregation. Unlike SCLC, the SNCC field representatives focused their attention on grassroots folks, not black professionals. In Albany they encountered problems from the local branches of the NAACP, who viewed the young upstarts as competition for members, and white officials who believed the whole campaign to register blacks was influenced by Communists.

As the registration drive intensified, more SNCC workers arrived in Albany, and by mid-December more than five hundred had been arrested. Dr. King, Reverend Ralph Abernathy, and Reverend Wyatt T. Walker, executive director of SCLC, arrived in Albany to support the movement. Dr. King and Reverend Abernathy were among 250 demonstrators arrested the next day. Dr. King vowed to stay in jail until Albany was desegregated. Meanwhile, there was turmoil in the ranks. The SNCC workers felt they were being upstaged by Dr. King and SCLC. Then began a series of cat-and-mouse tactics between Dr. King and the local sheriff. When Dr. King and Reverend Abernathy were found guilty, they chose to stay in jail instead of paying a fine. The sheriff, wise to their tricks, threw them out of jail, telling them that someone had paid their fines. He knew if they remained in jail, the problems in Albany would continue.

In the end, SNCC won a moral victory in Albany, though the schools remained segregated; the city closed the parks rather than integrate them, and after all the chairs were removed from the library, blacks were allowed to enter. SNCC had gained invaluable lessons in organizing from the Albany experience, which they would need later, particularly in Alabama and Mississippi.

MARTYRS OF THE MOVEMENT
—
Four Little Black Girls Dressed in White

Very few people remember the names of the four little girls killed in the cowardly bombing of the Sixteenth Street Baptist Church in Birmingham, Alabama, on September 15, 1963. Sometimes reporters and historians cite the wrong number killed or mistake the date, or debate whether they should be listed with other victims of Jim Crow. Carole Robertson, Cynthia Wesley, and Addie Mae Collins, all fourteen years old, and eleven-year-old Denise McNair are as much martyrs of the civil rights movement as any of those dedicated fighters who gave their lives.

The four were killed three weeks after the historic March on Washington, and the act was symbolic of the hatred and bigotry so deeply entrenched in some white southerners. Some of Dr. Martin Luther King's detractors blamed the deaths on the movement, which in their opinion was too aggressive. But King countered his critics: "What murdered these four girls? The apathy and the complacency of many Negroes who will sit down on their stools and do nothing and not engage in creative protests to get rid of this evil."

All of the young girls were dressed in white. Each of them had prepared a speech at the church's annual Youth Day program. They were engaged in a lively debate on the lesson topic, "The Love that Forgives," when the bomb exploded. The blast was so loud, it was heard miles from the church. Angela Davis, who grew up on the city's Dynamite Hill, so called because of the numerous bombings of black homes, and who knew most of the girls personally, was in France attending the Sorbonne when the tragedy occurred.

"I would like to remember not only the terror that claimed her life [Carole] and that of her Sunday-school friends, but also the positive lives they claimed for themselves as teenage girls," Davis wrote. We all should remember them and what they might have become. Among the mourners at three of the funerals were eight hundred Birmingham pastors of both races, making them many times over the largest interracial gathering of clergy in the city's history.

Viola Liuzzo

Viola Gregg Liuzzo, a white homemaker from Detroit and mother of five children, may not have been in Selma when James Reeb, a white minister, was clubbed to death, or when Jimmie Lee Jackson was shot and killed by a police officer in nearby Marion, Alabama, but she was in Montgomery to hear Dr. King's speech on March 25, 1965, after leading 4,000 marchers on the fifty-mile trek down Route 80 from Selma to Montgomery. She must have felt the goose pimples when King intoned: "However difficult the moment, however frustrating the hour, it will not be long, because truth crushed to earth will rise again. How long? Not long. Because you shall reap what you sow. How long? Not long . . . because the arc of the moral universe is long, but it bends towards justice. How long? Not long. Because mine eyes have seen the glory of the coming of the Lord."[64]

After the demonstration at the capitol, marchers were advised to leave the premises as quickly as possible. Liuzzo, who had taken an incomplete in her classes at Wayne State University in Detroit to join the march, was among those who volunteered to drive marchers back to Selma. She had made one trip, and with Leroy Moton, who had proudly displayed the American flag during the march, she headed back toward Montgomery for more passengers.

Driving her Oldsmobile down Route 80, Liuzzo was chased by a car occupied by four Klansmen. They pulled alongside Liuzzo's car and one of the men shot her twice point-blank in the face. Liuzzo was dead when her car crashed into a ditch. Moton, aware that the murderers were peering into the car, pretended to be dead. The murderers mistook Liuzzo's blood for Moton's. When they left, he got out of the car and flagged down a passing motorist, who happened to be another demonstrator. Later it was disclosed that one of the four men in the car, Gary Rowe, was an FBI informant.

On December 3 Collie Leroy Wilkins and two other Klansmen were convicted of conspiracy charges in the murder. They received ten-year prison sentences. A week later, the whites charged in the murder of Reverend James Reeb were acquitted. In the end, the march from Selma to Montgomery played a decisive part in convincing Congress to pass a voting rights bill, which President Lyndon Johnson signed August 6, 1965.

BETCHA DIDN'T KNOW

Although the MFDP (Mississippi Freedom Democratic Party) was denied seating at the 1964 Democratic National Convention and the all-white delegation was left intact, the newcomers (led by Fannie Lou Hamer) made such an impressive stand for electoral fairness that both major parties decided never again to seat a racially discriminatory delegation.

Murder in Mississippi

James Chaney, Andrew Goodman, and Michael Schwerner are perhaps the most discussed of the civil rights martyrs. Given the coverage they have received, a paragraph or two might be sufficient, but because of the distortions in the movie *Mississippi Burning*, roughly based on their tragedy, there is a need to set the record straight.

It is generally known that Hollywood has never allowed the truth to get in the way of a good story, and this is certainly the case with *Mississippi Burning*. The film's basic flaw is the rewriting of history in which the FBI agents are portrayed as good guys protecting and aiding civil rights workers. This cockamamie twisting of facts is pure Hollywood, as in the film *Red Ball Express* (1952), wherein most of the soldiers in the legendary trucking unit that played such a vital role in supplying battalions with matériel are white, when in reality this was mostly an all-black outfit, except for the officers.

"One of the greatest problems we face with the FBI in the South is that the agents are white southerners who have been influenced by the mores of their community," Dr. Martin Luther King, Jr., told the press in Albany in 1962. "To maintain their status, they have to be friendly with the local police and people who are promoting segregation. Every time I saw FBI men in Albany, they were with the local police force."[65]

And if Dr. King's impressions were credible for the situation in Albany, they probably were just as valid on August 4, 1964, in Philadelphia, Mississippi, where Goodman, Chaney, and Schwerner met their fate. Chaney, twenty-one, was a member of CORE, and a native of Mississippi. He met Goodman, a twenty-year-old volunteer and a student from Queens College in New York City, in conjunction with "Freedom Summer," a project in which thousands of students across the country were recruited to work in Mississippi as voter registration volunteers. Goodman arrived from a week-long orientation in Oxford, Ohio, with Michael Schwerner, twenty-four, a white man from Brooklyn. Schwerner and his wife, Rita, had established the CORE office in Meridian.

A day after meeting one another, they drove off to investigate the burning of a church in a nearby town. Returning from the site, they were stopped by Deputy Sheriff Cecil Price outside Philadelphia, Mississippi, and taken to jail for speeding; they were released later that night.

At this point the three young men were enveloped in that malevolent Mississippi night, and what happened next is a matter of conjecture. The three were reported missing June 21, and their bodies were not found until August 4 in an earthen dam on a farm a few miles from where they had been arrested by Sheriff Price. During the search for the volunteers, three other black bodies of nameless men were discovered. They were MIAs who were quickly forgotten. Chaney, Goodman, and Schwerner had been shot and killed by .38–caliber bullets. Chaney's skull, much like Emmett Till's, had been bashed in.

Four months later the FBI arrested twenty-one white Mississippians, including Deputy Sheriff Price. Only six of the accused received jail sentences, but for violating the victim's civil rights, not murder. The first interracial lynching in the United States ended as most of the others had in which only blacks were involved: Justice denied.

UNSUNG WORKERS
Dave Dennis

"I don't grieve for James Chaney," said Dave Dennis, delivering Chaney's eulogy. "He lived a fuller life than many of us will ever live. He's got his freedom, and we're still fighting for ours. I'm sick and tired of going to the funerals of black men who have been killed by white men . . ."[66] Dennis, head of CORE's workers in Mississippi, was a fearless leader who had faced down his share of angry mobs. He was also a key coordinator of the Council of Federated Organizations (COFO), which had spearheaded the Freedom Vote project of 1963.

Unita Blackwell

Ms. Blackwell, along with the esteemed Fannie Lou Hamer and others, was a principal organizer of the Mississippi Freedom Democratic Party (MFDP), which challenged the seating of the all-white delegation from that state to the Democratic National Convention in 1964. She is currently the mayor of Mayersville, Mississippi (the first black woman mayor in the state), the very place "the people used to arrest me every day and harass me every day," she recalled. "They turned cars upside down, burned crosses in my yard, threw homemade bombs at us."[67]

Bob Moses

Moses is often mentioned with other unsung workers such as E. D. Nixon, Willie Ricks (who many contend was the first to cry "black power" in Mississippi), Ruby Doris Robinson, and Diane Nash. He was certainly among the best and the brightest—and the most courageous—of the freedom fighters. In James Forman's book *The Making of Black Revolutionaries,* which is a sizzling document, detailing the struggle in the deep South during the civil rights period, no one is cited more than Moses.

Moses was a math teacher in New York City when he quit his job to go South. Willie Peacock filed this report of his arrival with Moses's at the SNCC's imperiled office in Greenwood, Mississippi: "We just walked in and Moses went ahead of me into the office. He didn't see anything ruffled up . . . so Bob turned the light on in the office, let the couch out, and put the covers on . . . turned the fan on, which makes a lot of noise, and went to bed. I was very—I was sacred. I just didn't understand what kind of guy this Bob Moses is, that could walk into a place where a lynch mob had just left and make up a bed and prepare to go to sleep, as if the situation was normal."[68]

Lucretia Collins

Among those who participated in the Freedom Rides in the early 1960s was Lucretia Collins, then a recent graduate of Tennessee State University. She was one of the courageous students from Nashville who continued the rides from Birmingham to Jackson after CORE members quit. "In Nashville, we had been informed that CORE was going to have Freedom Rides that would be carrying people all over the South," Collins told James Forman, "and their purpose was to test the facilities at the bus stations in the major cities.

"Later, we heard that the bus of the Freedom Riders had been burned on Mother's Day in Anniston, Alabama, and that another bus had been attacked by people in Birmingham. CORE was discontinuing the Freedom Ride, people said. We knew we were subject to being killed. This did not matter to us. There was so much at stake, we could not allow the segregationists to stop us. We had to continue that Freedom Ride even if we were killed in the process."[69]

She was not killed, but did go to jail in Jackson with the other riders.

James Forman

James Forman spent a considerable amount of time recording the deeds of other members who gave unstintingly to the struggle, but his own contributions on the front lines of the civil rights movement should not be ignored. Forman's background in the struggle began during World War II when he was an anti-Fascist youth. After four years in the armed forces, he entered Roosevelt University in Chicago when he was twenty-six.

Two years later, armed with press credentials, Forman took off for Little Rock, where the turmoil at Central High School would become the center of national attention. Fayette, Greenwood, McComb, Albany, were just a few of the southern outposts where Forman's organizing and tactical skills were critical. One of his most daunting tasks was not a standoff with a member of the Klan, but fighting to hold SNCC together, particularly as it splintered along racial lines.

"In the winter of 1966 at the Peg Leg Bates staff meeting in upstate New York, a motion was passed late one night stating that the Student Nonviolent Coordinating Committee should be an all-black organization," Forman recalled. "Along with others, I voted against this motion, stressing that a viable organization did not expel people from its ranks based on their skin color." It was a futile measure, and if there were a vapor of hope, it was washed away by the incipient cry of "Black Power!"[70]

THE DREAM DEFERRED

THE 250,000 BLACKS and whites assembled for the March on Washington in 1963 was perhaps the largest interracial gathering in the nation's history with the purpose of lobbying for passage of civil rights measures. It was a glorious moment, which Dr. Martin Luther King, Jr., enshrined with his memorable "I Have a Dream" speech. Midway through the five-minute speech, King offered a passage of particular poignancy for black and white marchers: "I have a dream that one day the state of Alabama, whose governor's lips are presently dripping with the words of interposition and nullification, will be transformed into a situation where little black boys and little black girls will be able to join hands with little white boys and little white girls and walk together as sisters and brothers."

The image of little black children and little white children coming together as sisters and brothers must have been especially alarming for those white segregationists who, within a few weeks, bombed the Sixteenth Street Baptist Church in Birmingham, killing four little black girls. Blacks and whites together was also upsetting to black separatists who, in their most organized form, were represented by the Nation of Islam (NOI).

KEY ANTIDISCRIMINATION LAWS ENACTED BY CONGRESS SINCE 1963

Voting Rights Act of 1963—Outlawed racial discrimination with respect to voter registration and voting.
Civil Rights Act of 1964—Outlawed racial discrimination in employment, public accommodations, and the federal funding of programs.
Civil Rights Act of 1968 (Fair Housing Act)—Outlawed racial discrimination in housing.
Voting Rights Act of 1982—Extended the 1965 act for twenty-five years, overturned at-large local election of public officials (*Mobile v. Bolden*), and extended for ten years the bilingual provisions of the original act.
Civil Rights Restoration Act of 1988—Outlawed federal funding of discrimination with respect to race, gender, disability, and age.

Civil Rights Act of 1991—Overturned several Supreme Court rulings by recodifying several equal employment opportunity laws (Title 7 of the Civil Rights Act of 1964 and Section 1981 of the Civil Rights Act of 1866).

—FROM *EMERGE* MAGAZINE

HISTORIC LEGAL DECISIONS

Scott v. Sanford—Dred Scott (ca. 1795–1858)—no, he didn't have dreadlocks—was a slave in Missouri who brought a suit for his freedom after his master had taken him into free territory. His case went to federal court after the Missouri state court ruled against Scott in 1852. In 1857 the Supreme Court ruled against Scott, finding that his status had been determined by the Missouri courts and further that Scott, as a slave, was not a citizen and therefore not entitled to sue in federal court. Later in the same year, Scott was acquired by means of a fictitious sale and emancipated. Scott continued to reside in St. Louis, working as a porter in Barnum's Hotel. He died of tuberculosis a year and a half later.

Plessy v. Ferguson—Homer Adolph Plessy was arrested for refusing to ride in the Jim Crow or "colored" railway coach on a sixty-mile intrastate trip from New Orleans to Covington, Louisiana, in 1896. Judge Ferguson was the defendant, who had conducted the trial on criminal charges. White lawyer Albion Tourgee was retained by Plessy as his counsel. In his brief, Tourgee, who was from New York but had served as a judge during the Reconstruction period, stated that "justice is pictured blind, and her daughter, the Law, ought at least to be color-blind." The court decided that the Louisiana law was not an interference with the power of Congress and required only that separate accommodations be equal. This sanction for segregation would be the law for fifty-eight years.

Herndon v. Lowry—In 1932 when the city of Atlanta cut 23,000 families from the relief rolls and eliminated benefits for hundreds of other families, young Angelo Herndon, a Communist organizer, led a protest march against the decisions. He was arrested on the grounds that he violated a Georgia slave law of 1861, and was charged with "attempting to incite an insurrection." Herndon was found guilty and sentenced to twenty years in prison. After four years of hearings and appeals, Herndon's conviction was reversed by the Supreme Court in 1937. Herndon was released and went north, where he continued to work with the Communist party.

Mapp v. Ohio—The Supreme Court ruled in 1961 that the Fourteenth Amendment applied Fourth Amendment protections against unreasonable searches and seizures to citizens in their dealings with individual states. The state of Ohio prosecuted Dollree Mapp for possessing illegal pornographic materials that officials had seized from her home without a search warrant. Mapp is currently working on her biography with writer Clarence Atkins in which she plans to explain the details of the case and its subsequent impact.

While not a legal decision, the *Rap Brown Act* has meaningful political implications. In 1968 H. Rap Brown, then head of the SNCC, was charged with inciting a race riot in Maryland, and was eventually sentenced to five years in a federal penitentiary for carrying a rifle across state lines while under criminal indictment. Congress passed the H. Rap Brown Act, despite the opposition of Attorney General Ramsey Clark, who stated that riot control was a local problem. This act was used by the Nixon administration to prosecute the Black Panthers and other dissenters. Most prosecutions under the act were subsequently overturned on appeal to higher courts.

SOUNDBITE

"Violence is as American as cherry pie."

—H. Rap Brown (Jamil Abdullah Al-Amin),
former head of SNCC[71]

MALCOLM X—
THE SHINING PRINCE
—

UNTIL THE ASSASSINATION of President John Kennedy, the Nation of Islam (NOI) appeared to be a powerfully united force. Since 1959, when the TV show "The Hate That Hate Produced" detailed the ascendance of Malcolm X, the Nation's membership grew astronomically. But all was not well; a whispering campaign against Malcolm X had been in motion for several months among the NOI leadership, and when Malcolm summarized Kennedy's assassination as a case of the "chickens coming home to roost," he was silenced for ninety days by Elijah Muhammad, the NOI's founder and leader.

The Nation of Islam was twenty years old when Malcolm X Little was released from Charlestown Prison, after serving six and a half years for burglary. It was founded in Detroit in the early 1930s by Wallace Fard, a Pakistani silk peddler who, according to Elijah Poole—soon to be Muhammad—was God incarnate. When "God" suddenly disappeared one day in 1933, Muhammad took over the small sect, but within a year he would move to Chicago, and it was there that the NOI began to elbow its way to recognition, quickly eclipsing a number of bickering black nationalist groups.

But not until Malcolm's arrival did the NOI become a household name. From 1953 when he was promoted to minister until 1963, Malcolm was a veritable blur, establishing mosques from coast to coast, founding a newspaper and radio stations, and generally being Muhammad's spokesperson. He never began a speech without invoking his mentor's "honorable" name. Malcolm had absorbed the complete spirit and letter of the NOI's creed and purpose. No one could so eloquently cite the sect's theology and myths, including the history of Yacub, a mad scientist who had learned to breed races scientifically. Exiled to the island of Patmos, Yacub, a black man, sought revenge on his enemies by creating a devil race—the white race. "From his studies," Malcolm explained in his autobiography, "the big-head scientist knew that black men contained two germs, black and brown. He knew that the brown germ stayed dormant as, being the lighter of the two germs, it was weaker. Mr. Yacub, to upset the law of nature, conceived the idea of employing what we know today as the recessive gene structure, to separate from each other the two germs, black and brown, and then grafting the brown germ to progressively lighter, weaker stages. The humans resulting, he knew, would be, as they became lighter, and weaker, progressively also more susceptible to wickedness and evil. And in this way finally he would achieve the intended bleached-out white race of devils." This myth or shards of cosmology was as serviceable as any for the lost-found members of the NOI.

As late as 1963, months before Malcolm was silenced, Muhammad told an audience at a rally in Philadelphia of his adoration for Malcolm. "This is my most faithful, hardworking minister," Muhammad said, embracing Malcolm before thousands of cheering followers. "He will follow me until he dies."

Muhammad's gift of prophecy was never anything to write home about, and his profligate ways would be even less admirable as Malcolm sought the truth to rumors that his noble leader was guilty of adultery. Malcolm accosted Muhammad and asked him if there was any validity to the charges he was fornicating with his young secretaries. "I'm David," Muhammad told Malcolm. "When you read about how David took another man's wife, I'm that David. You read about Noah, who got drunk—that's me. You read about Lot, who went and laid up with his own daughters. I have to fulfill all of those things."[72]

Malcolm was crushed. The one man he held above reproach, a man he had deified, not only had clay feet but chose to cloak his transgressions in biblical garb, aligning himself with the reprobate prophets of old. The next meeting Malcolm had with Muhammad would be his last. Muhammad silenced him for violating his edict not to comment on the president's assassination. For the second time within months, Malcolm was stunned.

His ghetto instincts told him that his comment was only an excuse for Muhammad to get rid of him.

Shortly thereafter, rumors surfaced that Malcolm was a marked man. Muhammad had given a direct order for his death. Attempts by Malcolm to reach his former leader were thwarted by Muslims loyal to Muhammad. There was only one thing left to do: Malcolm boldly proclaimed he was forming his own organization. Malcolm never formally announced his split from the NOI; he merely launched his own Muslim Mosque Inc., and later the Organization of Afro-American Unity.

Nineteen sixty-four was an eventful year for Malcolm, a year highlighted by two trips abroad, and none more exciting than fulfilling a lifelong dream of making the pilgrimage to Mecca. From this experience Malcolm was exposed to an orthodox Islam that preached a universal brotherhood with no distinction given to one's race. "My pilgrimage," Malcolm confessed, "broadened my scope. It blessed me with new insight. In two weeks in the Holy Land, I saw what I never had seen in thirty-nine years here in America. I saw all *races*, all *colors*—blue-eyed blondes to black-skinned Africans—in *true* brotherhood! . . . In the past, yes, I have made sweeping indictments of all white people. I never will be guilty of that again—as I know now that some white people *are* truly sincere, that some truly are capable of being brotherly toward a black man."[73]

Malcolm's expression of a more accepting humanism did not mean he was any less militant about confronting oppression. His nationalism had expanded—he was now an internationalist, encouraged by meetings with such esteemed African patriots as Gamel Nasser of Egypt, Milton Obote of Uganda, Jomo Kenyatta of Kenya, and especially Kwame Nkrumah of Ghana. During this last phase of his political development, his "Omowale" stage—the brother who has come home—Malcolm approached his full potential as a leader. He had elevated civil rights to human rights, and was preparing to take the plight of black Americans to the World Court when he was cowardly gunned down February 21, 1965, at the Audubon Ballroom outside of Harlem.

Nearly thirty years after his assassination, Malcolm's death is still cloaked in a shroud of mystery. There seems to be little doubt about who did the shooting, but who sent them and if they were part of a larger conspiracy to rid America of a major irritant are questions some of the Malcolm scholars cannot answer. Spike Lee's film provides some understanding of the murder, at least those last few hours as his assassins rehearsed their plan.

If there was one major omission in the film—and there were many redeeming aspects—it is Lee's failure to deal with Malcolm's dynamic last year. All of his previous years were merely preparation for the political promise that seemed so imminent before he was cut down. To some extent that promise—certainly his verve and audacity—was reprised in the next several years with the emergence of the Black Panther Party.

SOUNDBITE

"A man who tosses worms in the water isn't necessarily a friend of the fish."

—MALCOLM X,
HUMAN RIGHTS LEADER[74]

THE PANTHER PROWLS

MALCOLM X IS the most obvious precursor of, or link to, the black liberation movement of the 1970s, but the civil rights workers also played a decisive role, particularly the heroic devotion of Freedom Riders, and the voter registration drive volunteers. This selfless struggle to overthrow the menace and deprivation of Jim Crowism was exemplary, and this struggle took a more aggressive form when it arose in the northern ghettos where Malcolm's uncompromising stance and speeches resonated with militancy, and a resolve to succeed "by whatever means necessary."

One of the means was to pick up the gun. In 1966 Huey Newton and Bobby Seale were students at Merritt Junior College in Oakland, California, when they formed the Black Panther party for Self-Defense. "We need a program," Huey Newton told Seale. "We have to have a program for the people. A program that relates to the people. A program that people can understand."[75] They were tired of the open assaults on the black community by the police, tired of corrupt politicians, tired of the joblessness and the generally wretched conditions of black people. And they also felt that no relief could come from the cultural nationalists, or from clandestine organizations such as the Revolutionary Action Movement.

They laid out their aims in a ten-point program that in several ways resembled the NOI's demands and those of the Garvey movement back in the 1920s, just as the name they chose for their organization existed in another form in Lowndes County, Alabama, during the heyday of the voter registration campaigns.

THE BLACK PANTHER PARTY PLATFORM

—•—

1.   *WE WANT FREEDOM. We want power to determine the destiny of our Black Community.*

We believe that black people will not be free until we are able to determine our destiny.

2.   *We want full employment for our people.*

We believe that the federal government is responsible and obligated to give every man employment or a guaranteed income. We believe that if the White American businessmen will not give full employment, then the means of production should be taken from the businessmen and placed in the community so that the people of the community can organize and employ all of its people and give a high standard of living.

3. *We want an end to the robbery by the white man of our Black Community.*

We believe that this racist government has robbed us and now we are demanding the overdue debt of forty acres and two mules. Forty acres and two mules was promised 100 years ago as restitution for slave labor and mass murder of black people. [Only one mule was promised. Perhaps the Panthers were requesting an additional one as interest.] We will accept the payment in currency which will be distributed to our many communities. The Germans are now aiding Jews in Israel for the genocide of the Jewish people. The Germans murdered six million Jews. The American racist has taken part in the slaughter of over fifty million black people; therefore, we feel that this is a modest demand that we make.

4. *We want decent housing, fit for shelter of human beings.*

We believe that if the white landlords will not give decent housing to our black community, then the housing and the land should be made into cooperatives so that our community, with government aid, can build and make decent housing.

5. *We want education for our people that exposes the true nature of this decadent American society. We want education that teaches us our true history and our role in the present day society.*

We believe in an educational system that will give to our people a knowledge of self. If a man does not have knowledge of himself and his position in society and the world, then he has little chance to relate to anything else.

6. *We want all black men to be exempt from military service.*

We believe that black people should not be forced to fight in the military service to defend a racist government that does not protect us. We will not fight and kill other people of color in the world who, like the black people, are being victimized by the white racist government of America. We will protect ourselves from the force and violence of the racist police and the racist military, by whatever means necessary.

7. *We want an immediate end to POLICE BRUTALITY and MURDER of black people.*

We believe we can end police brutality in our black community by organizing black self-defense groups that are dedicated to defending our black community from racist police oppression and brutality. The second Amendment to the Constitution of the United States gives us a right to bear arms. We therefore believe that all black people should arm themselves for self-defense.

8. *We want freedom for all black men held in federal, state, county and city prisons and jails.*

We believe that all black people should be released from the many jails and prisons because they have not received fair and impartial trials.

9. *We want all black people when brought to trial to be tried in court by a jury of their peer group or people from their black communities, as defined by the Constitution of the United States.*

We believe that the courts should follow the United States Constitution so that black people will receive fair trials. The 14th Amendment of the U.S. Constitution gives a man a right to be tried by his peer group. A peer is a person from a similar economic, social, religious, geographical, environmental, historical, and racial background. To do this the court will be forced to select a jury from the black community from which the black defendant came. We have been, and are being tried by all-white juries that have no understanding of the "average reasoning man" of the black community.

10. *We want land, bread, housing, education, clothing, justice and peace. And as our major political objective, a United Nations–supervised plebiscite to be held throughout the black colony in which only black colonial subjects will be allowed to participate,*

for the purposes of determining the will of black people as to their national destiny.

When, in the course of human events, it becomes necessary for one people to dissolve the political bands which connected them with another, and to assume, among the powers of the earth, the separate and equal station to which the laws of nature and nature's God entitle them, a decent respect to the opinions of mankind requires that they should declare the causes which impel them to the separation.[76]

The Panthers' ten-point program goes on to incorporate further rhetoric from the Declaration of Independence to justify its strategy of armed struggle. This platform was later amended to conform to the party's adoption of a Marxist-Leninist class analysis; however, no revision was ever offered in the demand to have only *men* freed from prison or jail, nor is it clear why they requested two mules when only one was promised. It might have salvaged a number of lives if the government had acceded to these demands for reparations, although the granting of reparations would certainly have created some even more vexing problems.

But the immediate problem was the state and its vicious apparatus that systematically decimated the Panthers. To read the Panther paper was to read a spreadsheet of horror, and to see one obituary after another of dead Panthers. What is often ignored amid the blood and gore is the accomplishments of the party, some of which were long ago adopted by city administrations and the federal government. "The free lunches and breakfasts, diagnosis of sickle-cell anemia, free clinics, and legal assistance were all part of our survival program," recalled David Hilliard, former Panther chief of staff. "And these things are just as much a part of the Panther legacy as the war we waged against the state."[77]

In his autobiography, *This Side of Glory,* Hilliard, who joined the party almost from its inception, details its rise and fall, milestones that included its bodacious brandishing of arms in Sacramento on the floor of the assembly in the state capital in 1967, the incarceration of Newton and the subsequent

"Free Huey" campaign, the cold-blooded murder of two promising Panthers, Mark Clark and Fred Hampton, by the Chicago police in 1969, and Elaine Brown's succession of Newton as head of the party in 1974. The killing of Hampton was a devastating setback, for both the party and the country since he had in his few years demonstrated such an enormous social and political potential.

"Ours was truly a vanguard organization," Brown asserts in her recent memoir, "a small unit in a big endeavor, whose purpose was to trigger a step-by-step revolutionary process, to clarify the issues, develop the mass mind, solidify a base of struggle, prepare our people to achieve freedom as nonantagonistically as possible—or to prevail in a conflict decided by bloodshed."[78]

Brown was the caretaker of a moribund, totally beleaguered operation, one that signaled its death knell long before Newton was killed in a drug dispute on the streets of Oakland in 1989. The party left behind several memorable slogans, such as "off the pig" and "all power to the people," that would later be revised by other organizations and individuals opposed to racism, discrimination, and the abuses of state power, in the same manner that the flower children, Gray Panthers, White Panthers, feminists, and gay rights activists would appropriate the essence of "black power."

ALL THE PANTHERS ARE NOT DEAD

David Hilliard is a recovering drug addict and a representative for the United Public Employees' Union, Local 790, in Oakland, California.

Elaine Brown lives in France and is married to a French industrialist. Her book *A Taste of Power* offers a rare glimpse of the inner workings of the Panther leadership.

Bobby Seale works as a counselor at a youth-employment project in Philadelphia. Seale should also be remembered as the lone black of the Chicago Eight, who were tried under the so-called Rap Brown law (Seale's trial ended in a hung jury), an antiriot provision in the 1968 Civil Rights Act. Brown, then head of SNCC, was accused of inciting riots in 1967.

Eldridge Cleaver is a born-again Christian who unsuccessfully ran for political office in Oakland. He operates a recycling business in Oakland, California.

Kathleen Cleaver divorced Eldridge, received her law degree from Yale Law School, and is now a law professor.

Bobby Rush is a congressman from Chicago.

Michael McGee, a former alderman in Milwaukee, is now a community developer.

Emory Douglas, whose cartoons were a main feature of the Panther paper, works as a graphic artist at the *Sun Reporter* in San Francisco.

Dhoruba Bin Wahad resumed his status as an outspoken community activist in New York City after serving nineteen years in prison on trumped-up charges. He also is a tireless advocate for political prisoners, particularly in behalf of two former Panthers, Geronimo Pratt and Mumia Abu-Jamal, who is fighting to reverse a death sentence in Philadelphia.

Assata Shakur resides in Cuba, where she is working on another book.

Connie Matthews, after separation from Michael "Cetawayo" Tabor, in the mid-1980s, moved from Zambia to Jamaica. Before joining Tabor, she was a secretary to Eldridge Cleaver and then to Huey Newton.

Michael Tabor, who, along with Dhoruba Bin Wahad, was one of the Panther twenty-one who were charged with plotting to bomb various sites in New York City, including Macy's and Abercrombie & Fitch Department Stores, is a popular radio broadcaster in Lusaka, Zambia, where he has lived for nearly twenty years.

Paul Coates is the owner and publisher of Black Classic Press in Baltimore.

BETCHA DIDN'T KNOW

Filmmaker St. Clair Bourne formed his own film production company, Chamba, in 1971. Since then he has directed more than thirty documentaries, including *In Motion: Amiri Baraka* and *Where Roots Endure*, an evocative study of the Gullah culture in South Carolina.

BLACK ARTS

THE BLACK LIBERATION movement reached its apex near the end of the 1960s, buffeted along by a massive corps of black artists who did not have to be told to invest their creative productions with a political edge. Many of these writers, musicians, actors, dancers, painters, sculptors, and filmmakers were also teachers, and thus it was easy for them to blend the exigencies of the black aesthetic with the demand for black studies. The black arts movement flowered like the Harlem Renaissance on campuses from one end of the nation to the other—San Francisco State College, Howard University, Wayne State University in Detroit—and in community organizations. It took shape in theater groups such as Karamu House in Cleveland, Concept East in Detroit, Kuumba Theatre in Chicago, the Free Southern Theatre in New Orleans, the New Lafayette, Frank Silvera's Writer's Workshop, and the Black Arts Repertory Theatre in Harlem, where the plays of Lonne Elder and Lorraine Hansberry cast their spells. Literary works erupted from Broadside and Lotus Press in Detroit, Third World Press in Chicago, and from a plethora of magazines—*Black World, Freedomways, Black Scholar, Black Creations,* and the *Journal of Black Poetry*—which provided a forum for such writers and poets as Quincy Troupe, Eugene Redmon, Carolyn Gerald, Lance Jeffers, George Kent, Addison Gayle, Kalamu ya Salaam, and Carolyn Rodgers. Amiri Baraka's poem "Black Arts" caught the rhythm and the rhyme of those days:

> *We are unfair*
> *And unfair*
> *We are Black magicians*
> *Black arts we make*
> *in black labs of the heart*
>
> *The fair are fair*
> *and deathly white*
>
> *The day will not save them*
> *And we own the night*

Galleries overflowed with the photographs of Gordon Parks, Bert Andrews, Moneta Sleet; the paintings of Dana Chandler, Harold Neal, Charles White, Nelson Stevens, and the AfriCobra artists; and the clubs and lofts reverberated with the sounds of Ornette Coleman, Archie Shepp, Sun Ra, Eric Dolphy, and the Art Ensemble of Chicago. James Brown's "Say It Loud, I'm Black and I'm Proud" was part affirmation and part anthem, Curtis Mayfield echoed the claim with his "Choice of Colors" and "We're a Winner," Jimi Hendrix stole the show at Woodstock, Stevie Wonder talked about the "Music on His Mind," Marvin Gaye wondered "What's Goin' On," and the Last Poets informed us that the "Revolution would not be televised."

And positive images even appeared on television in "I Spy," "Mission: Impossible," and "Star Trek." Things were slowly opening in Hollywood, where films such as *Uptight* were providing at least a glimmer of revolutionary moxie prior to the vapidity of "blaxploitation" films only a few years away.

Black pride could be detected in the titles of books and

poems: *Black Music* (Amiri Baraka), *Think Black* (Haki Madhubuti), *I Am a Black Woman* (Mari Evans), and *We Are a BaddDDD People* (Sonia Sanchez). The Dance Theatre of Harlem and Alvin Ailey's company, with the superb interpretations of Judith Jamison, leaped into the fray. Black nationalism was at such a fever pitch that even the passing of cultural giants like Langston Hughes, John Coltrane, and Otis Redding in 1967 saw but a momentary pause. But there were still some of the old guard who took time to remind the new rebels during these heady times that their impulses and creations were part of a long continuum—and very much in the American grain.

"Don't write about the Negro, write about Americans," author John Oliver Killens advised his young protégés. "But surely the American Negro is the most uniquely American of all Americans, because he was created *here*, in this place, physically, psychologically, sociologically, culturally, economically. He is an American product. The Negro, in his black presence, is the barometer of this nation's Constitution, and all its democratic traditions yet realized."[79] From another sector of the black intelligentsia came Albert Murray's admonition and his summary of the new wave of political and cultural aspirations. "What U.S. Negroes themselves want," Murray wrote in his book *The Omni-Americans,* "it should be easy enough to see, is their share of the material benefits of U.S. life—and they intend to upset enough smugness to get it. For the rest, they are far more ambivalent about the so-called white world than white people seem to realize. Nor is this simply a matter of sociopolitical action. What Louis Armstrong has been doing to popular songs all these years is an infinitely more accurate index to fundamental U.S. Negro attitudes towards 'white culture' than are some of the embarrassingly superficial and contradictory gestures of alienation currently so popular among some black nationalists and 'Afro Zionists.' "[80]

An impudent Ishmael Reed seems to cry "a pox on both houses" in his neo-hoodooism where "dance and drums preceded the word. Thousands of years before the invention of the 'Novel' or the 'Short Story,' Thoth, the black Birdman of Egypt, 'invented letters' and 'gave names to things.' Magic/

religion came before 'criticism,' and words (nommo) were the rappings of not one but thousands of Spirits. Centuries before the 'literary capitals' of London, Paris, and New York, Ife, in Nigeria, was the home of the Necromancers, heavier than Solomon, conjurers of dread and joy." Reed and his cohorts were not interested in planting their flags on things— "We plant our flags on the seventies."[81]

I'VE SEEN THE PROMISED LAND

BUT BEFORE THE sixties were over, amid the celebration and epiphany, there were still some dues to pay. The paroxysms of rage and fire that engulfed the nation's cities in the early sixties were still simmering when ten urban centers exploded in the summer of 1967. What happened in Detroit was typical of the disturbances. They were not so much race riots as angry outbursts against the symbols of authority, most immediately the police, whose brutality often triggered the uprisings.

The reckless insensitivity of law enforcement officials may have ignited the riots, but the causes in most cases grew out of a stockpile of unattended grievances. Before the police raided a "blind pig" on Detroit's west side, there had been a number of incidents over a two-year period that had infuriated the black community. On the city's east side the summer before, the police only narrowly averted a riot after arresting several youths for disturbing the peace. A few weeks before the raid, on June 26, Danny Thomas, a young black man, was shot to death at a picnic defending his pregnant wife from the attack of seven white youths. His wife witnessed the slaying and miscarried shortly thereafter. All but one of the white youths were released.

On July 23, about 4:00 A.M., the police raided an after-hours joint where liquor was served. The blind pig was only five blocks from Danny Thomas's home. More than eighty persons were at the club celebrating the return of two Vietnam veterans. As the patrons were being escorted to police cars and van, a crowd of two hundred people assembled. When the police convoy drove away, neighborhood residents began throwing stones at the cars. Then rumors were circulated that the police had used excessive force. A black youth, Michael Lewis, whom the police called "Mr. Greensleeves," because he wore a green shirt, reportedly exhorted the crowd to riot. Four hours later, looting and violence were widespread, and by evening the riot had reached a peak level.

As the disorder increased, it became necessary to bring in National Guardsmen and then paratroopers to quell the upheaval. After four days the disruption was calmed. More than 7,000 persons had been arrested, and forty-three killed, thirty-three of them black. Property damage was estimated at $22 million, and on at least a couple of streets a full block of homes went up in flames.

Tampa, Newark, Atlanta, Cincinnati, and Plainfield, New Jersey, were among the other cities to experience widespread disorder. The nation was rocked, and President Lyndon Johnson established a commission to assess the damage and to determine why the riots had occurred. When the Kerner Commission issued its report, there was one basic conclusion that continues to echo without cessation: "Our nation is moving toward two societies, one black, one white—separate and unequal."[82]

Among the several recommendations made by the commission to improve the status of black Americans, those on the economic agenda were the most critical. "What the American economy of the late 19th and early 20th century was able to do to help European immigrants escape from poverty is now largely impossible," the report stated. "New methods of escape must be found for the majority of today's poor."[83]

To remedy this disparity, Dr. Martin Luther King, Jr., proposed even stiffer measures. "We must recognize that we can't solve our problem until there is a radical redistribution of economic and political power," King told his Southern Christian Leadership Conference staff in 1967. This was among the first signs of King's shift in analysis, an extension of his reformist aims into a revolutionary posture. "We are engaged in a class struggle," he would conclude by early 1968.[84]

King's social and political analysis, which had first shown signs of broadening as early as 1965, was by 1968 clearly a concern to his colleagues, and to the FBI, which stepped up its surveillance of the leader. His position against the escalating war in Vietnam became apparent in the summer of 1965, and now the FBI and the White House faced an even graver concern when King announced the mobilization of a Poor People's Campaign. The campaign, he told his chief aide and longtime associate Reverend Ralph Abernathy, would stress the need for "a guaranteed minimum wage in this country, so that no family will be without the means to buy the necessities of life. Second, we need vouchers or stamps for free food, so that the parents of those children can go to any grocery store and buy the right kind of food. And third, we need to do away with the commodity program where people are given whatever surplus food the government has—when they have it. All poor people get is starches and fats. No wonder so many of them have such short lives."[85]

But King's plan was opposed by members of SCLC's executive committee, principally Reverends James Bevel and Jesse Jackson, who believed the plan had too many shortcomings. Meanwhile, in Memphis, another event was shaping up to distract King from gaining support for his campaign. In March, the anticipated garbage workers' strike in Memphis emerged, and since it concerned the economic plight of poor people, it was grist for King's mill. He arrived in Memphis in late March, gave a speech, and promised to return to lead the embattled sanitation workers in a march. King never made it on the second occasion, but Reverend Abernathy filled in for him.

Finally, on April 3, King returned to Memphis in time to give the keynote speech at a rally at the Church of God in Christ. It was a rainy evening in Memphis, but the church was packed, and the media was out in full force. After a long introduction by Reverend Abernathy, Dr. King began his speech, moving from specific actions to general principles, and back again. And then came the prophetic finale:

> Well, I don't know what will happen now. We've got some difficult days ahead. But it really doesn't matter with me now, because I've been to the mountaintop. And I don't mind. Like anybody, I would like to live a long life. Longevity has its place. But I'm not concerned about that now. I just want to do God's will. And He's allowed me to go up to the mountain, and I've looked over, and I've seen the promised land. I may not get there with you. But I want you to know tonight that we as a people will get to the promised land. And so I'm happy tonight. I'm not worried about anything. I'm not fearing any man. Mine eyes have seen the glory of the coming of the Lord.

"I had heard him hit high notes before," Reverend Abernathy recalled of the speech, "but never any higher. The crowd was on its feet, shouting and applauding—even some of the television crew. It was a rare moment in the history of American oratory, something to file along with Washington's Farewell Address and the Gettysburg Address. But it was somehow different than those speeches because it was an eloquence that grew out of the black experience, with its similarities to the biblical story of captivity and hard-won freedom. Everyone was emotionally drained by what he had said, including Martin himself, whose eyes were filled with tears."[86]

There is no way to comprehend King's prophecy, though we do know he was under great stress at the time. His redemptive tears may have been for those who resisted his plans for the Poor People's Campaign, for the invaders who disrupted his first attempt to march in Memphis, for the war in Vietnam, or they may have welled up from sheer pressure and exasperation of his personal life and the insidious monitoring of his every move by the FBI. Rhetorically, King's emphasis on the mountaintop is reminiscent of Reverend Vernon Johns's great sermon "Transfigured Moments." What Reverend Johns did was to analyze the symbolism of mountains in the lives of Moses, Elijah, and Jesus Christ. "It is good to be the possessor of some mountain-top experience," Johns wrote, stressing the need to bind the inspiration of leaders with the needs of the common folk. "It is a heart strangely unChristian that cannot thrill with joy when the least of men begin to pull in the direction of the stars."[87]

King's assassination was like a shot to the soul of the nation, and nowhere did its shock resound more compellingly than in the realm of the black church. "The King of love was dead," Professor Gayraud Wilmore registered, "and with his death an era of interracial church social action and theological innocence came to an end. Everyone knew that the memory of his commitment and faithfulness would never be permitted to die in the Black Church, but for those church leaders and theologians retreating from a city ready to burst into a strange, elegiac violence, a new challenge to America had to be mounted, one more consonant with the pragmatic sensibilities of the religious experience and theological maturity of a proud Black people come of age."[88]

While Wilmore and other members of the clergy chose to contemplate in silence the meaning of King's life, the ghettos of America unleashed a savage reply, as black smoke curled over nearly every major city. It was a bitter and ironic response to the memory of a man who believed so strongly in nonviolence. The apostle of peace would have been further troubled by developments thousands of miles from Memphis, where the fighting in Vietnam, following the Tet offensive, was intensifying.

SOUNDBITE

"Injustice anywhere is a threat to justice everywhere."

—DR. MARTIN LUTHER KING, JR.[89]

NO VIETCONG EVER
CALLED ME A NIGGER!
—

ON DR. MARTIN Luther King's birthday in 1971, forty members of the Black Liberation Front of the Armed Forces held a demonstration at Long Binh Jail or, as the soldiers called it, LBJ, site of the bloodiest stockade riot in the war. Black soldiers on the battlefront now began to raise their voices with their sisters and brothers on the home front, protesting a war that with each year became more futile. Stateside GIs were also protesting. At Fort Hood, forty-three black soldiers refused to board planes for Chicago, where they were to put down the demonstration provoked by the Democratic party's presidential nominating convention. Earlier, in July 1967, during the rebellion in Detroit, black marines William Harvey and George Daniels called a meeting to question why black men were fighting "a white man's war." The request was equivalent to disloyalty, and they were court-martialed and sentenced to long terms in the stockade.

In 1963 when Private First Class Reginald Edwards arrived in Vietnam, there were only 16,000 U.S. troops scattered across the country, about 10 percent of them black, closely reflecting the ratio of blacks in U.S. society. Edwards was gung ho, wound tight with the notion that the Vietnamese were the enemy who had to be killed. "As a black person," he said, "there was no problem fightin' the enemy. I knew Americans were prejudiced, were racist and all that, but basically, I believed in America 'cause I was an American . . . The first person that died in each battalion of the 9th Marines that landed was black, and they were killed by our own people. Comin' back into them lines was the most dangerous thing then. It was more fun sneakin' into Ho Chi Minh's house than comin' back into the lines of Da Nang."[90]

Most black soldiers in Vietnam in 1967, according to Wal-

lace Terry, who was covering the war for *Time* magazine, supported the war effort. "They believed America was
guaranteeing the sovereignty of a democratically constituted
government in South Vietnam and halting the spread of Communism in Southeast Asia." But by the end of the war this
attitude had changed considerably. "The war," Terry continued, "which had bitterly divided America like no other issue
since the Civil War, had become a double battleground, pit-
ting American soldier against American soldier. The spirit of
foxhole brotherhood I found in 1967 had evaporated."[91]

Despite the interracial tension among the troops, the lack
of promotions, and thc assignmcnt to the worst hellholes in
Nam, blacks continued to reenlist twice as fast as whites. Many
young blacks, however, never went anywhere near a draft
board or military recruiter. "To conduct this war," Robert
Allen wrote in a letter in 1966, refusing to submit to induction
into the army, "the U.S. is drafting thousands of black men
to fight for 'freedom' abroad while their freedoms at home
are denied. These black men are forced to fight for white
imperialism in its attempt to destroy colored nations. They
are forced to fight for the sole benefit of their former slave
masters. These black men go to war knowing that their brothers and sisters at home will continue to be subjected to violent
attacks by racists which will go unpunished. An army which
will not protect black citizens at home and instead attacks
colored people in Vietnam is not an army in which any self-
respecting black man should serve. It is for these reasons that
I refuse to accept induction into the U.S. Armed Forces."[92]

Allen, now a noted author, editor, and teacher, was a
twenty-four-year-old graduate student at Columbia University
when he launched this missive. And the campuses of America
were hothouses of activism, hosting hundreds of antiwar sit-
ins and teach-ins. At Wayne State University in Detroit, students chose not to close down the university but to *open* it
up, and symposiums on the war and its perils were held as
alternatives to regular classes. It was only a matter of time
before the state would step in and stop the campus rallies.

In Ohio, at Kent State University in the spring of 1970, more
than six hundred antiwar demonstrators, protesting the U.S.

invasion of Cambodia, were fired upon by National Guardsmen. They were guilty of taunting the Guardsmen, sticking flowers in the muzzles of their rifles, hurling rocks at them, which necessitated the shooting, it was reported. Four students were killed and nine were wounded. The nation was aroused, and memorials were held for the students at nearly every college and university around the country. All of the Guardsmen were exonerated four years later. Eleven days after the Kent State massacre, demonstrators assembled at Jackson State, a historically black college in Mississippi, and two students were killed and twelve wounded by the state police. Media coverage of this attack was comparatively nonexistent.

FINALLY GOT THE NEWS
—

MEANWHILE, THE CONFLUENCE of organizations opposed to the war and the campus uprisings found a natural ally in black workers, many of whom were angry veterans, and many of whom were not, like General Baker, a Detroit factory worker. And Baker is a convenient bridge between the war resisters and the militant black labor unions in which he would play a vital role. He, like Robert Allen, had sent his draft board a letter of defiance. Baker told his board that when they were prepared to fight just wars of liberation, "then you can send for me and I'll be glad to fight," otherwise leave him alone.

Baker's roots in the struggle began in the 1960s when he traveled to Cuba as a member of the Venceremos Brigade, a radical cadre of black and white volunteers in support of the Cuban revolution. He may have had ties with the Fair Play for Cuba Committee formed in 1960, which gave impetus to the fledgling New Left. Baker was one of hundreds of workers at Dodge Main, one of Chrysler Corporation's largest and most dilapidated plants, who formed a wildcat strike and shut down the plant in May 1968. They were fed up with the increased speed of the assembly lines, which at one point amounted to the production of nearly a car a minute. Baker was fired, but he was by no means through with Chrysler or the United Automobile Workers union. In 1967, following the rebellion, Baker helped organize a corps of black workers who were tired of being consigned always to the most danger- ous, lowest-paying jobs with the least seniority and security.

By 1968 the group of workers had formed the Dodge Revolu- tionary Union Movement. It was a group equally opposed to the company and the UAW. In fact, after a while, to these work- ers, UAW meant "U Ain't White," clearly indicating the black workers' separation from the largely white union. Soon there were sister organizations sprouting up around the city, mostly at other auto plants, calling themselves ELDRUM (Chrysler's Eldon Avenue plant), FRUM (Ford's River Rouge complex), and CADRUM (General Motors' Cadillac plant). There were rev- olutionary union affiliates outside of the automotive industry, too, and they began to pop up all over the country. The United Black Workers at the Mahwah plant in New Jersey proclaimed that "the factories belong to the people and we workers are the people."

The constitution of DRUM extended this analysis: "We . . . understand that there have been previous attempts by our people in this country to throw off this degrading yoke of brutal oppression, which have ended in failure. Throughout our history, black workers, first slaves, and later as pseudo freedmen, have been in the vanguard of potentially successful struggles both in all black movements as well as integrated efforts . . . At this point we loudly proclaim that we have learned our lesson from history and we shall not fail . . . "[93]

DRUM's cadre was more than mere plant workers, however. Many of them—Mike Hamlin, Kenny Cockrel (who had won a national reputation for his brilliance in the courtroom, par- ticularly in his defense of a noted community activist, Hay- ward Brown), John Watson, Chuck Wooten, Marian Kramer, and John Williams—had come of age in a city vibrant with radical thought and politics. Detroit's history of labor unions, potent Communist party cells, and an advanced black artistic community combined to nurture these activists. Many of the early black political formations and thinkers, such as Freedom Now party, GOAL, Malcolm X, James Boggs, Charles Denby, and later Harry Haywood, provided additional stimulation. Out of this fertile incubator would come the Shrine of the Black Madonna (Yes, madonnas were black centuries before they were blonde.) or the Black Christian Nationalists, The Pan-African Congress, USA, The Republic of New Afrika, and activists associated with Robert Williams, who gained national attention after his armed stance in Monroe, North Carolina, and the Revolutionary Action Movement.

A good number of DRUM's members were also students at Wayne State University, most significantly John Watson. Watson, heeding the precepts of Lenin, founded the *Inner City Voice*, which reported on the activities of the various RUMs (Revolutionary Union Movements), along with a strong opposition to the war in Vietnam and advocacy of the Palestine Liberation Organization. Later, Watson was the editor of Wayne State's student newspaper, *The South End*, which resurrected the political line of the *Inner City Voice* after it folded, and often printed at the top of the paper: "One class conscious worker is worth a thousand students!"

In 1969 the several RUMs were united under the League of Revolutionary Black Workers (LRBW). The promise of workers' collectives, and a direct challenge to those who owned the means of production, unfortunately died abornin'. The formation of the League was a creative response to the problems of the RUMs' isolation and a need to consolidate for financial and operational reasons, but "the League did not succeed in confronting the problems of declining mass revolutionary sentiment, tactical maneuvers by management, and tactical errors by RUM leadership which were curtailing the in-plant revolt," concluded Ernie Allen, a former member of the League, and now a leading scholar in black studies. "But in 1969 and 1970 such *political failures* were masked by a false sense of organizational successes in other areas: the creation of the League film *Finally Got the News,* the proliferation of LRBW offices in the Detroit area, participation in a book-discussion project which had enrolled hundreds of liberal whites, as well as the growing media attention which the League was attracting nationwide."[94]

This growing celebrity only exacerbated many of the internal problems hampering the League's development, as the strong personalities of the organization's executive committee brought conflicting agendas to the table. The League was also beset with a definitional problem. Was it exclusively a labor union set up to meet the needs of black workers? Was it a political formation with an aim toward seeking elective office? Should it compete with the UAW and attempt to snare one of its locals? And how did white colleagues fit into the scheme of things? These questions were either never raised or could not be answered. After two years of activity, the League was tottering on the verge of extinction when James Forman, of SNCC fame, blew in from New York City with money raised from religious institutions. In 1969 Forman delivered his Black Manifesto as part of the Black Economic Development Conference convened in Detroit. He told the gathering that black workers had helped to make the United States one of the richest countries in the world, and that reparations were due.

Forman declared: "We are therefore demanding of the white Christian churches and Jewish synagogues which are part and parcel of the system of capitalism, that they begin to pay reparations to black people in this country. We are demanding five hundred million dollars from the Christian white churches and Jewish synagogues. This total comes to fifteen dollars per nigger. This is a low estimate, for we maintain there are probably more than thirty million black people in this country. Fifteen dollars a nigger is not a large sum of money, and we know that the churches and synagogues have a tremendous wealth, and its membership, white America, has profited and still exploits black people."[95]

From these reparations, which totaled $1 million, according to some accounts, Forman was able to finance certain programs sponsored by the League. Black Star, a printing press, was established, of which Forman's collection of essays was the most notable publication. Some of the money also helped to defray expenses allocated to making the film *Finally Got the News,* a documentary explaining the nature of the League and its goals. Efforts by the League to induce Jane Fonda and other Hollywood activists to join them on a film project never got beyond discussion.

When the League unraveled, the subsequent groups reflected the interests of the executive committee's dominant leaders. Those who were primarily based in the factories struggled to keep the League intact, and later would be centrally involved in the creation of the Communist Labor party; some gravitated toward electoral politics and confrontations with Detroit's killer cops, while others resumed their college lives, earning law degrees, master's degrees in education, and doctorates.

The UAW had quietly observed the black dissidents with interest, occasionally speaking out against them. Emil Mazey, a ranking UAW official, characterized DRUM and its members as a bunch of fanatical "black fascists whose actions are an attempt to destroy the union."[96] He compared them to the Communists of the past. Black trade unionists, especially those comfortably ensconced in leadership positions, kept their distance from the "Leagueites and Drummers," although there were some who studied the wildcatters and learned from their mistakes.

These trade unionists found their opportunity to organize in 1972 after the refusal of George Meany and AFL-CIO leadership to oppose the election of Richard Nixon. The Coalition of Black Trade Unionists (CBTU) was the organization, and it had a number of grievances. They sought an increase of blacks in the leadership ranks of the unions; an end to discriminatory hiring practices; more protection of black workers by union stewards; and a more serious regard by the union of black policy concerns. The CBTU was composed of forty unions, some within the jurisdiction of the AFL-CIO, including auto, steel, meat cutters, teamsters, government employees, and other service workers. The year following its founding, the Coalition would insist that "it is our challenge to make the labor movement more relevant to the needs and aspirations of black and poor people workers. The CBTU will insist that black union officials become full partners in the leadership and decision making of the American labor movement."[97]

No matter how fervent the demands, the white labor aristocracy, like its rank-and-file members, maintained its indifference, if not hostile resistance, to the inclusion and elevation of black workers in the nation's trade unions, although there were some black trade unionists who were die-hard loyalists.

"In my family [Jimmy] Hoffa was next to God," Brent Staples wrote in a *New York Times* editorial. "When my uncle Paul started driving in the 30's, he earned $50 a week. Health and welfare benefits were nonexistent. The work week was 48 hours; the first overtime came at hour 49. Then Hoffa slugged his way to power and organized the truckers. My uncles were eventually earning more a day than they had once earned in a week—with a health plan. The Staples brothers are grateful for the deal that Hoffa cut them. It bought the houses they live in, put shoes on their children's feet and sent some of them to college. 'Hoffa was the greatest thing to happen in my lifetime,' my uncle Paul said. 'Sure, he got something for himself, but he got something for the working man, too.' "

Still, as Staples noted, until his "disappearance" in 1975, Hoffa sat on his hands while his "mob-infested union" ripped off its constituents. Such accusations against union leaders were widespread in the late 1970s by rank-and-file members, sparking massive reform movements. With or without reform, most black workers retained that locked-out, underrepresented feeling that they had come to expect. A noted commentator observed in 1959 that "the Negro worker's historical experience with organized labor had not been a happy one," and the words were still accurate thirteen years later. The intransigence on the labor front was matched by the unchanging rigidity in the political arena for blacks in the early 1970s. It was time for a national black political agenda.[98]

SOUNDBITE

"When you become sentimental about power, you don't have it anymore."

—JOHN HENRIK CLARKE,
HISTORIAN AND PROFESSOR EMERITUS[99]

POLITICS IN COMMAND
—

BLACKS COULD POINT with pride in 1967 at the mayoral victories of Carl Stokes in Cleveland, Richard Hatcher in Gary, and Floyd McCree in Flint, Michigan, and Representative Shirley Chisholm's presidential campaign in 1972; nonetheless, the political picture was dismal. To rearrange this reality was one of the issues on the agenda of the National Black Political Convention at its first meeting in Gary, Indiana, in 1972. "The 1970s will be the decade of an independent black political thrust," predicted Mayor Hatcher, the host of the convention.[100] Over 3,000 delegates, representing an array of political tendencies, assembled for the convention, making it the largest in black history. Elected officials, businessmen and women, teachers, activists, and hundreds of civil servants were among the 12,000 people attending the various workshops. Only the NAACP, of the major organizations, failed to send a delegate. The cochairs of the event—Mayor Hatcher, Representative Charles Diggs of Michigan, and Pan-Africanist Amiri Baraka—were indicative of the cross section of participants. What was immediately evident was the tentative rapprochement between elected officeholders and community activists.

"We come to Gary in an hour of great crisis and tremendous promise for Black America," the convention's statement asserted. "While the white nation hovers on the brink of chaos, while its politicians offer no hope of real change, we stand on the edge of history and are faced with an amazing and frightening choice: We may choose in 1972 to slip back into the decadent white politics of American life, or we may press forward, moving relentlessly from Gary to the creation of our own black life. The choice is large, but the time is very short . . . A Black political convention, indeed all truly black politics must begin with this truth: *The American system does not work for the masses of our people, and it cannot be made to work without radical fundamental change.*" (their emphasis)[101]

The lengthy statement further noted that a black agenda recognizes that "white America moves towards the abyss created by its own racial arrogance, misplaced priorities, rampant materialism, and ethical bankruptcy." The convention delegates created a National Black Political Assembly (NBPA) to carry out some of the proposed demands. One issue would be a point of contention and cause mainstream politicians to reserve their support of the NBPA. Israel was condemned for its expansionist policy and forceful occupation of sovereign territory of another state. "The National Black Political Convention resolves to support the struggle of Palestine for self-determination."

A position supporting the Palestinians was, for most members of the three-year-old Congressional Black Caucus (CBC), a body of elected black officials, reprehensible, and akin to committing political suicide. "We vigorously oppose the efforts of any group that would seek to weaken or undermine Israel's right to exist."[102] Without the firm endorsement of the CBC, the NBPA had little chance of surviving, and the second convention in Little Rock, despite the resourceful leadership of Ron Daniels, who replaced Diggs as chairman, was a bust, with only 2,000 folks attending. As late as 1980 the NBPA, reduced in size and calling itself the National Black Independent Political Party (NBIPP), was still trying to make a go of it, but the window of opportunity had closed back in Gary, and the NBPA—in whatever form—resisted all attempts at revival.

One demand made by the NBPA in 1972 to support an international African Liberation Day did find some popular appeal. And this annual event was largely under the aegis of the African Liberation Support Committee (ALSC), a coalition of different organizations. After placing the subject of African independence squarely before the American people through a series of mass demonstrations and conferences, and raising significant funds for progressive liberation movements in Africa, the ALSC began to disintegrate from its own ideological heat. The narrow nationalists who insisted on the primacy of race as the principal contradiction in the oppression of black America almost came to blows with the mechanical Marxists and their ceaseless prattle about the importance of a class analysis. There were a silent few who saw the necessity of both lines as critical to working toward a solution to the problem, but they got lost in the debate as such major players as Owusu Sadaukai, Amiri Baraka, and Abdul Alkalimat gradually adopted a Marxism-Leninism perspective, shedding their dashikis, bubas, and other cultural nationalist trappings for working-class garb.

Suddenly the main contradiction in the struggle was the irreconcilable differences expressed by the warring sectors of the movement. It was fratricidal, Manning Marable opined. "Organizations collapsed beneath the weight of polemics; old friends turned against each other; marriages were broken over which African liberation organization one chose to support; individuals lost their jobs inside Black Studies Departments at universities, depending upon where they stood politically on the Leninist-cultural nationalist debate."[103]

The situation was tragic when it was not completely farcical, and many of the black radicals had less to do with Marxism than with a crude economic determinism and simplistic adaptation of the ideas of Mao Tse-tung, Marable continued. "Many black activists who *claimed* to be Marxists had never actually read Marx, and if they had, they had left undigested the rich corpus of modern socialist theory which concretely relates Marx to the unique conditions of social transformation under late capitalism."[104] The contending factions saved their most celebrated showdown for an international stage in Africa during the Sixth Pan-African Conference in 1974 at Dar es Salaam, Tanzania. In the end there was no clear victor because the schism was mutually destructive. They had met the enemy, and it was they!

SOUNDBITE

"The idea that black people can have unity is the most dangerous idea we've let loose."

—BAYARD RUSTIN (1910–1987),
CIVIL RIGHTS ORGANIZER[105]

CIRCLE THE WAGONS

POLITICAL PRESSURE FROM black militants during the early 1970s was felt at the polling booth and ballot box. By 1974 more than two hundred blacks sat in thirty-seven state legislatures, and seventeen served in Congress. Most significant was the presence of four women representatives—Shirley Chisholm of New York, Barbara Jordan of Texas, Yvonne Braithwaite of California, and Cardiss Collins of Illinois. And the proliferation of mayors was not confined to northern cities; the wave had reached several small southern towns. Overall, by the mid-seventies, there were 3,503 blacks in elective office out of some half million elected officials in the country. For every 100,000 blacks in the country, there were sixteen black officeholders, which was a vast improvement over the ratio of the previous decade.

Having flexed their political muscle in local, district, and statewide elections, black voters were now ready to take on a national task. In the 1976 presidential election blacks went to the polls and provided the margin of votes to propel Jimmy Carter into the White House. Carter extended his southern hospitality by appointing more blacks to government positions than any other president in history. Among his appointees were Drew Days (assistant attorney for civil rights), Andrew Young (ambassador to the UN), Patricia Harris (HUD secretary), and Eleanor Holmes Norton (chair of the EEOC). These appointments by Carter were heralded by civil rights organizations and the black media, but at best they were cosmetic and had little impact among the black poor, whose misery index remained unchanged. Unemployment reached record highs for the nation's black youth, and the attack on Andrew Young for his support of liberation movements in Africa and meeting with representatives of the PLO, as well as the backlash from the Bakke decision, which had a chilling effect on affirmative action measures, were sharp reminders that the euphoria from Carter's victory was ephemeral at best.

It was time to circle the wagons again, and the Congressional Black Caucus (CBC) sounded the bugle. The cadre at the core of the CBC was Charles Diggs of Detroit, whose breakthroughs as head of the House Committee on African Relations were widely acclaimed; Ron Dellums of Oakland, California, who would later chair the House Armed Services Committee; Detroiter John Conyers, Jr., later noted for his tireless campaign to make Dr. Martin Luther King, Jr.'s, birthday a national holiday; Augustus Hawkins of California, coauthor of the Hawkins-Humphrey Full Employment Bill; and Parren Mitchell of Baltimore, who spent six illustrious years in Congress, with a number of minority-related bills to his credit. The flamboyant Adam Clayton Powell, Jr., of Harlem would certainly have joined his colleagues in shaping strategy for the CBC during its initial stages, but Powell was near the end of his career, and in 1970 he was narrowly defeated by Charles Rangel.

Shirley Chisholm (1924–). Shirley Chisholm's elective political career began in 1964 when she became the first black woman state assembly member from Brooklyn. While in Congress, she ran for president, but lost the Democratic nomination to George McGovern in 1972. Her long tenure was distinguished by a strong advocacy of black and feminist causes. Among her many accomplishments was a public law she cosponsored that authorized the erection of a memorial to Mary McLeod Bethune in the District of Columbia—the first time federal dollars had been set aside to honor a black. In 1982 Chisholm, at fifty-eight, resigned her seat and, except for appearances to support Jesse Jackson's two presidential attempts, has remained outside the political arena.

Andrew Young (1932–). A native of New Orleans, Andrew Young was a member of the CBC from 1973 to 1977 as a congressman from Georgia. His early recognition, however, was earned during those turbulent days in the civil rights movement when he was an aide to Dr. Martin Luther King, Jr. Young is a graduate of Howard University, where he was a premed student. Upon leaving Howard, he switched from dentistry to the ministry, enrolling in the Hartford Theological Seminary. It was at Hartford that he fell under the influence of the Gandhian philosophy of nonviolence. In 1957 he moved to New York City to direct a youth work program sponsored by the National Council of Churches.

Four years later he relocated to Atlanta to oversee a voter registration project for the United Church of Christ, which put him in touch with members of the SCLC. After losing on his first attempt at elective office, Young won a congressional seat in 1972 and was reelected twice before leaving Congress in 1976 to join the Carter administration. Three years later, following charges that he conducted "unauthorized" meetings with members of the PLO, he resigned from his position as ambassador to the UN. In 1981 he was elected mayor of Atlanta, and again in 1985. He lost a gubernatorial race in 1990. No longer an officeholder, Young is still sought as a political consultant.

William Clay (1931–). Born in St. Louis, Missouri, Clay is a graduate of St. Louis University. It was during his tenure as a manager of a life insurance company in St. Louis that Clay became an active member of CORE. He led many marches for the desegregation of public accommodations. In 1959 (and again in 1963) he was elected to the city's board of aldermen from the Twenty-sixth Ward. He was business representative of the city employees' union from 1961 to 1964. And in January 1969 he was seated in the Ninety-first U.S. Congress as a Democratic representative from Missouri, and has been returned ever since. Clay was instrumental in starting the major push to establish the Congressional Black Caucus in 1969. In 1971 he offered his definition of the new black politics, which called for a revision of the old concept that what is good for the nation is good for minorities. "What is good for minorities is good for the nation," Clay said.

Barbara Jordan (1936–). "All my growth and development led me to believe that if you really do the right thing, and if you play by all the rules, and if you got enough good, solid judgment and common sense, that you're going to be able to do whatever you want to do with your life. My father taught me that."[106] And she was taught well, because by the time she was thirty, she was a member of the Texas Senate from Houston, her hometown. She was the first black senator to sit in that body since 1883, and later became president pro tempore. In 1972 she was elected to the House of Representatives and served with distinction for three terms. Since 1979 she has been a professor at the Lyndon Baines Johnson School of Public Affairs at the University of Texas in Austin.

Ron Dellums (1935–). Son of an organizer for the Brotherhood of Sleeping Car Porters, Ron Dellums was born in Oakland, California, and attended city college there. Later he received an M.S.W. degree from the University of California at Berkeley. Until 1970 he was a psychiatric social worker at various community and youth centers. That year he was elected to the U.S. House of Representatives from the Seventh Congressional District of California. At one time an avowed socialist, Dellums has consistently supported progressive issues. Dellums was a particularly vocal opponent of the U.S. involvement in the war in Vietnam. "I consider our involvement in Indochina illegal, immoral, and insane,"[107] Dellums said from the floor of Congress.

SOUNDBITE

"An effective strategy for empowerment . . . must begin with the recognition that the American electoral political system was never designed to uproot the fundamental causes of black oppression."

—MANNING MARABLE,
POLITICAL SCIENTIST AND CHAIR OF
THE INSTITUTE FOR RESEARCH IN
AFRICAN AMERICAN STUDIES AT
COLUMBIA UNIVERSITY[108]

COSBY'S FORMULA

THE CONGRESSIONAL BLACK Caucus celebrated its second anniversary in June 1971 by inviting comedian Bill Cosby as a guest speaker. "Good evening," Cosby began his speech, "I think all you niggers . . ." And he let the phrase hang in the air for a few seconds. Meanwhile, gales of laughter erupted from the audience. With his impeccable timing, Cosby continued: "I say good evening, niggers, because that's what a lot of you are going to be when you leave this room. And I mean the white people sittin' there too. Niggers come in all colors."[109] The applause was deafening.

Poking fun at serious politicians and getting them to loosen up was not the usual patter of Cosby's stand-up comedy routine, but he was changing, and so was black comedy since he broke into the business right out of Temple University in 1962. Cosby's style was based on storytelling, no seething, snappy one-liners of a Dick Gregory and Moms Mabley or "blue routines" popularized by such predecessors as Redd Foxx, Slappy White, and Pigmeat Markham, or the whimsy rhymes of Nipsey Russell. What he sought was a different way to the funny bone, and to those fans who insisted he sprinkle a few Dick Gregory–like barbs on racial matters into his act, Cosby politely told them: "Rather than trying to bring the races together by talking about differences, why not bring them together by talking about similarities?"

Whether consciously or not, crossover and appealing to as broad an audience as possible was always a Cosby objective. Cosby's method of comedy had a classic ring, too, something akin to the Mark Twain stories his mother read to him when he was a child. But instead of nineteenth-century Hannibal, Missouri, or the Mississippi River, Cosby gleaned his material from the ghetto of Philadelphia and the Temple University environs where he led a triple life as an aspiring comedian, a talented if not gifted athlete, and a part-time employee with a host of menial jobs. When he first caught the eye of critics and colleagues, he was doing a series of brief stints at small clubs, polishing up sketches like Noah and the Ark:

"NOAH."

"Who is that?"

"It's the Lord, Noah."

"Right!"

Finally convinced he's talking to the Lord, Noah is nonetheless puzzled.

"I want you to build an ark."

"Ri-ght. What's an ark?"

"Get some wood. Build it three hundred cubits by eighty cubits by forty cubits."

"Right. What's a cubit?"

Then the Lord tells him he is about to destroy the world. Noah is wide-eyed with wonder and asks, "Am I on 'Candid Camera'?"

"I'm gonna make it rain four thousand days and drown them right out."

"Ri-ght. Listen, do this and you'll save water. Let it rain for forty days and forty nights and wait for the sewers to back up."

"RIGHT."[110]

This was the Cosby approach at its memorable best. Nothing obscene, vulgar, or risqué, just old-fashioned storytelling with a clever twist. Take a common situation or a well-known story, look for the comic edges, mix in a few funny voices, and deliver it all in a laid-back manner with an assortment of changing facial expressions—this was the Cosby formula. "I'm tired of those old jokes about stereotyped Negroes," Cosby told a reporter. "You know what I *mean?* I don't miss 'Amos 'n' Andy,' I'm tired of those people who say, 'You should do more to help your people.' I'm a comedian, that's all. My humor comes from the way I look at things. I am a man. I see things the way others do . . . A white person listens to my act and he laughs and he thinks, 'Yeah, that's the way I see it too.' Okay. He's white. I'm Negro. And we both see things the same way. That must mean that we are *alike*. Right? So I figure this way I'm doing as much for good race relations as the next guy."[111]

This search for racial similarities, the merging of black and white experience or characters, was the overall thrust of "I Spy" (1965–1968), the hit TV series with Cosby as Robert Culp's costar. Though rough around the edges at the start, the show eventually settled into an easy, inoffensive, but highly entertaining adventure series. "My people would just like to enjoy an hour of TV where a Negro isn't a problem," Cosby explained. "People can see I'm a Negro; we don't need to say anything else." Culp added: "We're two guys who don't know the difference between a colored man and a white man. That's doing more than a hundred marches. We're showing what it could be like if there had been no hate."[112] Cosby's greatest success was still in front of him on TV as Dr. Cliff Huxtable on "The Cosby Show," where he would be the head of a wholesome black family, and stay among the most popular shows in TV history.

Elsewhere, Flip Wilson, Richard Pryor, and other comedians were competing for America's laughter. Some of the rivalry was neutralized when Pryor and Wilson had cameo roles in *Uptown Saturday Night* (1974), in which Cosby shared top billing with Sidney Poitier. An essentially uneven, chaotic comic romp, the film was not without moments of sheer hilarity, and, as noted critic Donald Bogle observed, a long way from the "outrageousness of a Tim Moore (Kingfish on "Amos 'n' Andy") or a Mantan Moreland screaming, 'Feets, do your stuff!' "[113] Still, by the mid-1970s Pryor began raking in the Emmys, weaving his comic spell that relied on his stock of unforgettable characters, such as Mudbone, and his compellingly unique way of invoking them. Like Cosby, he crossed over with tremendous success, but without losing any of his black fans. But Pryor liked flirting with danger and destruction, and soon his life commanded the front pages of newspapers and magazines. In 1980 Pryor was allegedly freebasing or smoking cocaine when he accidentally ignited himself. He suffered third-degree burns over half his body. By the mid-1980s Cosby was once more riding a crest, and on his way to amassing the megabuck salaries that would make him among the richest black men in America. While others laughed, he laughed loudest and last on his way to the bank.

TEN MAJOR SPORTS STORIES OF THE MID-SEVENTIES

FORMER ATHLETES SUCH as Bill Cosby were doing all right off the field and outside the arena, but the mid-seventies really belonged to several top performers in boxing, baseball, tennis, basketball, and football.

1. *April 8, 1974.* **Henry "Hank" Aaron** of the Milwaukee Braves hits career home run 715, breaking the record held by Babe Ruth. Aaron, a native of Mobile, Alabama, began playing professional baseball with the Mobile Bears, an all-black team, and then went on to star for another black franchise, the famous Indianapolis Clowns. The Milwaukee (now Atlanta) Braves signed him as a shortstop, but by 1954 Aaron was a regular in the outfield, leading the Braves to two pennants. He won the National League's Most Valuable Player award in 1957, blasting forty-four home runs.

2. *September 10, 1974.* Perennial National League all-star **Lou Brock** of the St. Louis Cardinals stole his 105th base against the Philadelphia Phillies and broke the major league record for stolen bases in a season, set by Maury Wills in 1962. Brock finished the season with a National League career record of 753 stolen bases.

3. *October 3, 1974.* **Frank Robinson,** the only player in baseball history to win Most Valuable Player awards in both the National and American Leagues, was named baseball's first black manager by the Cleveland Indians. As a player, Robinson was a superb all-around athlete, accumulating nearly

3,000 hits and 574 home runs. "If I had one wish today," Robinson said upon breaking the color barrier, "that wish would be to have Jackie Robinson here to see this happen . . . I don't think I could have stood the pressure or have gone through what Jackie had to."[114] Jackie Robinson, harassed and insulted during his debut with the Brooklyn Dodgers after being signed as the first black player in the major leagues in 1947, was not related to Frank Robinson. He died in 1972.

4. *October 29, 1974.* **Muhammad Ali,** born Cassius Clay in 1942 in Louisville, Kentucky, defeated George Foreman in Kinshasa, Zaire, regaining his heavyweight boxing title. Ali, thirty-two, knocked out Foreman in the eighth round of a scheduled fifteen-round bout. It was the richest title fight in history, with both fighters earning $5 million. Ali, a convert to the Nation of Islam, had been stripped of his title in 1967 after being convicted of draft evasion. Four years later the conviction was overturned by the United States Supreme Court. As a amateur, Ali, then Clay, won a gold medal in the 1960 Olympics. He was unbeaten in his first nineteen professional fights, dethroning heavyweight champ Sonny Liston in 1964. In 1975 Ali was voted Athlete of the Year by the Associated Press, and later, in October, he would successfully defend his title against Smokin' Joe Frazier in a classic fight billed as the "Thriller in Manila."

5. *July 4–5, 1975.* **Arthur Ashe** became the first black tennis player to win the men's singles title at Wimbledon. Born in Richmond, Virginia, Ashe began playing tennis under the tutelage of Dr. Robert "Whirlwind" Johnson. He won the national junior indoor singles title in 1960 and successfully defended it the following year. In 1963 he was the first black member to be selected for the American Davis Cup team. At UCLA, from which he graduated in 1966, Ashe led the school's team to the NCAA singles and doubles titles in 1965. Two years later he was the American clay-court champ. Ashe was the first African-American to win a major title when he achieved the national amateur men's singles championship in 1986; he won the Australian Open in 1970.

6. *July 12, 1976.* A change in the baseball reserve clause was agreed to by major league owners and players. The new rule allowed players to become free agents after five years. the history of the ruling can be traced back to 1969 when all-star outfielder **Curt Flood** of the St. Louis Cardinals, after being traded, refused to report to the Philadelphia Phillies. He brought a suit against the National League, challenging the reserve clause, under which a player remains the exclusive property of the club owning his contract unless the club trades him to another club or releases him outright. His suit reached the Supreme Court in 1972, but it was rejected. Flood lost the battle but ultimately won the war for other players.

7. *1975 and 1976.* Ohio State University halfback **Archie Griffin** wins the coveted Heisman Trophy two years in a row. The trophy is emblematic of the top college football player in the nation. Griffin went on to star in professional football for the Cincinnati Bengals.

8. *1975 and 1976.* Running back **Franco Harris** of the Pittsburgh Steelers is selected the Most Valuable Player in the Super Bowl. Wide receiver **Lynn Swann** of the Pittsburgh Steelers received the same award the following year.

9. *1974.* **David "Skywalker" Thompson,** a six foot four-inch guard at North Carolina State University is awarded the Most Valuable Player trophy for leading his team to the NCAA championship. An exceptional leaper, Thompson starred first in the old American Basketball Association before joining the Denver Nuggets in the NBA.

10. *1974 and 1976.* Center **Kareem Abdul-Jabbar** (Lew Alcindor) was named the NBA's Most Valuable Player, first with the Milwaukee Bucks in 1974 and then with the Los Angeles Lakers in 1976. Abdul-Jabbar played his collegian ball at UCLA, leading his team to the national championship in 1966. Not until he was injured in 1968 did UCLA taste defeat, but they did go on to win their third straight NCAA championship. In Milwaukee he established his dominance at center, and by 1971 he was averaging more than thirty points a game. He won league MVPs in 1971 and 1972.

SOUNDBITE

"Float like a butterfly and sting like a bee."

—BUNDINI BROWN,
BOXING TRAINER[115]

HALEY'S COMET

TOWARD THE END of the 1970s black athletes were highly visible, and when the big game was televised, particularly in basketball and football, amateur or professional, black faces were right in the thick of things. In 1977, for at least eight fantastic nights on prime-time TV, blacks continued to monopolize the screen, only this time it wasn't a sport—it was "Roots." Author Alex Haley's book on the saga of his family, in which he traced his roots back to a village in Africa, was adapted for television. And if D. W. Giffith's *Birth of a Nation* was, in the words of Woodrow Wilson, "history written with lightning," then "Roots" was sociology reduced to electronic impulses, and for more than a week, a twelve-hour program held 130 million Americans (120 million of them white) captive.

Why so many white people? Was it an opportunity for white America to relieve its collective guilt? Maybe they watched because the programs just happened to be on during one of the coldest, snowiest weeks of the year. Or were they induced to watch out of some psychological motivation, finding sexual connotations in the idea of one person owning another, as one journalist observed? Was "Roots" successful because of the heavy promotional campaign, the fact that it was aired on consecutive nights, or was it just the right show at the right time? David Wolper, the producer of "Roots," believes there may be some validity in all the preceding reasons, although "I feel that the main reason "Roots" was a success was because it was a very strong drama about people," Wolper asserted. "It went beyond just a black story—it dealt with universal truths and human emotions that everybody could respond to. It endowed this black family that we were watching with all the qualities that we admire in all human beings—faith, courage, honor and family devotion."[116]

As compelling as the TV version of "Roots" was, it is the book on which everything rests. It was as a boy in Henning, Tennessee, sitting at his grandmother's feet, that Haley first heard the magnificent stories about his family. She told him about her parents and her parents' parents, and all the way back to the mysterious "African." This African, she told Haley, had been out in the forest chopping wood when he was kidnapped by slavers and brought to America.

Haley never forgot these stories, and after establishing his writing career and assisting Malcolm X with his autobiography, he began his twelve-year search to authenticate his grandmother's stories, and to find the one ancestor who could unlock the door and give him the missing pieces. This long odyssey took him thousands of miles from home to a small village called Juffure in the Gambia. After several frustrating days, Haley was finally taken to the *griot* or oral historian who could provide the connection to his African past. For two hours the aged *griot* recited the history of Haley's forebears, mentioning the name of Kunta Kinte, the missing link the author had been seeking. "I sat there as if I were carved of stone," Haley wrote at the end of his book. "My blood seemed to have congealed. This man whose lifetime had been in this back-country African village had no way in the world to know that he had just echoed what I had heard all through my boyhood years on my grandma's front porch . . . of an African who always had insisted that his name was 'Kin-tay'; who had called a guitar a 'ko,' . . . and who had been kidnapped into slavery while not far from his village, chopping wood, to make himself a drum.''[117]

Roots was a phenomenal success, selling 1.6 million copies in the first six months, but Haley's research, which he called "faction"—part fact and part fiction—was soon under attack, and charges of plagiarism were hurled by black and white writers, most notably Margaret Walker and white author Harold Courlander. Walker charged that Haley had lifted actual passages and based characters on material from her book *Jubilee.* Courlander, an expert in African and African-American folklore, leveled similar accusations about Haley's theft from his chronicle *The African.* Both writers brought suits against Haley, but only Courlander was granted any relief, as Haley settled the matter out of court. Though the actual sum of the settlement was never disclosed, it was speculated to have been close to a half million dollars.

Haley admitted that he was in part culpable, but most of the blame was shifted to research assistants who provided material whose sources he, in the rush to complete the book, failed to check thoroughly. Later, historians came forward to challenge the veracity of Haley's African contacts; his *griot* was, according to several writers, a fraud, and Haley knew it all along. The debate raged on for several months with no resolution, not that anything could have ever been proved conclusively. It should be noted that even the Pulitzer Prize judges were somewhat puzzled about the category in which to honor Haley in 1977, finally designating his award under "Special Citation."

BETCHA DIDN'T KNOW

In 1978 James Alan McPherson was the first black author to receive a Pulitzer Prize in fiction for his collection of short stories, *Elbow Room.*

KEEP IT IN THE FAMILY

WE SHOULD NOT be fooled by the number of blacks in the cast and production credits of "Roots"—blacks were still conspicuously absent in the TV industry, and at the managerial level they could be counted on E.T., the extraterrestrial's, fingers. And the general picture was no better. According to the Equal Employment Opportunities Commission (EEOC), in 1979 only 7.2 percent of the managerial workforce was minority, which meant that perhaps 4 or 5 percent were black. And if corporate America is the presumed training ground for the potential black business owners of the future, then grim, too, is this prospect, although many minority entrepreneurs and companies, such as RMS Technologies, Inc., Stop Shop and Save, The Maxima Corporation, and Network Solutions, are apparently undaunted by the statistics, forging ahead against the odds.

In 1977 there were over 230,000 black-owned businesses in America, and much of this can be attributed to the rise in black purchasing power, which was estimated at $30 billion in 1968 and $70 billion in 1978. This relative increase in the number of black-owned businesses, however, was offset by encroachments from large white companies who sought to compete in the manufacture of hair and skin care preparations and cosmetics. Even in the publishing industry, where black newspapers and magazines had been holding their own, there was an invasion from white companies seeking to capitalize on what they viewed as a growth industry.

But there were a few long-standing black-owned businesses that continued to prosper, despite economic downturns. The Booker T. Washington Insurance Company of Birmingham, Alabama, is indicative of this staying power. Established in 1932 by A. G. Gaston, BTW continues to extend its corporate reach, purchasing two radio stations in 1975. That BTW refuses to rest on its laurels stems largely from Gaston, who was born in a log cabin in Demopolis, Alabama, in 1892, and has tirelessly pursued his "dream to be rich" since he was a young man doing all sorts of odd jobs. His idea to form a burial society was an outgrowth of other business activities that the enterprising young man conducted among his fellow employees at the Tennessee Coal and Iron Company. Not only did he sell them box lunches prepared by his mother, he lent them money at an interest rate of twenty-five cents on the dollar every two weeks.

Gaston's big break occurred in 1923 when Reverend S. H. Ravizee of Hopewell Baptist Church, no longer interested in collecting burial fees among his flock, sent them instead to Gaston. Subsequently the burial society acquired the mortuary that became the home of Smith and Gaston Funeral Directors, and in 1932 it was incorporated as Booker T. Washington Burial Insurance Company. Seven years later, Gaston, recognizing another need in the black community, founded the BTW Business College. And then for the next three decades BTW expanded in several directions, acquiring property, setting up investment companies, opening motels, and constructing housing. Like the man whose name his company bore, Gaston was a firm believer in the power of success—and money. "Money has no color," he told a reporter. "If you can build a better mousetrap, it won't matter whether you're black or white, people will buy it."[118]

The multimillionaire has other homilies he dispenses to those seeking a successful business venture: Take no chances with your money. A man who has no money to lose has no business gambling; never borrow anything that, if forced to, you can't pay back. These rules may have been known and followed by John H. Johnson when he launched his publishing business in 1942. Johnson started his company after borrowing five hundred dollars from his mother. In order to raise the money, his mother allowed him to pawn some of the furniture. Berry Gordy also began his record company after securing a loan from his parents. And this practice of keeping it in the family has been widely copied in the black community. Earl Graves and his family have made *Black Enter-*

prise one of the leading black magazines. The Gardners of Chicago control a major company supplying hair products and cosmetics. The Herman J. Russell family of Atlanta has kept its construction company profitable for three generations. J. Bruce Llewellyn, who was told by his father that "this is a great country with great opportunity, but you're going to have to work twice as hard to get half as much,"[119] heeded the advice and set up a thriving network of businesses, including the Coca-Cola Bottling Company of Philadelphia.

The Sengstacke family of Chicago, like the John H. Johnson family, is also the keeper of a journalistic empire. At the foundation of the Sengstacke dynasty is Robert Abbott. Born in 1868 in Georgia, Abbott was the center of a custody struggle after his father died and his mother fought her in-laws to retain her son. She was helped in this successful legal battle by John H. Sengstacke, the offspring of a German merchant and a slave girl. He had returned to America from Germany—where he had been taken to avoid being reared as a slave—to inquire about his father's inheritance, of which he was defrauded. After the custody fight, he married Robert's mother.

Robert's first brush with journalism may have come when his father became a translator for the *Morning News,* a Savannah newspaper. He briefly attended Hampton Institute, but left to work for the Savannah *Echo,* where earlier he had worked in the print shop. Meanwhile, his father was starting up his own newspaper, the Woodville *Times,* where Alexander, Robert's brother, became editor after their father's death. With one eye on the print and another on a law book, Robert eventually acquired a law degree but was not admitted to the bar. By this time he had changed his name back to Abbott, dropping his stepfather's name.

Residing in Chicago at the turn of the century, Abbott founded the *Chicago Defender* in 1905, first as a daily and then as a weekly. His total capital was twenty-five cents, which he spent on paper and pencils. The paper was printed on credit. It took World War I to get the paper truly off the ground after several years of muckraking and sensational journalism. The *Defender* provided the clarion call for blacks to leave the

South "and come North where jobs and opportunities are plenty." More than 100,000 black migrants answered the call, settling in what were to become the ghettos of Chicago. Soon the paper was on its way to prosperity, buying a press and then a building. It became the first unionized paper as well as the first to employ an integrated staff. With the Depression the paper suffered financially, and Abbott struggled to overcome personal setbacks, especially the death of his mother.

In 1939, at seventy-one, Abbott decided it was time to relinquish his grip on the paper and willed two-thirds of the estate to his nephew, John, his brother's son, and a third to his second wife, whom he married in 1934. A year later Abbott died. The paper was floundering when John took over, but he quickly set it on an even keel, utilizing skills he had gathered as a student at the Chicago School of Printing and Northwestern University. Shortly thereafter, he sought to expand the paper, developing a chain of small newspapers around the country. The *Michigan Chronicle* in Detroit is part of the Sengstacke chain. John's son, Robert, became president of Sengstacke Enterprises.

These industrious black families have taken their cue from a business format that faded from the scene at the close of the last century. They have convincingly shown that it is possible to succeed if the family gets involved in an enterprise and works with dedication. Even such renowned economists as Lester Thurow have applauded the practice, endorsing it as a possible route out of dependency.

BETCHA DIDN'T KNOW

The C. H. James Company of West Virginia, an $18 million wholesale food distributor founded in 1916, is the oldest African-American business in the nation.

SOUNDBITE

"Most people don't really believe in success. They feel helpless before they even begin. 'Whitey's' not keeping blacks down. He's not keeping us from jobs and education. We have the power to make it in this society, and we can't blame the system for everything. It is the fear of failure that gets into the way."

—JOHN H. JOHNSON,
FOUNDER AND CEO OF THE
JOHNSON PUBLISHING COMPANY[120]

"WE ARE THE REVOLUTIONARIES!"

TO BE SURE, some black families, some elements of the black elite, prospered, as they always have, but the majority of black people were hopelessly snared in the mangrove of poverty. The plight of the black community was a common litany voiced by social scientists, aired through the media, and experienced by countless residents in rural shacks or in crowded inner cities, living in dilapidated housing and killing each other for space and possibility. Seeking a route of escape from such dire circumstances, poor blacks grabbed on to whatever hope there was, often succumbing to the siren song of false prophets of doom such as Reverend James Jones, whose followers—the majority of them black—committed mass suicide in their jungle estate in the countryside of Guyana in 1978 after their leader told them it was the only way to end the harassment by government agents.

Other blacks, with their backs against the wall, chose another option in relieving the numbing oppression. Their answer to exploitation and racism was armed struggle, and in 1977 when Assata Shakur was convicted, it marked one of the final episodes in the militancy of the so-called Black Liberation Army (BLA). The genesis of the BLA can be traced to the ashes of the Black Panther party and the murder of George Jackson. In 1969 the police, in a predawn raid of a Chicago apartment, executed Fred Hampton and Mark Clark. Law enforcement officials had killed a number of Panthers around the country, but these were the most devastating, and it epitomized the aims of COINTELPRO (Counter Intelligence Program) and the FBI "to expose, disrupt, misdirect, discredit, and otherwise neutralize"[121] black nationalist organizations and their leaders. Other groups targeted by the FBI were RAM (Revolutionary Action Movement), CORE, the Nation of Islam, and the Deacons for Defense and Justice, a paramilitary group from out of the South.

On August 21, 1971, George Jackson, twenty-nine, a widely admired revolutionary, while running across the yard of San Quentin Prison with a gun in his hand, was shot and killed. Jackson was in prison after a lifetime of crime. But gradually his activities in prison, which included all kinds of strong-arm tactics to control drugs, booze, and gambling, took a political turn. Always a voracious reader of Marx, Lenin, and African freedom fighters, and later author of *Soledad Brother*, Jackson began to tutor members of his prison gang, the Wolf Pack. After three black prisoners at Soledad were killed in cold blood by guards, Jackson avenged their murders, beating and killing one of the guards. His case, along with two other men who were falsely accused, became a cause célèbre among black militants and white leftists. For them and others, Jackson symbolized prison resistance, and he was viewed as the personification of revolutionary fervor.

He was certainly idolized by his sixteen-year-old brother, Jonathan, who made a bold move to liberate him. On August 7, 1970, Jonathan, brandishing an arsenal of weapons under his coat, entered a courtroom in San Rafael, near the San Quentin Prison. "We are the revolutionaries," Jackson cried to the startled people in the courtroom. He freed three prisoners and took five hostages, including the assistant district attorney and the judge, and then scurried across the Civic Center parking lot to a waiting van. The nine people were not in the van five minutes before they were surrounded by the police, who opened fire. Jackson, the judge, and two of the prisoners were killed. His plan to hold the judge as ransom for his brother had tragically backfired.

Shortly after his brother's death, George Jackson, by now a field marshal for the Panther party but still in prison, formed his "people's army." They trained in the Santa Cruz mountains in preparation for another attempt to free Jackson, but it never materialized, although members of the army continued to smuggle matériel into the prison for Jackson. When Jackson was not confined to solitary, he was allowed a few visitors. White Attorney Stephen Bingham was granted an interview with Jackson, and on his way to meet Jackson was handed a briefcase at the last moment by a young white woman. She had entered the prison under an assumed name.

"As Jackson was being returned to his cell," wrote Jo Durden-Smith in his book *Who Killed George Jackson?*, "an attempt was made to kill him. The gun he had been supplied did not work; the guards had one that did. Jackson was to be killed with this gun, which would then be identified by the guards as the gun he had been smuggled. The other, unworkable gun would be removed."[122]

Their setup, however, went awry. Jackson overpowered the guard with the gun, and then proceeded to free other prisoners in the Adjustment Center. Two guards were killed immediately, then a third who arrived later. Realizing he and the others were doomed, Jackson chose to sacrifice his life, running out into the yard, where a bullet to the brain killed him instantly.

The audacity of the Jackson brothers spread throughout the prison system, with an intense impact in California institutions such as Chino, Soledad, and Vacaville. One inmate at Vacaville who undoubtedly absorbed George Jackson's spirit, if not his politics, was thirty-three-year-old Donald D. De-Freeze. In 1973 DeFreeze, then at Soledad and an instructor in political and cultural awareness programs, escaped with another prisoner, and formed the Symbionese Liberation Army (SLA), an interracial band of revolutionaries. Later they kidnapped newspaper heiress Patty Hearst, and pulled off a series of bank robberies.

By this time DeFreeze had promoted himself to field marshal, reminiscent of Jackson's title, and chosen a new name: Cinque. DeFreeze's choice of a name was fitting in one way since Joseph Cinque, an African captive, had led a mutiny aboard the slave ship *Amistad* in 1839. Cinque and his cohorts killed the ship's captain and three of the crew, and tried to steer the vessel to the coast of Africa. But the Spaniard they had spared to serve as navigator tricked them. Believing they were in a "free country," the Africans surrendered to the United States Navy off Montauk Point on Long Island. Their case aroused national attention. Two years later, in a long and brilliant closing argument during the trial, ex-president John Quincy Adams won the Africans acquittal before the Supreme Court. Adams contended that Cinque and the others were within their rights to use whatever means necessary in their bid for freedom. The Africans were freed, and assisted by the American Missionary Association, returned to their homeland.

The twentieth-century Cinque did not fare as well. With Patty Hearst as a hostage, the SLA demanded seventy dollars in food for every needy person in California. The Hearst family responded, launching a $2 million food giveaway program on February 22, 1974. Meanwhile, Patty Hearst, in a tape sent to authorities by her abductors, declared she was joining the SLA of her own free will, denouncing her family as "capitalist pigs." She was later captured on film participating in the robbery of a San Francisco bank. A federal grand jury indicted her for this crime. On May 17, 1974, the police located the hideout of the SLA, surrounded it, and torched it with flamethrowers. During the ensuing shootout, six of eight SLA members were killed, including Cinque. Patty Hearst and William and Emily Harris, wanted for bank robbery, were not in the building at the time of the attack. But by September 1975, after a nineteen-month search, Hearst was captured and she was indicted with the Harrises on charges of assault, robbery, and kidnapping in connection with a 1974 shoplifting incident.

At about the same time as DeFreeze was assembling the SLA, Assata Shakur lay in a hospital, close to death with her median nerve severed, handcuffed to her bed, as law enforcement officers hovered near, trying to interrogate her. They finally had the woman they had been seeking for at least two years for her alleged role in a number of serious robberies by the Black Liberation Army, of which she was a member. Above her picture in posters plastered in newspapers, subways, and post offices was a headline announcing a ten-thousand-dollar reward for information leading to her capture and conviction. "Everywhere I went," Shakur said in her memoir, "it seemed like I would turn around to find two detectives following behind me. I would look out my window and there, in the middle of Harlem, in front of my house, would be two white men sitting and reading the newspaper. I was scared to death to talk in my own house."[123]

Having won acquittals in two previous trials, despite damning misinformation, Shakur was again facing charges after being arrested on the New Jersey Turnpike with fellow BLA members Sundiata Acoli and Zayd Malik Shakur. A state trooper and Zayd were killed in the shootout; Assata and another trooper were wounded. This time, though, she was convicted as an accomplice to the murder of a New Jersey state trooper and of atrocious assault on another. The state had manipulated facts and fabricated a tale to guarantee her conviction. Although even if she had participated in the turnpike shootout in the manner claimed by the prosecutors, her actions were armed self-defense and not "terrorism." Assata and Sundiata were convicted for the death of the state trooper in separate trials. Both were sentenced to "life plus thirty years consecutive."

Because of their political backgrounds, Assata and Sundiata were subjected to the harshest prison conditions imaginable. After six years of inhumane confinement, the BLA liberated

Assata from the Clinton Women's Prison in New Jersey. Later, Mutulu Shakur, not related to Assata, and white revolutionary Marilyn Buck were convicted of aiding Assata in her escape. Buck was a former member of the Students for a Democratic Society, which was aligned with the white radical extremist group the Weather Underground.

SOUNDBITE

"Brethren arise, arise! Strike for your lives and liberties. Now is the day and hour ... Rather die free men than live to be slaves ... Let your motto be resistance!"

—HENRY HIGHLAND GARNET (1815–1882), ABOLITIONIST AND MINISTER TO LIBERIA[124]

A CHRONOLOGY OF FIRSTS

1979

Audrey Neal is the first black woman, or woman of any ethnic group, to become a longshoreman (or longshore-woman) on the eastern seaboard. Neal works at the Bayonne Military Ocean Terminal in New Jersey.

1980

Dr. Levi Watkins, Jr. performs the first surgical implantation of the automatic implantable defibrillator in the human heart. The device corrects an ailment known as ventricular fibrillation, or arrhythmia, which prevents the heart from pumping blood.

1981

Dr. Lenora Cole-Alexander becomes the first black to head the U.S. Labor Department's Women's Bureau.

Pamela Johnson is named publisher of the *Ithaca Journal* and becomes the first black woman to hold such a position with a major newspaper.

Dr. Ruth Love becomes the first black to serve as superintendent of the Chicago school system. Before her appointment to this post, Dr. Love held the same position in Oakland, California.

Lillian Roberts is named the first black woman to head the New York Labor Department. She was appointed commissioner of the department July 2.

Vanessa Williams, Miss New York State, becomes the first black Miss America in the sixty-two-year history of the Atlantic City pageant. The first runner-up is **Suzette Charles**, representing New Jersey, who coincidentally is also black and the first black Miss New Jersey. She would eventually assume the title after **Miss Williams** surrenders the crown following disclosures she posed nude for *Penthouse* magazine. It's just the matter of an *s* between reigning and resigning.

1985

Lieutenant Commander Donnie Cochran becomes the first black pilot in the U.S. Navy to fly with the navy's elite special flying squadron, the Blue Angels. The precision flight team was formed some forty years ago and has performed its highly skilled aerobatics in air shows here and in Europe.

IN THE SHADOW OF THE GREAT WHITE WAY

—

ANOTHER SIGNIFICANT FIRST of the early 1980s was accomplished by playwright Charles Fuller. His Pulitzer Prize in 1982 for *A Soldier's Play* was the second time a black had won the award. Two years later Fuller adapted the play—renamed *A Soldier's Story*—for the screen, retaining much of the vigor and power of the stage production. Fuller's achievement marked a decisive advance for blacks on Broadway from one perspective, but there was nothing new about the general presence of blacks on the "Great White Way"; in fact, it was black laborers who widened an old "Indian" path through the wilderness, forming that conduit from the Battery to the Bronx. Previously we discussed the impact of black performers during the 1920s when *Shuffle Along* was the rage, and was followed by a string of hit musicals, mostly by white writers, but featuring black singers and dancers such as the captivating Florence Mills.

White writers would continue this trend in the 1930s with productions by the Gershwins, Rodgers and Hart, Oscar Hammerstein, Jimmy McHugh and Dorothy Fields, Vernon Duke, and others. The Depression era also brought a solid dose of social realism to the American theater. Emerging from the traditional Jewish theatre came the Group Theatre under the stewardship of Lee Strasberg, whose productions countered the superficialities of a *Green Pastures* on Broadway. Such efforts were, however, paradoxical in that while they provided blacks with work, they also spawned another round of indelible stereotypes that would spill over into other areas of the entertainment business, adding more confusion to the nation's already troubled race relations.

During the next score of years, *Shinbone Alley* with Eartha Kitt and *Jamaica* with Lena Horne were most memorable. Sammy Davis, Jr., starred in *Mr. Wonderful* and *Golden Boy,* marvelously demonstrating his versatility. *No Strings,* with Diahann Carroll as the centerpiece, began a trend away from all-black casts toward integrated shows built around black stars.

Duke Ellington's *Beggar's Holiday,* an integrated musical featuring white vocalist Alfred Drake, was typical of this trend. The sets were by Perry Watkins, Broadway's only black set designer. Before Ellington's appearance, the black composer had been absent from Broadway for quite a while. In 1947 Langston Hughes collaborated with composer Kurt Weill, a naturalized citizen who immersed himself in the Broadway scene of the late 1930s, writing the lyrics for the "first Broadway opera," *Street Scene,* with the book by Pulitzer Prize–winning author Elmer Rice. Although Hughes's lyrics to "Moon Faced, Starry Eyed" were the rave of the season, another song from the musical, the hauntingly beautiful "Lonely House," was also effective:

> *At night when everything is quiet*
> *The old house seems to breathe a sigh*
> *Sometimes I hear a neighbor snoring*
> *Sometimes I hear a baby cry*
>
> *Sometimes I hear a staircase creaking*
> *Sometimes a distant telephone*
> *Then the quiet settles down again*
> *The house and I are all alone*
>
> *Lonely house, lonely me*
> *Funny, with so many neighbors*
> *How lonely it can be*
>
> *Lonely street, lonely town*
> *Funny, it can be so lonely*
> *With all these folks around*
>
> *I guess there must be something*
> *I don't comprehend*
> *Sparrows find companions*
> *Even stray dogs find a friend*
>
> *The night for me is not romantic*
> *Unhook the stars and take them down*
> *I'm lonely, in this lonely*
> *house in this lonely town.*

Despite a reasonably congenial and productive working relationship with Weill and Rice, Hughes had his personal problems with them, and with the overall constrictions of Broadway. "The only way for colored to do much down on that street without outside influences diluting the product," he complained quietly about Broadway, "will be for the race to open a theater of its own."[125]

As early as 1935, actress Rose McClendon, who had a role in Hughes's *Mulatto*, anticipated the playwright's suggestion with her Negro People's Theatre, which was located at the Rockland Palace in Harlem. When the government began subsidizing theater projects around the country, blacks jumped on the bandwagon and a Federal Theatre Project was established at the Lafayette Theatre. Canada Lee's riveting performance in an exotic version of *Macbeth*, adapted and directed by Orson Welles and John Houseman, was widely acclaimed. By the 1940s black theater was beginning to cast a longer shadow outside the Great White Way. And the American Negro Theatre (ANT), formed by remnants of the McClendon Players, Abram Hill, and Frederick O'Neal, was competing against the likes of Paul Robeson *(Othello)*, Ethel Waters *(Mamba's Daughters)*, Gordon Heath *(Deep Are the Roots)* and Jane White *(Strange Fruit)* in dramatic presentations on Broadway, and Pearl Bailey *(Arms and the Girl* and *God Sends Sunday)*, Dooley Wilson *(Bloomer Girl)*, and Todd Duncan *(Lost in the Stars)*.

Anna Lucasta, Philip Yordan's play, was adapted for an all-black cast and was ANT's first major production, with standout portrayals from the gorgeous Hilda Simms, Alice Childress, who was on her way to becoming a fine writer as well, her brother Alvin Childress, who played Amos on TV's "Amos 'n' Andy," Earle Hyman, whose career received a boost in the 1980s as Bill Cosby's father on "The Cosby Show," and Herbert Henry. Theodore Ward and Owen Dodson, who was also an accomplished poet, were among a small but talented group of playwrights struggling for recognition. Ward's play, *The Big White Fog*, is considered one of the most underrated plays in black history. They would blaze the trail for Louis Peterson and his *Take a Giant Step* (1953), Lorraine Hansberry's *Raisin in the Sun* (1959), and Ossie Davis's *Purlie Victorious* (1961).

Except for an occasional production here and there—Alice

Childress's adaptation of Hughes's *Simple Speaks His Mind,* for example—the black theaters in Harlem were dark, and the lights would not come on again until the cataclysm of the late 1960s. Meanwhile, there was much more action on Broadway with Jean Genet's *The Blacks,* which was stocked with future greats—James Earl Jones, Roxie Roker, Louise Stubbs, Louis Gossett, Jr., Cicely Tyson, Helen Martin, Roscoe Lee Browne, Cynthia Belgrave, Maya Angelou, and Michelle Nichols. This farce launched more notable black performers than *Show Boat* and *Porgy and Bess* combined. Charles Gordone's *No Place to Be Somebody* (1970) and *For Colored Girls Who Have Considered Suicide/ When the Rainbow Is Enuf* (1978), by Ntozake Shange, were like bookends to the 1970s, though the latter was the source of a long-simmering controversy for its bold assertions about the relationship between black men and women.

Zooman and the Sign, written by Charles Fuller and directed by Douglass Turner Ward, introduced the charismatic Giancarlo Esposito, later one of several actors in Spike Lee's stable, and a strong supporting cast headed by Mary Alice, Carl Gordon, and Ray Aranha. Ron Milner's *Season's Reasons* (1980), Shange's *Boogie Woogie Landscape* (1980), Laurence Holder's *Zora* (1981), and Elizabeth Van Dyke's *Love to Lorraine* (1982) were some of the top plays of the early 1980s. Woodie King's Henry Street Settlement, the Billie Holiday Theatre in Brooklyn, Barbara Ann Teer's National Black Theatre, and Evelyn Robinson's AUDELCO (Audience Development Committee) were some promising signs that the 1980s might be another boom decade for black theater.

BETCHA DIDN'T KNOW

For his play *No Place to Be Somebody* (1970), Charles Gordone was the first black to receive the Pulitzer Prize for drama.

BLACKS BEHIND BARS
—

THE POSSIBILITY OF being somebody while incarcerated in America's prisons is not very likely, and thus there were thousands of such black "nobodys" in jails and penitentiaries. In fact, since the mid-1980s more blacks were arrested and incarcerated in the United States than in South Africa. Of the more than 500,000 men, women, and youths behind bars in some 6,500 penal institutions of various types in this country in 1982, it was estimated that 80 to 90 percent of these inmates were blacks. It should be noted that during this same year one third of all blacks in the labor force were jobless at some point in the year. The correlation between unemployment and the incarceration of blacks is particularly alarming among black youths, where perennially 50 percent of them are without jobs.[126]

Other economic factors are critical to this index, too. "Blacks constitute 12 percent of the United States population," sociologist Robert Staples observed in his *Urban Plantation* (1987), "but 36 percent of them are officially classified as poor. Blacks also make up about 30 percent of those arrested for three property crimes in the FBI's Index (burglary, larceny theft, and auto theft). For violent crimes, black percentages are even higher. According to 1981 FBI reports, blacks represented 57 percent of those arrested for robbery, 48 percent of those arrested for murder or rape, and 37 percent of those arrested for aggravated assault."[127]

But as Staples reminds us, the relationship between crime and race is a spurious one; the more salient relationship is between race and class. Blacks are systematically denied job opportunities in the primary sector and relegated to unstable secondary sector jobs. Consequently, compounding the reality that they are the "last hired and the first fired" is their lack of technical skills and training, which limits the possibility of

216

advancement and promotion to primary sector jobs. Then there is the traditional double standard of the criminal justice system that operates as conduit, funneling thousands of black men and women into the nation's prisons, then and now a booming growth industry.

"Someone black and poor tried for stealing a few hundred dollars has a 90 percent likelihood of being convicted of robbery, with a sentence averaging between 94 and 138 months," said Lennox Hinds, former national director of the National Conference of Black Lawyers. On the other hand, he continued, "A white business executive who has embezzled hundreds of thousands of dollars has only a 20 percent likelihood of conviction, with a sentence averaging about 20 to 48 months."[128] The disparity between the punishment meted out for so-called blue-collar crimes and white-collar crimes is another vector in the race and class relationship. In effect, white middle-class Americans are arrested generally for relatively minor property crimes, while blacks are herded off to prison for committing violent crimes.

A young black person with a "rap sheet" or criminal record is effectively stigmatized and virtually eliminated from ever being gainfully employed and meaningfully participating in mainstream society. And the drug epidemic has only cast a wider net, ensnaring even more black youths. Statistics show that the majority of drug users and those who profit from sales are white; blacks are arrested in almost disproportionate numbers. The black community is becoming increasingly aware that the war on drugs does not target the suppliers and distributors, but those users at the bottom end of the process.

As Clarence Lusane shows in *Pipe Dream Blues,* there is an inextricable link between drugs and racism. "Judges, politicians, police officers, the CIA, and other authorities, as well as organized racists, are involved in drug trafficking, money laundering, or payoffs. It's virtually impossible, in fact, to have the magnitude of drugs that flow into the black community without official and semi-official complicity. Federal narcotics agents have been charged and arrested on numerous occasions for such crimes."[129] One need only peruse the Mollen

Commission findings in New York City in 1993 to note the depth of police corruption.

SOUNDBITE

"From what I see, from what I hear on the street, the fear of the penitentiary is no big thing because the penitentiary is so full of black men, so full of people that people know, it's like a reunion."

—DAVID LEMIEUX,
A CHICAGO POLICE OFFICER[130]

A LUTA CONTINUA—
THE STRUGGLE CONTINUES

THE MAJORITY OF black Americans were obviously not behind bars, but the millions menaced by poverty, escalating unemployment, and the ravages of police brutality certainly felt they were confined within larger societal boundaries. Persistent oppression and the blatant denial of justice hovered in the background when Liberty City, an enclave of Miami, exploded in the spring of 1980. After an all-white jury acquitted four white deputy sheriffs in the brutal murder of Arthur McDuffie, a black insurance executive, thousands took to the streets, breaking windows and looting stores, overturning cars and torching them, expressing their rage and anger in a variety of ways. It took 7,000 troops, including National Guardsmen, state troops, and local and metropolitan police forces, to quell the two-day disturbance, which left in its wake sixteen people killed, hundreds injured, and eleven hundred arrested. Property damage exceeded $100 million. In July, two months after Liberty City's "racial time bomb" went off, Miami experienced another rebellion in which forty people were injured.

McDuffie was just one of several blacks slain by overzealous police officers. In Philadelphia a young black man, William Green, was gunned down; in New Orleans, Lawrence Lewis was a victim of police abuse; in Boston, Brooklyn, and Wrightsville, Georgia, young black youths consistently found themselves in the crosshairs of guns wielded by law enforcement officers. The daily atrocities committed by the police and rightist terror groups were key issues on the agenda when the National Black Political Assembly (NPBA) met in August 1980 in New Orleans. An all-out effort was also summoned to revive the NPBA, which, since its peak period in 1974, was dormant, if not completely collapsed. More than 196 delegates attended the meeting, but no principles of unity were forged. It was reported that such issues would be discussed at the convention that coming November.

But November brought even more pressing issues, and of paramount importance was the presidential election. In October, black disenchantment with President Jimmy Carter began to surface—this time, however, not from the grass roots but from the black elite. Two former civil rights leaders from the Southern Christian Leadership Conference, Reverend Ralph Abernathy and Hosea Williams, after declaring that Carter had not kept his campaign promises, openly endorsed Ronald Reagan's candidacy. "Though I endorsed him," Reverend Abernathy would later explain, "I can honestly say that I didn't vote for Ronald Reagan."[131] Nor did millions of black voters, but apparently they didn't vote for Carter either, as some three million blacks who voted in the 1976 presidential election did not vote in 1980.

When the votes were finally tallied in 1980, Carter received nearly 90 percent of the black vote, whose overall numbers were down since the last presidential campaign, as they were for white voters. Only 54 percent of the voting-age population went to the polls, so that, of the total who were eligible to vote, 27 percent voted for Reagan. Clearly, as one pundit put it, the largest party in the election was the "party of nonvoters."

With Reagan's victory fresh in mind, more than 1,300 blacks assembled in Philadelphia at the end of November to form the National Black Independent Political Party (NBIPP). Meanwhile, in New York City, Reverend Herbert Daughtry of the House of the Lord Church in Brooklyn was at the helm of the National Black United Front (NBUF), which was struggling valiantly to expand its political base. Any possibility of a merger between the two organizations was snuffed when Reverend Daughtry stated that the position of the leadership of NBPA was opposed to the idea "of the NBPA devoting its energies to developing a black independent political party, and we being the mass-based movement."[132]

On another front, such prominent activists of the black liberation movement as Jamil Abdullah al Amin (H. Rap Brown), Kwame Ture (Stokely Carmichael), and Afeni Shakur (Alice Williams), a New York City Black Panther who was framed on bomb conspiracy charges, called on the Congressional Black Caucus to convene hearings on the FBI's domestic counterintelligence program (COINTELPRO). Assisted by noted white radical attorney William Kunstler, the activists charged that the FBI campaigns were responsible for the decimation of black leadership and organizations in the 1960s and 1970s. Much of the impetus for this new appeal for investigation of COINTELPRO stemmed from New York City Black Panther party leader Dhoruba bin Wahad, who was at the time still incarcerated. The documents revealed a campaign of forged letters, anonymous telephone calls, and other illegal tactics designed to undermine the New York Panther chapter.

Nineteen eighty-one was hardly a month old when it was reported that three black youths in Miami had been convicted of beating three whites to death during that city's rebellion. By spring, more disturbing news emerged from the racially tense communities of Buffalo and Atlanta, where blacks were being mysteriously abducted and killed. Over thirty black children were killed during a two-year period in Atlanta, and many residents were not convinced that Wayne Williams, arrested and charged for the crimes, was actually guilty. Community organizations pointed to the Klan as the culprit, noting its continuous public call for the mass murder of blacks.

If things were not bad enough among the nation's impoverished, the Reagan administration dumped on more despair. In rapid succession, it eliminated the Comprehensive Employment Training Act (CETA) program, which had been originally funded at $3.1 billion, thereby summarily ending more than 150,000 federally supported jobs; then cut by $1.7 billion the child nutrition program, designed to feed hungry urban children, and to make things even worse, plans were being formulated to trim nearly a half million families from the welfare rolls. Retrenchment and rollback, the watchwords of the Reagan administration, were at hand.

Responding to Reagan's drastic cuts, on September 19, 1981, a massive 300,000 demonstrators from labor and civil rights organizations protested the social policies of the Reagan administration in a Solidarity Day march in Washington, D.C. A month before in Chicago, the National Black Independent Political party held its first meeting under the banner of a similar theme: "Fight Reaganism, Racism and Economic Reaction." The 800 delegates representing 3,000 members in fifty-eight chapters were also concerned about "reawakening the freedom struggle throughout the black community."

While some activists were hashing out strategy and tactics in the nation's capital, others were marching: in Selma, Alabama, an old civil rights battleground, 5,000 marched in support of voting rights extension, another gain threatened by the Reagan administration; in Mobile, some 100 miles south, 9,000 marched for the same cause; in Harlem 20,000 gathered in the streets to challenge Reaganism; 7,000 rallied in Jersey City, 5,000 in Washington, D.C., and in Milwaukee, 10,000 marched in opposition to the police murder of Ernest Lacy. All the marching, however, did little to halt the rampant spread of racial hostility, which was reaching epidemic proportions. Some of the violence was obviously random, but far too much of it was deliberately fomented and carried out by white supremacist groups, which were in many instances aided and abetted by law enforcement officers.

Instead of investigating these attacks on blacks, the FBI and its agents were too busy plotting ways to further neutralize or destroy black organizations such as the separatist Republic of New Afrika (RNA), which they characterized as a "terrorist organization." On October 27 two hundred FBI and SWAT team officers surrounded Sunny Ali's house in Gallman, Mississippi, armed with high-powered rifles and backed up by four army tanks. The FBI claimed that Ali, through her husband, was linked to the attempted Brinks robbery the previous week in Nyack, New York. Ms. Ali was arrested, and her attorney, Chokwe Lumumba, vice president and grand counsel for the RNA, was at first not allowed to visit her. This attack was just the first of many earmarked for militant black nationalists and members of the Black Liberation Army.

Black activists, workers, students, and other progressives could have used the FBI's help as they boldly confronted the renewed efforts of the Klan to intimidate and frighten them. In Athens, Georgia, over four hundred University of Georgia students held a vigil against the Ku Klux Klan. In Detroit, the Klan postponed a rally after hundreds of concerned citizens gathered at downtown Kennedy Square. Through the National Anti-Klan Network a well-coordinated monitoring of Klan activity was devised. It was now possible, on a nationwide basis, to observe and report Klan movements and to alert forces to oppose them.

Given the vast number of marches and demonstrations that had occurred across the nation since the ascendancy of Reagan and his pernicious policies, it was perhaps inevitable that by 1983 a massive March on Washington would occur. The first public mention of such a march, commemorating the twentieth anniversary of the historic event in 1963, came from within the SCLC, which under the leadership of Dr. Martin Luther King, Jr., had played such a pivotal role in the first one. It was a call that, if not greeted with mass enthusiasm, nonetheless struck a responsive chord in most radical, progressive, and black nationalist circles. Several black conservative detractors criticized the plan, charging that not enough money was available to finance such a march, and that it would not attract the numbers needed to make it an overwhelming success.

But the voices of dissent were muffled by the unanimous

roar from labor, the black church, and, unlike 1963, from black nationalists and revolutionary socialists. Indeed, black militants and leftists were reluctant to participate at first, observing that the mobilization was basically controlled by "black bourgeois and petty bourgeois" leaders, but by midsummer most had agreed to take part—it was, as one black nationalist commented, "too large an event to ignore." Activist/artist Amiri Baraka echoed this sentiment: "When the black masses move forward in any shape and forceful manner, the whole society must feel the impact."[133]

On August 27 the impact began to reverberate as 300,000 people, assembled at the mall under banners that proclaimed "Jobs, Peace, and Freedom," cheered on such speakers as Benjamin Hooks, Dorothy Height, Audre Lorde, Bella Abzug, Andrew Young, Louis Farrakhan, Jesse Jackson, and Harry Belafonte. Singer/actor Belafonte was especially forceful in his call for global peace and the assertion that "racial injustice is still our crippling burden and America's shame."[134]

There is no way to assess accurately the overall impact of the march, but it certainly sent a message to the White House. Some political analysts suggested that the mobilization led directly to Jesse Jackson's presidential bids and contributed as well to the successful mayoral campaigns of W. Wilson Goode in Philadelphia and Harold Washington in Chicago.

SOUNDBITE

"Divide and conquer, in our world, must become define and empower."

—AUDRE LORDE (1934–1993),
POET, AUTHOR, AND TEACHER[135]

RAPPER'S DELIGHT

EMPOWERMENT WAS DEFINITELY taking shape on the cultural or entertainment front by 1983, if Michael Jackson's achievements were any barometer. Jackson, ably assisted by his producer, Quincy Jones, won an unprecedented seven Grammys with his megahit album *Thriller.* Of course, gathering his share of awards was nothing new for the "King of Pop"; he had been among the top recording artists since the late 1960s with "I Want You Back." Hot on Jackson's heels was a colorful whirlwind from the St. Paul–Minneapolis area, Prince. A devotee of James Brown, Prince gave soul music a unique spin, adding considerable portions of Jimi Hendrix, Little Richard, Sly Stone, and Duke Ellington to his new funky mixture.

Whether Jackson or Prince were aware or not—though they were hardly threatened—a new concept was looming larger and larger on the horizon. By 1983 the musical concept of rap was about four years old, providing we mark its emergence in 1979 as a brainchild of Sylvia Robinson. Robinson was at a party at the Harlem International Disco when "all of sudden I heard these three guys rapping over the microphone," she recalled. "Something hit me—I thought they were fantastic. An inner voice said to me, 'That's a concept.'"[136] And Robinson had the experience to recognize a marketable concept when she heard one. A veteran of the music industry, Robinson first gained national attention as half of the team Mickey and Sylvia whose "Love Is Strange" was the rage in 1957. During the 1970s she and her husband, Joe, owned the All-Platinum record label, where they produced and wrote such hits as "Love on a Two-Way Street," by the Moments, and "Pillow Talk," which Sylvia recorded herself. With their operational base in place, they secured backing from Morris Levy, the late

Mafia-connected New York music mogul, and launched their new Sugar Hill label.

The Robinsons recruited their teenage son, Joey, told him what they had in mind, and sent him to assemble some talent for their "Rapper's Delight" project. All three of the young men who would become the Sugar Hill Gang had experience as hip-hop disc jockeys and emcees. "Rapper's Delight" was an immediate favorite in the States and then swept across Europe, where it reached the top of the charts in Sweden, Holland, and West Germany.

Grandmaster Flash, a hip-hop deejay from the Bronx called the "Toscanini of the Turntables," gave rap its next boost onto the national scene. From a Jamaican friend, Kool Herc, Flash added the cutting and scratching technique, at the same time rapping. Then came DJ Hollywood, Afrika Bambaataa, and Melle Mel, all of them to some extent influenced by the Jamaican dub artists and deejays I-Roy and Big Youth. A more detailed chronology of rap's evolution would include the early jazz scat and jive singers, the "dozens," or getting the best of someone by talking about a member of the family, and the "blue comedians" such as Redd Foxx and Rudy Ray Moore.

Smelling the money falling from the rap tree, it was not long before the major companies entered the game. When Mercury signed Kurtis Blow, a Harlem-born rapper, the floodgates were opened. His 1980 hit "The Breaks" was a seminal solo innovation and was widely imitated. Although Sylvia and Joe Robinson kept abreast with these insurgents, soon Russell Simmons and Rick Rubin jumped in the mix and pushed the concept to a new height. Now, with its top act Run-D.M.C. off and running, Simmons and his Rush label established a new plateau. Rap was about to explode and they were on the launching pad.

SOUNDBITE

"The best way to explain rap is that it's a conversation going on between two people from the same neighborhood. I rap to someone who has the same lingo as me and the record buyer is tapping into our phone line."

—ICE-T,
RAP ARTIST, AUTHOR, AND ACTOR[137]

HOMEGIRLS AND HAND GRENADES
—

RAPPERS WERE NOT the only wordsmiths kicking up a ruckus. Black writers of fiction and nonfiction were stirring up things on the literary scene in the early 1980s, especially black women authors, who began to assert themselves with an uncompromising vigor. Barbara Chase-Riboud's *Sally Hemings* (1980) was the decade's first shot across the bow. Chase-Riboud, who has resided in Paris since 1961 and first achieved acclaim as a visual artist, has taken the alleged liaisons between Thomas Jefferson and his slave mistress and woven a tale that bristles with credulity. The book is well researched and written with such an engaging poetic voice that if the slave master and his mistress did not have those trysts, they missed a grand opportunity.

Mary Helen Washington's *Midnight Birds: Contemporary Black Women Writers* (1980) is a perceptively conceived anthology widely used in literature classes all over the country. The stories and essays by these writers touch on a number of pertinent issues as they grapple with the complexity of relationships among black women. In *Ain't I a Woman* (1981) bell hooks extends this thrust in her always provocative analysis. Hooks is a thoughtful writer who is as versatile as she is current on problems that bedevil the black community. And these themes are given scholarly insight and a poetic turn in June Jordan's *Civil Wars* (1981) and Jayne Cortez's *Firespitter* (1982), respectively.

Fantasy and realism are deftly fused in Toni Morrison's *Tar Baby* (1981) There has never been any doubt about Morrison's grasp of black folklore, but to show its effectiveness in other climes gives this novel an additional universal appeal. Identity and affirmation are at the center of Audre Lorde's *Zami: A New Spelling of My Name* (1982) and Gloria Naylor's *The Women of Brewster Place* (1982), which, when adapted for television, retained its immediacy and poignancy.

The Color Purple (1982) was also lifted from the page, but this adaptation was for the screen, and it was as if Alice Walker's Pulitzer Prize–winning novel was rediscovered. For several months after the movie appeared, the black community was still dividing into warring camps of disagreement about the film's content and intent. Not since Michele Wallace's take-no-prisoners treatise *Black Macho and the Myth of the Superwoman* (1979) had there been such an outcry over a work of art. Many of the movie's detractors were upset over the unbalanced treatment of black male characters. Except for Mister—and only near the end after he has gone through a transformation—is there an admirable black man, the critics wailed. Walker was airing our dirty linen in public, was the attitude many of her defractors held. Others contended that Walker's portrayal was a reality, and representative of the abuse of black women by black men. "The novel and the movie show that male brutality against women is endemic to an entire way of life that believes in the natural supremacy of men over women," asserts Calvin Hernton in *The Sexual Mountain and Black Women Writers*.[138] Even today, if you want to start an argument in a roomful of black thinkers, break the ice with an opinion on *The Color Purple*, and then sit back and watch the fur fly.

Much less controversial but no less rewarding is Paula Giddings's *When and Where I Enter* (1984), a sumptuous assemblage of black women's history and accomplishments. Giddings's journalistic prowess is never better displayed as she recounts the background of fairly well-known women such as Ida Wells Barnett and Mary Church Terrell, and the relatively obscure achievers like Mary Shadd Cary and Anna Julia Cooper. And perhaps the only reason Giddings offered no discussion on Harriet Wilson is that her book *Our Nig* (1984) was just being readied for publication after being rescued from oblivion by Henry Louis Gates, Jr. First published in 1859, *Our Nig* is the story—and probably autobiographical—of a young mulatto woman who works as an indentured servant for a white family in Boston. Despite the book's dramatic power and literary merit, it mysteriously lay dormant until recovered by Gates in 1982. For some reason, possibly its theme, the book appealed to neither black nor white readers.

BETCHA DIDN'T KNOW

Our Nig (1859), by Harriet Wilson, was the first novel written by an African-American woman.

HE'S GOTTA HAVE IT

BLACK MALE FICTION writers were not exactly null and void during the early 1980s—David Bradley's *Chaneysville Incident* (1980), Ishmael Reed's *The Terrible Twos* (1982), Charles Johnson's *Oxherding Tale* (1982), and John Edgar Wideman's *Brothers and Keepers* (1984) fell short of creating a wave of sensation, but they did cause a slight ripple on the literary lake. The big noise from black male artists was coming from Hollywood, and although Richard Pryor and Eddie Murphy are noted for writing their own material, it was their appearances in forgettable schlock that were earning them some public notice and heftier bank accounts.

Both Pryor (*Stir Crazy*, 1980, and *Superman III*, 1983) and Murphy (*48 Hours*, 1982, and *Trading Places*, 1983) were cast in films ostensibly as sidekicks. In these comedy films, neither of the actors got a real chance to strut his stuff. Their parts ran the gamut from silly to farce without ever transcending the predictable sight gags and horrendous dialogue. Pryor, who had been such a commanding presence in three rather ordinary films—*Car Wash* (1976), *Greased Lightning* (1977), *Which Way Is Up?* (1977), all by black director Michael Schultz—was now trying to get back to the top of his game after a close run-in with death. But he hit rock bottom as a plaything for a white child in *The Toy* (1982).

Murphy, meanwhile, found a star vehicle in *Beverly Hills Cop* (1984), a film that offered him at least a few scenes to unload his comedic arsenal. In a memorable sequence Murphy's timing is superb, and with one expression, "A-Salaamu Alaikum" (Peace be unto you), he eludes a sticky situation and connects, especially with black viewers. The roles may have been mindless and the scripts without hope, yet Murphy was getting over, and waiting for the moment when he could take control of a production, or at least let fly some of the pizzazz that made him such an attraction on TV's "Saturday Night Live."

Murphy's fortune took a turn for the worse in *Golden Child* (1986), and unlike Spike Lee, he was still caught in the Hollywood shuffle, and unable to call his own shots. Lee's small, independent production *She's Gotta Have It* (1986) was both a critical and commercial success. A graduate of New York University Film School, Lee was heralded as the black Woody Allen, a comparison he abhors, when his first feature film made everybody sit up and take notice, although the vote from black women about Nola Darling's behavior was fifty-fifty. More than anything this breakthrough film set the stage for other black independent filmmakers to sell their projects and treatments to Hollywood studios and producers.

The silver screen had its share of dusky invaders, and so did the Great White Way, thanks to the smooth, inexhaustible pen of August Wilson. *Ma Rainey's Black Bottom* (1985) was the beginning of a series of historical plays by Wilson, each one representing a particular decade—this one takes place in the 1920s—and dramatizing a cultural or political issue. The black artist's encounter with the racist recording industry is one theme in this energetic romp. Wilson shifted gears in *Fences* (1985), a drama for which he won a Pulitzer Prize. A father and son are at odds over the question of identity and values in this play that occurs in the 1950s. In the major Broadway production, James Earl Jones, the father, and Courtney Vance, the son, are fenced in by societal pressures and their own deteriorating family, and their exchanges were so heated, it was inevitable that they would soon come to blows.

SOMEBODY OVER THE RAINBOW

THERE WAS ALSO plenty of hot breath between Reverend Jesse Jackson and Senator Walter Mondale as they vied for the Democratic nomination during the presidential primaries in the summer of 1984. Jackson called his political army the Rainbow Coalition, but there was no pot of gold waiting at the end of the campaign. Jackson surprised many pols who predicted his results would be embarrassing by running a strong third behind Mondale, garnering over three million votes. His election bid was marred by his comment that New York City was "Hymietown," and his association with the fiery Minister Louis Farrakhan of the Nation of Islam.

Jackson's verbal blunder was an off-the-cuff remark picked up and circulated by black reporter Milton Coleman of the

Washington Post. The gaffe led to charges that Jackson was anti-Semitic, forcing him to take a defensive posture. Farrakhan exacerbated the situation by allegedly threatening Coleman's life. Suddenly the man known for exclaiming he was "somebody" was on his way to being a nobody. Later, Jackson apologized to the Jews and distanced himself from Farrakhan, who was gathering his own notoriety. In 1988 Jackson made another bid for the Democratic nomination; he fell short once more, but 6.7 million voters liked what they saw and heard during his campaign.

What Farrakhan was saying, though, was causing migraines and conniptions from Los Angeles to Madison Square Garden. Pulling in large crowds wherever he spoke, Farrakhan became one of the most recognized black men in America. But for many Jews he was among the most despised after his injudicious, backhanded praise of Adolf Hitler and his chastisement that "Judaism is a gutter religion," in which he claims he was quoted out of context. Compared to Jackson, who was often considered a loose cannon, Farrakhan was a runaway freight train, barreling pell-mell from debacle to fiasco. Even black intellectuals were baffled by Farrakhan's defiance. Les Payne, an editor at *Newsday* newspaper, Reverend Calvin Butts of Abyssinian Baptist Church in Harlem, activist-writer Paul Robeson, Jr., and Abdul Wali Muhammad, a spokesperson for the Nation of Islam, assembled on Gil Noble's "Like It Is" TV show to discuss the ramifications of Farrakhan's bluster. Robeson did not bite his tongue. In his opinion Farrakhan was guilty of "irresponsible and dangerous rhetoric." Maulana Ron Karenga, an educator and theorist who formulated the Kwanzaa celebration and Nguzo Saba or the Seven Principles of Kawaida, voiced a similar concern and chided Farrakhan for his inability to operate within a unified context: "Farrakhan lacks historical experience in working in a black united front and therefore appears to lack sufficient appreciation for his allies' goals and the need to compromise at crucial junctures."[139] And "compromise" may be the operative word, because Farrakhan is not known for compromising on anything, least of all his "principles."

SOUNDBITE

"I know in the past [Farrakhan] has given the impression that the Honorable Elijah Muhammad is still living in some kind of form. But I say he is saying one thing to appease or to make people who believe in the old teachings of the Mothership and all that feel comfortable and feel that he is representing them too."

—WARITH DEEN MUHAMMAD,
SON OF ELIJAH MUHAMMAD AND
LEADER OF THE AMERICAN MUSLIM MISSION[140]

DESPOTS IN THE DIASPORA, FIRE IN PHILADELPHIA

BY 1983 REAGAN was comfortably in the White House, and the rest of the world, particularly the Third World, waited, expecting the worst from an administration seeking an opportunity to flex its military muscle. When internal turmoil ripped the Caribbean island nation of Grenada apart, the Reagan regime had its first hapless sparring partner. The Grenadian revolution, inaugurated in 1979, began to unravel months before ultraleftists within Maurice Bishop's New Jewel movement staged their coup. What began as a glorious extension of the Cuban revolution, and a model for a multiracial Socialist society, ended with a bang, not a whimper. Don Rojas, former press secretary to Prime Minister Bishop, offered this analysis of the coup: "What happened . . . was that the New Jewel party took a leap forward so drastically, so dramatically, as a result of rampaging ultraleftism that it very quickly alienated itself from the broad masses of the Grenadian people."[141] Not since the toppling of Kwame Nkrumah in Ghana in 1966, and the recent assassination of Walter Rodney in Guyana in 1980, had there been such sorrow and dismay among revolutionary black nationalists.

In effect, the revolution outran the people it had sworn to serve, opening the door to reaction and invasion. The actual details of what happened on October 13, 1983, "Bloody Wednesday," remain a mystery. A crowd marched on Bishop's residence, he was seized, and later executed along with several other cadre members. A faction formerly connected with the People's Revolutionary Government, now calling itself the Revolutionary Military Council (RMC), took control of the country and imposed a curfew. But only a small percentage of the Grenadian people recognized the RMC. With the government now in chaos and totally destabilized, Washington made its move.

Under the pretext of safeguarding the lives of some 1,100 U.S. citizens, mostly students at the medical college, U.S. armed forces invaded Grenada on October 25. Nearly 2,000 marines and rangers led the invasion. And soon these troops were bolstered by contingents of navy SEALS and other U.S. troops totaling 6,000. Within a week hostilities were subdued. Hundreds of Grenadians were killed and over a thousand held in detention. U.S. casualties were listed as 16 killed and 115 wounded. It was a comparatively easy exercise in troop deployment in the Caribbean Basin and a successful display of intimidation. "What happened in Grenada," Rojas noted further, "was part of the rapid militarization of countries in the eastern Caribbean and the intensification of anti-Communist hysteria sweeping the region. This Communist witch-hunting is going to spill over into a rejuvenated, right-wing-orchestrated campaign against progressive people in the United States itself."[142] And the actions over the remaining months of the year would verify Rojas's prescience.

The stepped-up campaign of repression aimed at the black

community in general and militants in particular took two forms. Most obvious was the malicious police brutality, which was no more than business as usual. Police abuse and misconduct were so rampant during this period that Congressman John Conyers (D-MI), chair of the House Subcommittee on Criminal Justice, was compelled to initiate a hearing on police brutality in Harlem. This was the first New York hearing on police brutality since 1980. Conyers's inquiry grew out of a number of citizen and civic leaders' complaints. According to the National Black United Front (NBUF), "deaths of black citizens at the hands of New York police officers have risen to over a thousand."[143] Since 1979, NBUF claimed, about seventy blacks had been killed by police officers; many of those slain were minors. The climate of police abuse enshrouding this period would remain the same through 1984 and 1985, with the well-publicized murders of Eleanor Bumpers, Michael Stewart, and Edmund Perry by New York police and transit officers indicative of the persistence of state-sponsored violence that was a horrifying, though familiar fact of black peoples' lives.

And the assault on black life was not only random; some targets of police repression were more glaring. On October 18, 1984, five hundred agents of the Joint Terrorist Task Force, in coordinated raids from Queens, New York, to parts of Massachusetts, rounded up eight blacks who, according to U.S. Attorney Rudolph Giuliani, were plotting revolution and were linked to the Black Liberation Army (BLA). Yes, eight blacks were threatening to overthrow the U.S. government! The activists, all of them highly skilled professionals, faced a sixty-one-count indictment and over 150 years in jail each for conspiring to rob armored cars and assist in prison breaks. During the trial, which began in the summer of 1985, it was revealed that the defendants had all been under surveillance for nearly two years, ever since the attempted hijacking of a Brinks truck in Nyack, New York, by three white members of the Weather Underground in alliance with the BLA. It had taken almost a year to seat a jury and to reach a verdict for the New York eight-plus, and they were all exonerated on the conspiracy charges, but they still faced possible sentencing for possession of illegal weapons and carrying false identification.

If the harassment and eventual arrest of the New York eight-plus had a chilling effect on the plans of black extremists, the barbarous attack by the Philadelphia police on the back-to-nature group MOVE made it unequivocally clear that law enforcement officials were more inclined to use force than to negotiate. For about two years city hall and residents had been discussing ways to end the way MOVE was "turning the neighborhood into a living hell."[144] Residents claimed MOVE had blocked off the rear driveway, were running up and down on the roofs and threatening people, and were playing loud music all through the night. Because MOVE refused to dispose of garbage, the group was blamed for the increased rat population. "But the worst part of it all," one resident said, "is that our children are being negatively affected by MOVE."[145] They called on Mayor Wilson Goode to do something about the intolerable conditions.

This was not the first time MOVE was the center of debate. In 1978 there was a shootout between the police and members of MOVE. One police officer was killed and nine members of MOVE were imprisoned. Remembering the previous incident, Mayor Goode, into the second year of his first term, delayed any action against MOVE, hoping calm would return to Osage Avenue. Things got worse. The media joined the outcry, and residents insisted that city hall take action, or they would. Mayor Goode called a special meeting of Ed Rendell, the district attorney; the police commissioner, Gregore Sambor; the managing director, Leo Brooks; and council member Lucien Blackwell. Upon being told there were outstanding warrants against members of MOVE for parole violations and assault, the mayor decided that the warrants supplied him with the legal right he needed to confront MOVE.

Troubled by his decision, Mayor Goode sought the advice of all his associates, who assured him the plan could work. Still, he was a bit concerned about his police commissioner, and his possible overzealousness. On Sunday evening, May 12, 1985, five hundred well-armed police officers slipped into position surrounding the MOVE house. Inside the house, nine women and children huddled in the basement garage nervously awaiting the raid. Rhonda, Ramona, and Theresa Africa were the women; the children were Birdie, Tree, Netta, Tomaso, Phil, and Delicia. Conrad, Frank, and Raymond, along with the founder of MOVE, John Africa, were the men located in other parts of the house, anticipating the siege.

Aware of the police encircling the house, MOVE defied them, daring them to attack. "Send in the CIA! Send in the FBI!" a voice boomed from a loudspeaker on the rooftop. "Send in the SWAT teams. We have something for you."

That Monday morning at six o'clock the police advanced on the house to serve the warrants. Shots rang out. Firemen began unleashing high-powered hoses on the wooden bunker on top of the house, hoping the intensity of the spray would bring it down. Suddenly things quieted down. The water tactic was not working. It was time to regroup.

It is still uncertain if Mayor Goode knew that Police Commissioner Sambor and other city officials had met and decided that the only way to dislodge the bunker was with explosives. Leo Brooks informed the mayor of the plan. "This was the first time I had heard the word *explosives*," Goode wrote in his autobiography. Before he could say anything further about the plan, it was too late. A helicopter, armed with illegal C-4 explosives, was circling the house. Goode watched the bombing on television, horror-struck at the menacing spread of fire that engulfed the block. He could see no firemen putting out the blaze, which was soon out of control. He knew his career was going up in that smoke. "Sadly," Goode said a week after the incident, "I realized that the police had killed two birds with one stone—MOVE and me."[146]

In the aftermath of the firestorm, eleven members of John Africa's family were killed—Ramona was the only adult to survive, Birdie the only child—and sixty-one homes were destroyed. Black activists were incensed. They called for an inquiry into the bombing, and soon a National Committee of Inquiry on the Philadelphia Crisis was formed. Among those involved were poet Sonia Sanchez, Dr. Francis Cress Welsing,

Professor Molefi Asante, Haki Madhubuti, Ron Walters, and William Strickland. More support might have emerged if people had been aware that MOVE had modified much of its inflexibility and had, by 1985, reduced its confrontational approach in the neighborhood.

To offset the move by community activists, and possibly to clear his name, Goode appointed his own commission to investigate the incident. Only the most naive of Philadelphians failed to see the transparency of such a commission. Even Goode admitted later that it might have been better to let an impartial grand jury look into the matter. Whether hand-picked or not, the commission found that the mayor, while absolved of any criminal liability, had been "grossly negligent" and had displayed a "reckless disregard for life and property."

Easily the most heart-wrenching testimony taken by the commission was delivered by thirteen-year-old Birdie Africa. "We was just sitting down there with the covers over our heads," Birdie began, ". . . and then we heard them putting gas, something, I think they was climbing up on the roof, then they started sticking gas in that pipe . . . then they put a match in there, then that's how we knew the house was on fire . . ."

> *elegy*
> *(for MOVE and Philadelphia)*
>   *1.*
> *philadelphia*
>   *a disguised southern city*
> *squatting in the eastern pass of*
> *colleges cathedrals and cowboys.*
> *philadelphia. a phalanx of parsons*
> *and auctioneers*
>   *modern gladiators*
> *erasing the delirium of death from their shields*
> *while houses burn out of control.*
>   *2.*
> *c'mon girl hurry on down to osage st*
> *they're roasting in the fire*

> *smell the dreadlocks and blk/skins*
> *roasting in the fire.*
>
> *c'mon newsmen and tvmen*
> *hurryondown to osage st and*
> *when you have chloroformed the city*
> *and after you have stitched up your words*
> *hurry on downtown for sanctuary*
> *in taverns and corporations*
>
> *and the blood is not yet dry.*
>   —SONIA SANCHEZ

FROM BEARDEN TO BEARDEN
◆

AND SANCHEZ WAS not the only artist inspired to commemorate the MOVE tragedy. Performance and conceptual artist Lorenzo Pace of New York City installed an exhibit that included burnt wood and rubble rescued from the actual fire in Philadelphia. The exhibit ran for several weeks at the Jamaica Arts Center in Queens, New York, in 1987. Pace's creativity was typical of the surprising advances in black visual arts in the late 1980s. While it was a season afloat with joy and the fresh creations of Martin Puryear, Emilio Cruz, Betye Saar and her daughter Alison, Adrian Piper, McArthur Binion, Cheryl Hanna, Gilda Snowden, David Hammons, Catti, Houston Conwill, Al Loving, and Howardena Pindell, it was also one of sorrow with the deaths of the eminent Romare Bearden, who died in March 1988 at seventy-five, and twenty-seven-year-old Jean-Michel Basquiat, who died of a drug overdose in August 1988.

Bearden is best known for his collaged images of the black experience, where pieces of history, folklore, music, and myth vie for a viewer's attention. A native of Pittsburgh, Bearden was raised in Harlem, a community where his mother, Bessie, was a political mover and shaker. Consequently young Bearden was privileged to meet all the top entertainers at his home, including Duke Ellington, Langston Hughes, and other artists associated with the Harlem Renaissance.

While working on a degree in mathematics at New York University, Bearden submitted cartoons to a campus humor magazine. This avocation led to his enrollment at the Art Students League, where he studied under George Grosz. During the 1930s he had a studio on 125th Street in Harlem and had among his colleagues such esteemed artists as Augusta Savage, Norman Lewis, Jacob Lawrence, Aaron Douglass, and Charles Alston. Later, at the Sorbonne in 1950–51, he discovered the works of Brancusi, Braque, Picasso, and other Cubists. Bearden experimented with several forms, including oil, photomontage, and other media, before devoting himself almost exclusively to collages.

Retrospectives of Bearden's work are usually the highlight of an artistic season, and they have been held recently in galleries and museums all over the world. His prints are among the most sought after by collectors, and his major pieces can be found in the permanent collections of the Whitney Museum of American Art, the Museum of Modern Art, and the Schomburg Center in Harlem.

Basquiat was just beginning to hit his stride as an artist when he died. Embraced by some of the leading artists and art critics, Basquiat experienced a meteoric rise to celebrity, which is all the more astounding when you consider his background was essentially as a graffiti artist. He was born in Brooklyn of a Haitian father and a Puerto Rican mother, and dropped out of high school in the eleventh grade. Although he had developed somewhat of a following with his "SAMO" graffiti, his real breakthrough occurred with solo shows in Europe. And then came an exhibition with Andy Warhol, Mr. Pop Art himself, and his name gathered international clout.

That he was an artist to be reckoned with was evident in 1985 when he was the subject of a cover story for the *New York Times Magazine*. Only the white artist Keith Haring possessed as distinctive a style and displayed as much potential as Basquiat.

Despite the setbacks, black artists could not afford to linger too long in sorrow, nor to sit on their laurels. Shows by sculptors Richard Hunt and Mel Edwards, both renowned pacesetters, were consistently fine and absorbing; Pat Ward Williams offered a stunningly new installation, *Ghosts That Smell Like Cornbread,* which combined photo and mixed media; and Faith Ringgold continued her love affair with the past through her lavishly embroidered story quilts. There were also several exhibits that surveyed the contributions of Hughie Lee Smith, Camille Billops, Herbert Gentry, Robin Holder, Benny Andrews, Hale Woodruff, Archibald Motley, Elizabeth Catlett, Eldzier Cortor, and Henry O. Tanner. Printmakers, especially those who clustered around Robert Blackburn's New York Workshop, included Michael Kelly Williams, Vivian Browne, and Camille Billops. A few folk artists—Joseph Yoakum, Bessie Harvey, Bill Traylor, and Richard Burnside—flourished. Ty Guyton's impressive urban structures in Detroit provoked discussion and were featured in several magazine and newspaper spreads.

And black galleries and museums prospered along with the artists, taking up the slack of the major museums to present the work of African-American artists. In New York, the Studio Museum in Harlem celebrated its twentieth anniversary in 1988, and became the first African-American institution accredited by the American Association of Museums. A year earlier, Mary Schmidt Campbell, its former director, was appointed to head New York City's Department of Cultural Affairs. Another enduring New York art venue, Kenkeleba Gallery, located in the East Village, frequently mounted exhibits of significant quality, as did the commercial gallery Cinque run by June Kelly.

Though there was a proliferation of black-artist-initiated shows at black venues, black curators did not avoid the mainstream. Alvia Wardlaw was appointed an adjunct curator of African-American Art at the Dallas Museum of Art, making her the first holder of such a position by a black woman. Along with her firm grasp of representational forms, Wardlaw is also quite adept in the field of photography, having curated a landmark show for Roy DeCarava in 1975.

DeCarava was among several noted black photographers who had solo exhibits in the late 1980s. Anthony Barboza, Moneta Sleet, Jr., Eli Reed, Jules Allen, Jeffrey Scales, Chester Higgins, Jr., and Dawoud Bey all had their photos featured in top magazines, including *Life*. Michel duCille, a photojournalist for the *Miami Herald*, won his second Pulitzer Prize with a feature on the effects of urban decay and drugs on a local housing project. Lorna Simpson and Carrie Mae Weems were both recipients of sizable grants from Polaroid and the Artist Foundation in Boston, respectively.

Jazz bassist Milt Hinton's candid photographs of his fellow musicians, taken over a fifty-year period, were widely praised and exhibited. The Schomburg Center for Research in Black Culture presented a panorama of contemporary visual artists living and maintaining studios in Harlem. Among the photographers were Pat Davis, Joe Harris, Hakim Mutlaq, Hugh Williams, Pat Phipps, Ed Sherman, and Shawn Walker. The exhibit was curated by Deirdre Bibby. At the Firehouse Gallery in Houston, Texas, *Herstory: Black Women Photographers* was an engrossing display of autobiographical works, featuring Millie Burns, Joan Eda, Collette Fournier, Coreen Simpson, Clarissa Sligh, and Fern Logan. Deborah Willis, one of the nation's foremost authorities of photography, curated the show. And in Atlanta, Georgia, at the APEX, Collections of Life and Heritage, Jim Alexander's photos traced the life of African-American music and its attending idioms.

Any one of these excellent photographers would have had a visual feast if they had attended a performance of *The Magic of Katherine Dunham*, dedicated to the dance pioneer by the Alvin Ailey Dance Company, and presented in 1987 at the City Center in Manhattan. Dunham (1909–), though hobbled a bit, presided over the reconstruction and rehearsal with a group of her former dancers—Tommy Gomez, Vanoye Aikins, Lucille Ellis, Pearl Reynolds, and Glory Van Scott. "Shango" (1945) and "Afrique" (1950) were among the Dunham works showcased by such Ailey regulars as Gary DeLoatch, April Berry, and Rodney Nugent. Dunham, vivacious as ever, divides her time between Haiti and East St. Louis, where her dance theater and school is regarded as a city treasure. The woman is a national monument.

That other internationally acclaimed dance company, the Dance Theatre of Harlem (DTH), under the direction of its founder, Arthur Mitchell, also had a bountiful season in 1987–88, gaining additional exposure from its television performance of *Creole Giselle.* The appearance helped the company raise the funds needed to defray expenses for a tour of Russia, where they performed in Moscow, Leningrad, and Tbilisi. DTH's Russian engagements, in which Garth Fagan's "Footprints in Red" was among the highlights, were well received.

Other companies staging memorable works included the Rod Rodgers Dance Company, Jackie Hillsman Experimental Dance Company, Diane McIntyre, whose use of jazz themes and musicians such as Olu Dara gives her performances a special zest, Charles Moore Dance Theatre, and Eleo Pomare Dance Company. Nanette Bearden, the wife of the late painter, collagist, and songwriter Romare, used the music of pianist/composer Mary Lou Williams to provide an evening of riveting choreography. Mel Tapley of the *Amsterdam News* said it "was an excellent showcase for dancers and choreographers with great jazz music. Both Romare Bearden and Mary Lou Williams would have liked the results of their inspiration and admiration."[147]

Dancers Judith Jamison, Debora Chase, Lula Washington, Virginia Johnson, Desmond Richardson, and Raquelle Chavis were delightful in solos and ensemble routines, particularly when leaping and spinning to the planned movements of Donald Mccall, Pearl Primus, Talley Beatty, and Chuck Davis. Tappers, too, made some headway, as Gregory Hines, Jimmy Slyde, Bunny Briggs, the Copasetics of Detroit, Honi Coles, and the sensational young star in ascendance, Savion Glover, slid and glided across the hardwood on, off, and miles from Broadway.

At the end of the 1980s and the early 1990s black classical musicians were widely featured in several sterling productions and were carrying on a tradition firmly established by Marian Anderson, Roland Hayes, Leontyne Price, and Grace Bumbry.

The robust soprano Jessye Norman, performing at Avery Fisher Hall in September 1989, was magnificent as Isolde in Wagner's *Tristan und Isolde*. During the same season Priscilla Baskerville led an exuberant cast in a newly staged *Porgy and Bess*. She delivered her songs with control and passion, much in the same manner as her triumph earlier as Bess in a Berlin production. Herbert Perry in *Turandot* and his twin bother, Eugene, in Anthony Davis's *Under the Double Moon* were as exciting as they had been together in a modernized version of *Don Giovanni* on public TV. Simon Estes, Kathleen Battle, Gordon Hawkins, Terry Cook, the late Ben Holt, bass Mark Doss, Cynthia Harmon, André Watts, all had splendid performances throughout the season. So did a few of tomorrow's stars, pianists Karin Hutchinson and Nina Kennedy.

SOUNDBITE

"I tell you what, by the white man's own method he's degraded his own self because he made himself the weaker one. He said, 'If there's one drop of your blood in my veins, then I am what you are.' "

—JOHNNY SHINES,
BLUES ARTIST[148]

THE GORGEOUS MOSAIC

BARRIERS WERE FALLING on New York City's artistic front in the late 1980s, so it was predicted that some precedents might soon occur in the political arena. One big, historic first arrived on November 7, 1989, when David N. Dinkins, sixty-two, became the city's first black mayor. It had taken New York City, often lauded as a bastion of liberalism, over a hundred elections to turn Gracie Mansion over to a person of color. By this time Mayor Coleman Young of Detroit had remodeled Manoogian Mansion three or four times, the late Harold Washington had come and gone as mayor of Chicago, and Atlanta had elected two different black mayors. Even a comparatively conservative city such as Los Angeles had experienced twenty years of black mayoral leadership under Tom Bradley.

A traditional club politician who gathered his wily smarts under the tutelage of the "Harlem Fox," the late J. Raymond Jones, Dinkins had risen from city clerk to Manhattan borough president to ride the will and desire of the "gorgeous mosaic"—a term he coined—to mayoral victory. There are two ways to interpret his notion of the gorgeous mosaic: On the one hand it is a general description of the rainbow of colors in the city's ethnic makeup. On the other hand, it was the electoral coalition—blacks, Jews, Latinos, Asians, feminists, gays, and lesbians—who rallied behind him to defeat Ed Koch in the primaries and to provide him with a narrow triumph over Rudy Giuliani in the finals. Dinkins beat Giuliani by a four-point margin or some 40,000 votes. It was the closest mayoral race in New York City since 1906.

For Dinkins to finagle this victory, there were a number of key events in the preceding years. Reverend Jesse Jackson's two bids for the presidency certainly loosened up the tight, almost conservative white vote in the city. Koch facilitated his political demise by sharply criticizing the city's police commissioner, Benjamin Ward, and insulting Reverend Jesse Jackson. Compounding these unnecessary abrasive remarks was his inept handling of incidents like the vigilantism of Bernhard Goetz, the Howard Beach affair, and the murder of Yusuf Hawkins.

Goetz, a seemingly mild-mannered white man, pulled his gun and shot four black youths on a New York City subway in 1985. Goetz was exonerated of all charges. One of the youths he shot, Darrell Cabey, is an invalid for life. Michael Griffith, a twenty-three-year-old black man, was killed on the

Shore Parkway in Howard Beach, New York, while fleeing a gang of white toughs. Griffith and two other black men, including his stepfather, Cedric Sandiford, were attacked by the mob of white men after leaving a pizza shop in the area. The whites shouted, "Niggers, you don't belong here!" Griffith and his companions first entered the neighborhood in search of a tow for their disabled car, which they had abandoned on the freeway. Yusuf Hawkins, sixteen, was shot and killed in the predominantly white Bensonhurst section of Brooklyn, New York, on August 23, 1989. Seeking a used car advertised in the newspaper, Hawkins and three friends encountered a mob of thirty whites brandishing baseball bats, chains, golf clubs, and at least one gun. The gang of whites thought the three had come to visit a white girl in the neighborhood. Six white youths were arrested in connection with the murder.

All of these events were fodder for Dinkins's campaign, and he used it masterfully during the primaries. On the same day Dinkins achieved his pinnacle, L. Douglas Wilder was making history as the first black governor of Virginia and the first elected black governor ever in the United States. Ironically, Wilder was sworn in 117 years later on the same day that P.B.S. Pinchback of Louisiana, the first appointed black governor, withdrew from office. Wilder, a fifty-eight-year-old Democrat, who had been the state's lieutenant governor, won by a narrow margin of 7,000 votes over J. Marshall Coleman, his Republican opponent. In typical racist fashion the media made hay of Wilder's victory, painting him as the polar opposite of Jesse Jackson. Wilder represented a more reassuring profile for a black man: Even during the turbulent 1960s, Wilder was far more concerned with amassing wealth (he is now a millionaire) as a trial lawyer than with civil rights. The article could have also mentioned that he was the grandson of a slave, an experienced state senator, and the winner of a Bronze Star in Korea.

Dinkins and Wilder had overcome tremendous odds in their climb to the top. They were victorious at a time when only three percent of the country's national, state, and local elected officials were people of color. To some degree, though Dinkins and Wilder both received more than 90 percent of the black vote in their elections, they were "cross-over" candidates who obviously seemed less threatening to whites. In their rhetoric they have both learned how to appeal to two disparate audiences without arousing rancor. And during their run for office both kept possible spoilers like Jesse Jackson (Wilder) and Louis Farrakhan (Dinkins) a safe distance from their campaigns. Other successful crossover candidates were Mayor Norm Rice in Seattle and Mayor Kurt Schmoke in Baltimore.

But gaining control of the mayor's office in various cities does not automatically confer power to the black community. For the most part, none of these black mayors has been able to break the vise and decolonize the black community, communities that can be compared to many Third World countries where the economy remains in the hands of outsiders, though the colonial forces have been sent a-packing. In short, a black mayor is the titular head of the city, but blacks do not control major public and private institutions in the city and county, nor has the management of these resources been transferred to black supervision.

BETCHA DIDN'T KNOW

During her run for the White House in 1988, Dr. Lenora Fulani of the New Alliance Party was the first black woman presidential candidate to receive federal matching funds for her campaign, and was awarded $800,000.

CHRONOLOGY—1988

January 27—Reverend Al Sharpton, a noted New York City activist, is arrested along with eleven other demonstrators at New York's La Guardia Airport after blocking traffic lanes outside a terminal building in protest of racial injustice in New York City.

February 10—Outspoken civil rights lawyer Alton Maddox, Jr., discloses to an audience in Ossining, New York, the trials and tribulations of Tawana Brawley, a sixteen-year-old girl from Wappingers Falls. Brawley claimed that she was abducted and raped in November 1987 by six white men, including at least one police officer. A grand jury report would later conclude that the whole thing was a hoax perpetrated by Brawley and perpetuated by Maddox, Reverend Al Sharpton, and attorney C. Vernon Mason.

February 27—Debi Thomas, a world-class figure skater, wins a bronze medal in the Winter Olympic Games in Calgary. She is the first African-American ever to win a medal in the Winter Games.

April 15—In Durham, North Carolina, more than five hundred black and white students at Duke University stage a rally in support of eight members of the faculty committee who resigned from the committee after other faculty members rejected their recommendation that each department hire at least one black faculty member by 1993. It was reported that there were only 31 black faculty members at Duke out of a total of 1,399, and 14 of these were in the university's medical school. More than 35 departments at Duke report no black faculty members.

August 16—Founded by freed slaves and once the largest black university west of the Mississippi River, Bishop College of Dallas, Texas, closes its doors after 108 years of service. The school was over $12 million in debt.

August 20— Mayor Tom Bradley of Los Angeles revs up his campaign for a fifth term. Bradley, a former police officer, was the first black mayor of a major city in which blacks were a minority.

October 5—The Supreme Court hears an affirmative action case involving the constitutionality of Richmond, Virginia's, set-aside program in the construction industry. The case, *City of Richmond v. J. A. Croson Co.*, will likely resolve a number of questions and will affect hundreds of millions of dollars in set-aside contracts in at least two thirds of the states and 190 cities, and affirmative action programs in general.

November 4—Actor Bill Cosby and his wife, Camille, donate $20 million to Spelman College in Atlanta, the largest single contribution ever made to a black college and one of the largest donations in recent years to any school. Cosby said he hoped their act of charity would serve as a model for others to emulate.

December 21—Ron Brown, a former top aide to Reverend Jesse Jackson's 1988 presidential candidacy, is endorsed by New York Governor Mario Cuomo and New Jersey Senator Bill Bradley to be the new chairman of the Democratic National Committee.

December 23—Broadcast journalist Max Robinson, the nation's first black network television anchor, was eulogized at the Shiloh Baptist Church in Washington by his close friend, the Rev. Jesse L. Jackson. Robinson died December 20 at Howard University Hospital of complications due to AIDS.

December 29—In Washington, D.C., Mayor Marion Barry denied he used drugs with an acquaintance whom he visited. "I believe that one is innocent until proven guilty," Barry said at a press conference at City Hall.

AMANDLA!

—

LIKE THE DAYS on which Dr. King and Malcolm X were assassinated, the day Nelson Mandela stepped from the Victor Verster Prison is a memorable one. The symbol of the South African liberation struggle was released after serving twenty-seven years in prison on February 11, 1990, and it touched off a worldwide celebration. From one corner of the globe to another, eyes were glued to televisions, watching Mandela take the first steps toward freedom, waiting for his first words.

"I stand here before you not as a prophet," Mandela told a throng of people at a Cape Town rally the day after his release, "but as a humble servant of you, the people. Your tireless and heroic sacrifices have made it possible for me to be here today. I therefore place the remaining years of my life in your hands."[149] "Tireless" and "heroic" are words he chose to describe his friends and comrades in the struggle against apartheid, but they are applicable to his own life, which began July 18, 1918, in Umtata, Transkei.

"My political interest was first aroused when I listened to my elders of our tribe in my village as a youth," Mandela recalled in his book *The Struggle Is My Life*. By the time he was twenty-three he fled the tribal life with its strict rituals and settled in Johannesburg, where he worked as a clerk before studying to be a lawyer. He had turned his back on his patrimony, and vowed never to rule over an oppressed people. "In 1944," he wrote, "I joined the African National Congress. The movement grew and in 1952 I was elected President of the Transvaal branch. The same year I became Deputy National President. I was ordered to resign in 1953 by the Nationalist Government. In 1953 I was sentenced to a suspended sentence of nine months' imprisonment for my part in organizing the campaign for the Defiance of Unjust Laws. Then in 1956 I was arrested on charges of high treason.

The case lasted for five years and I was discharged in March 1961. Early in April 1961 I went underground to organize the May strike, and have never been home since."

He would later write in an open letter to the press explaining the hardship of going underground: "I have had to separate myself from my dear wife [Winnie], and children, from my mother and sisters, to live as an outlaw in my own land. I have to abandon my profession and live in poverty, as many of my people are doing ... The struggle is my life," he concluded.[150]

After his release the indefatigable Mandela rested a moment and then set off on an international tour. His reception in New York City as part of a ten-day tour across the United States was typical of the thousands who turned out to welcome him. On June 20, 750,000 people jammed downtown Manhattan for a ticker-tape parade. He told the cheering crowd that apartheid was "doomed" in South Africa and he profusely thanked the efforts of the people in the United States for their commitment. "We have made the government listen, and we have broken the walls of the South African jails," he said.[151] But the struggle was not over, he reminded the celebrants, and he insisted that the sanctions stay in place until complete freedom is granted and the last vestige of apartheid was removed.

In Washington, D.C., five days later, Mandela was welcomed by Randall Robinson, founder and head of TransAfrica, an organization that had spearheaded the antiapartheid movement in the United States, and which was chiefly responsible for keeping the sanctions against South Africa on a steady course. Since 1977, TransAfrica has been in the forefront of efforts to pressure this government to promote a more progressive human rights policy. "Sanctions must remain in place," Robinson declared, "and it would be a mistake ... at this juncture for President Bush to invite President de Klerk to visit the U.S."[152]

Supporting TransAfrica's call for continued sanctions, Virginia's Governor L. Douglas Wilder demanded all of his state's agencies and institutions divest themselves of business investments in companies "not substantively free" of economic activity in South Africa. Like most states, a bulk of Virginia's investments in related business in South Africa came from the pension funds for retired state employees. In New York City Mayor David Dinkins said he would abide by Mandela's mandate and would not invest over $40 billion in pension funds it controlled in companies that do business with South Africa.

Meanwhile, on another international front that figured prominently in TransAfrica's goals was the situation in Haiti. In December 1990 despotism bit the dirt as the Haitian people overwhelmingly chose Reverend Jean-Bertrand Aristide as the first democratically elected president in the country's history. The dark days under the boot of the Duvaliers were gone. Aristide, a mild-mannered Catholic priest who speaks eight languages, writes poetry, and plays the guitar, would appear an unlikely candidate to run a country where the menace of political thugs is a part of daily life. It was too good to be true, and then the dream abruptly ended seven months after he was sworn in. Father Aristide was suddenly president-in-exile seeking political asylum in the United States. Within a few months he had set up his government-in-exile from rented apartments in Georgetown.

In October 1994, a year after his scheduled return, Aristide arrived in Haiti and assumed his rightful place at the head of the government. The military junta, headed by Raoul Cedras, which had blocked Aristide's entry, relinquished power and within several days Cedras was forced to leave the country. He currently resides in Panama.

The peaceful restoration of Aristide was facilitated by President Clinton's negotiation team, led by former President Jimmy Carter. Meetings with Lt. Gen. Cedras followed the arrival of more than 7,000 U.S. Marines and soldiers to the island nation. According to government sources, the U.S. troops will soon be replaced by a United Nations security contingent, which will include 2,000 American soldiers.

What lies ahead for the newly installed Aristide government is anybody's guess, but two things are certain: Continued unrest from the Haitian middle class who will assail the new government as it curtails its traditional privileges, and impatience from the downtrodden masses, who will protest that change is not occurring rapidly enough.

DAUGHTERS OF THE DUST
—

MANDELA'S AFRICA AND Aristide's West Indies are conveniently meshed by film director Euzhan Palcy, who was born in Martinique and directed the antiapartheid movie *A Dry White Season* (1990). Given her gender and the type of films she makes, Palcy is not exactly representative of the flock of new black filmmakers grabbing the headlines and marquees in the early 1990s. Many filmgoers and some critics feel that Palcy's first feature film, *Sugar Cane Alley* (1983), for which she won the Silver Lion prize at the Venice Film Festival, was superior to *A Dry White Season*. It did not help that her second film focused almost exclusively on the travails of white South African liberals. None of the formidable black South African actors in the film—Zakes Mokae, Winston Ntshona, and John Kani—was given meaty roles. Nevertheless, Palcy is a powerful filmmaker with an abundance of savvy and political awareness, and it is easy to predict that her work will always warrant a second look.

More than two viewings may be required to sort through the layers of myth and mysticism in Julie Dash's *Daughters of the Dust* (1991). Before the film made it to the mainstream, it had gathered a cult status—either viewers liked it very much or walked away puzzled by its meaning. Simply put, the film is about a Gullah family at the turn of the century, who dwell on one of the Sea Islands near Charleston, preparing for an exodus by boat to the mainland. The tension occurs between members of the family who resemble the *sankofa* bird—they face forward but they look back—and others who are ready to put the past behind them. Author/critic Toni Cade Bambara offers this insight: "Standing near the front of the boat is a woman in a long white dress and a large veiled hat. The image is familiar from dominant cinema's colonialism-as-entertainment genre. But we notice that this woman stands hipshot, chin cocked, one arm akimbo. These *ebonics* signify that filmmaker Dash has appropriated the image from reactionary cinema for an emancipatory purpose. She intends to heal our imperialized eyes."[153]

Less ambitious and far easier to decipher were other top releases from 1991, including Mario Van Peebles's *New Jack City;* Matty Rich's *Straight Out of Brooklyn;* the underrated and sadly neglected *The Five Heartbeats,* written and directed by Robert Townsend; *House Party II,* by the Hudlins (Reginald and Warrington); Charles Lane's *True Identity; A Rage in Harlem,* directed by Bill Duke, from a book by Chester Himes; *To Sleep with Anger,* directed by Charles Burnett; and Keenan Ivory Wayans's *I'm Gonna Git You Sucka.* Of course, Spike Lee was back again, as he has been doing almost each year since *She's Gotta Have It* in 1986, with a new film, *Jungle Fever.* Lee was out to recover from the rash of nasty reviews of *Mo' Better Blues* (1990), but he went from the blues to a fever, and he only made some critics sicker.

On the other hand, a brash newcomer, John Singleton, was hogging the spotlight, and some would say rightfully, with his debut feature *Boyz N The Hood.* For the motif of this film Singleton mined his own turbulent past, particularly his strained relationship with his father. What is most evident, though, is the movie's nitty-gritty nihilism, which pervades South Central L.A. Laurence Fishburne and rap star Ice Cube portray strong characters, and it would have been interesting to see them have more than a passing encounter on-screen.

The nineteen black films released in 1991 surpassed the total count of the 1980s. Why suddenly so many black films by black directors? Was Hollywood experiencing its own special case of perestroika and glasnost? Or was this just another temporary flirtation with the black experience at a time when Hollywood needed a quick fix, a shot of ethnic adrenaline? Warrington Hudlin, a Yale graduate, believed that Hollywood was sniffing around because of an interest in fresh themes and new blood—make that bloods. "They are all tapped out," Hudlin told the *New York Times.* "How many sequels can you do? Very few of our stories have been told. People want to see them."[154]

Hollywood needed a quick fix, a shot of ethnic adrenaline? Warrington Hudlin, a Yale graduate, believed that Hollywood was sniffing around because of an interest in fresh themes and new blood—make that bloods. "They are all tapped out," Hudlin told the *New York Times*. "How many sequels can you do? Very few of our stories have been told. People want to see them."[154]

But there are a slew of "exotic" untapped cultures to exploit—why black America? That answer can be found in demographics. The moguls of Hollywood are certainly aware that blacks represent 25 percent of America's movie-house

BETCHA DIDN'T KNOW

Actress/comedienne Whoopi Goldberg won an Oscar for her supporting role in the movie *Ghost* (1991), only the second black actress awarded the coveted gold statue.

CAN'T WE JUST GET ALONG?

NOT TOO FAR from the Hollywood sound stages, another drama was unfolding, and while it, too, was being filmed, the reality of the scenes would ultimately have a devastating impact on the city of Los Angeles—and other parts of the country. There was nothing unique about Rodney King's brutal beating by the Los Angeles police, except it was captured on film. Two years earlier, cited Charles Simmons, a journalism and law professor at California State University at Los Angeles, Donald Jackson, a black police officer, was the victim of a similar abuse by white cops. White cops cursed him and smashed his head through a store window, all of which was taped by a film crew and shown on national television the next day. "At the subsequent hearing and trial," Simmons wrote, "the accused police claimed that Jackson had thrown himself through the window as a tactic to make the white officers look bad. They were acquitted."[155]

And so were the four cops who stopped motorist King that March evening and beat him senseless, clubbing him with batons fifty-six times within eighty-one seconds while other cops looked on. Amateur filmmaker George Holliday caught the entire scene on videotape, and there was a collective gasp when it was shown on the evening news. The officers, who had arrested King after a high-speed chase, said the beating was justified since King was resisting arrest.

The King trial, as it was popularly known, took place the following April in Simi Valley, a pristine suburb of Los Angeles and a haven for retired police officers, but it could have been in Money, Mississippi, in 1955, considering the results. All four cops were exonerated, and the next verdict belonged to the people who exploded in a rebellion that only Hurricane Andrew exceeded in death and destruction. During the three-day rampage, Korean store owners felt the brunt of looting. Some blacks were still angry about the killing of an unarmed young black girl, Latasha Harlins, by a Korean grocer. Michael Dinwiddie, a resident of mid-Wilshire who had experienced the Detroit riot of 1967, was not fazed when he heard folks were running amok. "The minute I heard looting had started," he told a reporter, "I knew what to do. Get a full tank of gas and some extra groceries."[156]

When calm was finally restored, following the entry of federal troops, fifty-eight people were dead and thousands injured, including white trucker Reginald Denny, who was mercilessly beaten by black marauders, and property damage ran to $550 million. Nearly 4,000 buildings were destroyed and some 10,000 more were burned. Now it was time to analyze what had happened, to assess blame, and to launch the massive cleanup campaign. "A racist, exploitative, capitalist society is responsible for the rebellion," said political activist

Ron Daniels. "The ancestors' exhortation is to be self-reliant, to take seriously the task of building viable, African-centered cultural, educational, economic, and political institutions, to be uncompromising in our revolutionary commitment in breaking the chains of white supremacy and white domination over the lives of our people and the lives of the oppressed."[157]

The "City of Angels" was still trying to recover its heavenly visage when Rodney King won the right to a second trial for the violation of his civil rights. Folks and the city braced again for the outcome of the trial, which was a fifty-fifty decision. Two of the officers were acquitted, while Sergeant Stacey Koon and officer Laurence Powell await sentencing. They could get up to ten years in prison and hefty fines, but don't count on the maximum, which will probably occur when the verdict is rendered for the two black men charged with the beating of Reginald Denny.

TO TELL THE TRUTH
—

SUPREME COURT JUSTICE Thurgood Marshall had no idea that his retirement from the nation's highest bench would set off a firestorm of national debate over the veracity of a black man and a black woman; their encounter, the charge and countercharge, would eventually become part media circus and part soap opera. On June 27, 1991, Justice Marshall, eighty-three, the first black appointed to the Court, decided his nearly twenty-five years of service were sufficient and stepped down. He had amassed an enviable record both as a jurist and as a lawyer. A fierce advocate of the First Amendment of the Constitution and civil rights, Marshall was the author of several important opinions. Black America moaned when they heard that he would no longer be there for them.

And more of them moaned and groaned when they heard that Judge Clarence Thomas was being considered as his re-

placement by President George Bush. In less than a month
after Justice Marshall announced his retirement, Bush nominated Thomas, forty-three, a conservative federal appeals
court judge, to replace him. The nomination was received
with mixed emotions. On the one hand, the black community—mostly those who had no idea who Thomas was or what
he represented, though something could have been deduced
by the character of the nominator was proud to have another black man on the Supreme Court. Those more informed, however, protested loud and long, denouncing Bush
for his shrewd machinations, and declaring that Thomas was
not qualified legally or morally to fill the shoes of the esteemed Marshall.

In the midst of Thomas's confirmation hearings before the
Senate Judiciary Committee, a bombshell was dropped. Its
origins began in August 1991 when a former Yale classmate
of Anita Hill, a University of Oklahoma law professor and
erstwhile assistant at the Education Department and the
Equal Employment Opportunity Commission, tipped off a
staff member of Senator Howard Metzenbaum (Democratic
senator from Ohio) of the Judiciary Committee that Thomas
had sexually harassed Hill. Confronted with the information,
Hill was at first reluctant to testify before the Committee, and
then after a series of contacts with various Senate investigators
and the FBI, she agreed to appear. But this occurred after
the Committee split its confirmation vote seven to seven.
Thomas's nomination went forward without recommendation
from the Committee.

Before long the media caught wind of the secret negotia-
tions. Hill's name and at least a portion of the FBI report
about her allegations were leaked to *New York Newsday* and
National Public Radio. Thomas denied the charges and requested a delay in the Senate vote. The Committee postponed
the vote for one week to investigate Hill's allegations. On
October 11 the hearings reopened and were carried live on
all the major TV networks. With an opening jab, Thomas
denied the charges and asserted that his reputation was being
ruined by unfair proceedings. Hill took the stand and provided the Committee with graphic testimony about sexual

comments that Thomas made about pornographic films and his own sexual prowess. Later that evening Thomas unleashed the first salvo, claiming the hearing was "a high-tech lynching for uppity blacks." Witnesses were called for both sides, and four of Hill's friends testified that she had told them several years before about Thomas's behavior. Hill's counsel released a lie detector test she took and passed.

After all was said and done, the Committee could reach no conclusion on whether Thomas or Hill was telling the truth. On October 16 the Senate voted fifty-two to forty-eight to confirm Thomas as associate justice of the Supreme Court. And yet, as Robert Chrisman and Robert Allen wrote in their introduction to *Court of Appeal: The Black Community Speaks Out on the Racial and Sexual Politics of Thomas vs. Hill,* "The deeper meaning and true impact of the hearings remained cloudy and unresolved. A vote for Clarence Thomas could be seen as either a liberal or a conservative gesture; as a pro-black or anti-black statement; or as an absolution of Thomas from the charges of sexual harassment."[158]

Reverend Benjamin Hooks, executive director of the NAACP, expressed the feelings of thousands of blacks who believed that Justice Thomas was not only an improper successor to Justice Marshall, but that his very presence on the Court was a blemish on Marshall's legacy. Before the hearings were over, Hooks stated: "We believe that Judge Thomas is part of the announced intention of the Reagan-Bush political establishment to 'pack' the Supreme Court—indeed, the federal judiciary—with persons sympathetic to the political and social views of the far right. We earnestly desire the appointment of an African-American to the Supreme Court bench. But if there is a reason to believe the African-American nominee would join in the further and continued erosion of threatened civil rights gains, we don't need that appointee."[159] Polls showed that the majority of black people supported Thomas's confirmation, including such personalities as poet Maya Angelou, Niara Sudarkasa, president of Lincoln University in Pennsylvania, and Reverend Joseph Lowery, executive director of the SCLC. None of them was apparently aware of Thomas's connection to paid South African agents through J. A. Y. Parker and his right-wing Lincoln Institute.

Hooks's worst fears about Justice Thomas surfaced almost immediately, as the conservative jurist sided with Justice Antonin Scala and Chief Justice William Rehnquist to form a solid conservative core on the Court. Practically all of his early opinions have veered to the right. He decided against a prisoner who had been handcuffed and beaten by a prison guard, finding the treatment was not cruel and unusual punishment as proscribed by the Eighth Amendment. And Thomas ruled against a paranoid schizophrenic who was forced to take large doses of medication months before his trial, producing a behavior that was seemingly sane. The drugging concealed his condition, the man claimed, thereby denying him due process. While the court found for the prisoner, seven to two, Justice Thomas was one of the dissenting votes. Later, Thomas would rule against Haitian refugees seeking asylum in the United States and against laws approving the design of districts to empower minorities. Only on one occasion during his first months on the bench did Thomas stray from the conservative line, and that case was on a segregation matter in Mississippi, which was too obvious for the justice to circumvent.

Most Supreme Court watchers were not surprised by the decisions of its newest member; what was a bit unexpected was the political flak from his showdown with Professor Hill. In the aftermath of the hearings several women seeking elective office were successful. None more stunning than Carol Moseley Braun's triumph in Illinois, making her the lone black in the Senate. She was sworn in with three other women. Women in the House of Representatives increased by nearly 70 percent after the 1992 tallies. Hill's actions also prompted other abused and harassed women to speak out and to seek redress.

Thomas's refusal to cave in may have emboldened the already highly visible black conservatives and neoconservatives to push for even more exposure in the media. Among the coterie of black conservatives are Glenn Loury, Thomas Sowell, Anne Wortham, Shelby Steele, Alan Keyes, Robert Woodson, Tony Brown, and Gloria Toote. In numbers they are small, but they carry a wallop disproportionate to their size, given their access to op-ed columns in major newspapers and magazines, and their appearances on TV talk shows. What is a black conservative? Well, there is no reliable litmus test, but normally they oppose affirmative action measures—"It's morally corrupting," Shelby Steele is known to bellow. These conservatives are quick to blame the poor and dispossessed for their own predicament; in their "victimization," conservatives charge, the downtrodden are responsible for their situation because America is a color-blind society and racism is nonexistent.

SOUNDBITE

"Do not take arsenic today because you may be confronted with strychnine tomorrow."

—CARL ROWAN,
A NATIONALLY SYNDICATED COLUMNIST[160]

OPERATION DESERT STORM
-

WHATEVER THE MENACE of black conservatives, it was light compared to the black troops deployed to frontline positions during Operation Desert Storm, the war to free Kuwait from Iraq during the summer of 1990. Black activists (and some black reservists) charged that blacks were being placed on battlefronts at a much higher rate than their white counterparts. Moreover, black America was perturbed by the exorbitant amount of money being siphoned from an already strapped

U.S. budget to pay for the massive deployment of some 400,000 troops, of which 30 percent were African-Americans, to Saudi Arabia and the Persian Gulf in the first months of 1991. "Think of the good that $1 billion could do for black America and poor white America," said the Reverend T. J. Jemison, president of the nearly eight-million-strong National Baptist Convention USA, the largest black organization in the country.[161] For Reverend Jemison and other critics, the U.S. dollars would be better spent mounting a full-fledged war against drugs and poverty instead of provoking a war in the Middle East. And the only thing different about this skirmish is that for the first time, black troops would be in combat knowing a black man, General Colin Powell, was the Chairman of the Joint Chiefs of Staff.

Powell had diligently worked his way up through the ranks, beginning as a captain in the Vietnam conflict. Born in Harlem and raised in the South Bronx, Powell was an average student who excelled in the ROTC (Reserve Officer Training Corps). When he graduated from City College in 1958 he was commissioned an army second lieutenant. Then there was a succession of military schools as he chose the military as his career. During his second tour of duty in Vietnam he earned the Bronze Star for bravery and the Soldier's Medal for heroism.

In 1971 Powell received a master's degree in business administration from George Washington University, Washington, D.C.; the following year he won a coveted White House Fellowship, which placed him solidly inside the Beltway and into the corridors of power. After distinguishing himself in several Pentagon assignments, Powell was appointed a national security advisor by President Reagan in 1987. Two years later, President Bush named Powell to chair the Joint Chiefs of Staff. No black soldier had ever risen this high in the service. Powell would also oversee the troops dispatched to famine-torn Somalia in 1992, ostensibly to assist in the distribution of food and to protect relief workers, but also to suppress the feuding armed warlords. One fifth of the 25,000 troops sent to this East African nation were blacks. Powell's term ran to September 1993, which brought his thirty-five-year military career to a close. He's currently writing his memoirs and lecturing.

GREEN MONKEYS AND KEMRON
—

CONSIDERING GENERAL POWELL'S effectiveness during Operation Desert Storm and in the Somalia relief effort, he might have been useful in the fight against AIDS (acquired immuno-deficiency syndrome). In 1991 the United States Centers for Disease Control called the AIDS epidemic a major health threat to black Americans. For black Americans between the ages of fifteen and forty-four residing in New Jersey and New York, AIDS was the leading cause of death. From 1981 when the Centers first began charting the disease, it has risen steadily. Of the 24,576 cases reported by 1986, 25 percent or 6,192 were blacks. Black men accounted for 23 percent of the 22,648 cases, and black women accounted for 51 percent of the 1,634 cases.[162]

These statistics told a grim tale, and many people in the black community who cavalierly ignored the disease, believing it to be restricted to white and black homosexuals, were stunned by the reports. Even more alarming, health officials were predicting 179,000 AIDS-related deaths by 1991. It was estimated that one to two million men and women have been afflicted with the virus and that they can be infectious.

Suddenly a topic that had been taboo in the black community was the source of much discussion, with some contending that the disease was man-made and part of a biological warfare scheme aimed at exterminating undesirables in the national population. Such conspiracy theories are perhaps understandable in view of the Tuskegee experiments in which black men infected with syphilis were delayed treatment to facilitate research. Others, including several reputable scientists and health agencies, pointed to Africa as the place where

AIDS originated. "Epidemiological studies conducted in central Africa by European, U.S. and African scientists revealed a high incidence of AIDS in Zaire and among west and east-central African countries," Dr. Beny Primm wrote in a special report on AIDS in 1987. "It is estimated that 50,000 people have died from the disease called 'slim' (AIDS) in central Africa since its confirmed appearances in the late 1970s. Privately some leading AIDS researchers say the death toll to date is several hundred thousand."[163]

Reports such as this give credence to those who point to Africa as the culprit. Of course, the charges are familiar. Since the earliest times Europeans and Americans have been quick to blame Africa and African-Americans for the deleterious aspects of culture while they take credit for all the various medical and technical advances. At the bottom of these assertions is a virulent racist notion that Africans are inherently promiscuous and unable to control their sexual desires. It was reported a few years ago that a black businessman traveling back and forth between Africa and Europe was responsible for spreading AIDS among European housewives. Even if such a case existed, there remains the problem of who gave it to him, and why these housewives were available to him.

To suggest, however, that it is only dyed-in-the-wool racists who see AIDS as beginning in Africa would be a mistake. Elaine Baldwin, a spokesperson for the National Institute of Health in Washington, D.C., believes that AIDS began in Africa. "The consensus in the scientific community is that AIDS originated in Africa from the green monkey," Baldwin explained. She contends that the AIDS virus may have been transmitted through the blood of the monkeys, which were often killed for food. "We can't be certain of any of this since the studies are still inconclusive," she continued. "It is hard to determine the genetic sequences of the virus since it mutates so fast and seems to follow no predictable pattern. That's why it's been so difficult to develop an effective vaccine."[164]

Baldwin is not sure how the virus got from monkey to humans, but she disagrees adamantly with those, like Dr. Francis Cress-Welsing, who hold that the virus is man-made. Despite their differing opinions, there is one thing that Baldwin and

Dr. Welsing have in common: the vervet or green monkey. In a lecture in 1991 at the Third Annual Holistic Retreat in Chicago, Dr. Welsing insisted "that AIDS was a man-made disease." Citing evidence gleaned from a book published in 1969, she wanted to know how a virus whose source we say we didn't know, and that started among Africans and Haitians, was written about in 1969 . . . From the very beginning it has been clear," she said, "that most of the statements about the origins of the AIDS virus were instances of deceit and outright lying or what is now referred to, euphemistically, as disinformation."

This man-made virus was developed "for the purpose of a systematic depopulation agenda," she asserted, specifically targeting the African-American community, white homosexuals, and other nonwhite drug abusers. The idea for such a disease, she said, came from scientists working at Fort Detrick, Maryland. On this point, Dr. Welsing quoted directly from the report: "The question of whether new disease could be used is of considerable interest. Vervet monkey disease may well be an example of a whole new class of disease causing organisms." This is "none other than the green monkey," Dr. Welsing exclaimed, "the African green monkey that the public is now being told is in the chain of causation eventuating in the present AIDS epidemic. The same monkey that was mentioned in a 1969 book discussing a fatal blood, tissue and venereally transmitted virus that is of biological warfare interest; this discussion being in a book surveying chemical and biological warfare."[165]

In perhaps less hysterical terms, Dr. William C. Douglass makes the same point but ups the ante by declaring that the World Health Organization (WHO) "had 'triggered' the AIDS epidemic in Africa through the WHO smallpox immunization program," that Africans were used as guinea pigs for the deadly man-made virus. He concludes in his article "WHO Murdered Africa" that the green monkey business was a lie to confuse the world and play down the epidemic while blaming Africans for its origins. And in an attempt to put an end to the monkey business, Dr. Douglass stated that an examination of the gene structure of the green monkey reveals "that it is not genetically possible to transfer the AIDS virus from monkeys to man by natural means," he said.[166]

Argument and wasted energy over the origins of a disease is purposeless if it sheds no light on a cure. And while Africa has been the center of this debate about the origins of AIDS, it may also be the place where a cure is found. A small breakthrough has been the source of some controversy. Dr. Davy Koech, Kenya's top medical scientist and director of the Kenyan Medical Research Institute (KEMRI), has developed a drug, Kemron, that boosts the number of immune cells in AIDS patients, although it does not dramatically reverse the symptoms of the disease. Apparently the WHO has endorsed Dr. Koech's achievements, but there is growing opinion that because the steps toward a cure are coming from Africa, the racism embedded in the U.S. medical community will stifle its acceptance and use. And to what degree will the transnational pharmaceutical industry get involved to either block or monopolize the distribution of Kemron?

The politics of AIDS, the allocation of research funds for treatment and to find a cure, is a tangled mess, and to date the only truly effective weapon against the disease is prevention. Parents, church groups, civic organizations, and community leaders must take an active role in disseminating factual information about AIDS. What we have to understand is that we are currently experiencing only the tip of an even worse calamity farther down the road. The real tragedy of AIDS will not be evident until the next century. Indeed, AIDS may not have started in Africa, but we know where it is now, and the crucial thing is to marshal the wherewithal, the knowledge, to combat it, so that one day we may have the luxury to sit around and argue about who developed the first cure for it.

BETCHA DIDN'T KNOW

Dr. David Satcher, formerly the president of Meharry Medical College, is now the director of the Centers for Disease Control and Prevention in Atlanta. Dr. Satcher is one of eight children raised by self-taught farmers whose education ended in elementary school.

RAPTIVISTS, GANGSTAS, AND THE HAMMER

To FIGHT THE rapacious spread of AIDS, hundreds of entertainers have volunteered their time in performances all over the world, and as they gain financial standing and power, rap artists are getting involved. Although no rap star has yet put out a disk with a strong AIDS message, the potential is definitely there. Since its appearance on the music scene in the late 1970s, rap has grown in stature, but not without rancor, backbiting, and internal dissension.

If the music's legitimacy is measured in record sales, then rap hit the big time in 1990–91 with M. C. Hammer's *Please Hammer Don't Hurt 'Em.* This album, his second, stayed at number one on *Billboard*'s pop album chart for twenty-one weeks, eventually selling ten million copies. It appeared at number one or number two for a total of thirty-six weeks, longer than any LP since Michael Jackson's *Thriller.* During 1990 it became the first album to surpass U.S. sales of eight million in a single calendar year since Prince's *Purple Rain* in

1984. These were quite astonishing accomplishments for a young man who had once been a batboy for the Oakland A's baseball team in his hometown, and also an evangelist known as the Holy Ghost Boy.

Whether from envy or rejection of his broader vision of the hip-hop genre, Hammer was the target of severe "dissing" or put-down by other rappers, and the music had its first sign of internal bickering. Sure, there had been some bad blood between Kool Moe Dee and LL Cool J, but the attack against Hammer resembled the old-fashioned game of the "dozens" or signifying on records. "You can swing a hammer," charged LL Cool J, "but you can't bust a glass." Hammer did his best to stay above the fray, but he snapped back with vitriol of his own: "I consider that a last cry for help."[167]

Rap gained national attention in 1992 when "raptivist" Sister Souljah's remarks about "black people killing white people" were reported by the *Washington Post* and then harped on by Democratic presidential hopeful Bill Clinton. It was reminiscent of the earlier brouhaha over 2 Live Crew's *As Nasty as They Wanna Be,* which a judge declared to be obscene. Hard-core rappers such as NWA (Niggas With Attitude), Ice Cube, Ice-T, and Public Enemy made it clear where they stood when the lines were drawn between those rappers who were determined to keep the politics up front and those who were not. And among their supporters are such prominent intellectuals as Cornel West, a professor of religion at Princeton and a best-selling author. "There's something that I like about Ice-T, Ice Cube and Paris and the so-called gangster rappers," West told a reporter recently. "They attempt to do what I attempt to do, as a public intellectual. And that is, to tell the truth . . . and anytime you tell the truth it's based on one's own experiences . . . Now, I'm deeply critical of misogyny, of the homophobia, of the preoccupation with the machismo identity that is associated with violence . . . but in telling the truth they do, in fact, express these kinds of unjustified sensibilities."[168]

Still other B-boyz and gangstas were less interested in social commentary, obsessing on "bitches" and "ho's." This denigration of black women in particular and black culture in

general sparked a reaction from Reverend Calvin Butts of
Abyssinian Baptist Church in Harlem. In the spring of 1993
Reverend Butts called a press conference and promised to
run a steamroller over a pile of indecent CDs in midtown
Manhattan in front of a major record company. Several rappers challenged Butts's project, saying they had a constitutional right to say anything they wanted to.

"I am not an opponent of free speech or a proponent of
censorship," Reverend Butts told a crowd gathered for the
crushing, "but something has to be done to stop the spread
of lyrics that demean our women and ridicule our culture."[169]
Counterprotesters yelled back at him and blocked the use of
the steamroller. Reverend Butts then asked his supporters to
stomp the pile of CDs, cassettes, and records, which they did
with great verve and rhythm. Since that encounter with rap
resisters, Reverend Butts has agreed to a meeting, and the
parties planned a major conference on the issue. Columnist
Ken Cockrel, Jr., of the *Metro Times* in Detroit slams some rap
music because the songs are irredeemably and relentlessly
violent. "Once you've heard your 345th song by a crotch-
grabbing goon boasting about how he's ready to 'peel a nig-
ga's cap back' the whole thing starts to seem pretty moronic,"
Cockrel observed. And many of the gangsta rappers are also
hypocritical, he wrote. "How else can Ice Cube label white
people as devils with lyrics like 'I hate the devil with a passion
and when I see the whites of his eyes I start blastin' ' from
his *Horny Lil Devil* and then tour before predominantly white
audiences with Seattle grunge rock royalty like Pearl Jam and
Soundgarden during last year's Lollapalooza tour? How else
can Dr. Dre do a song called 'The Day the Niggaz Took
Over,' where he exhorts his homies to 'break the white man
off somethin' lovely,' and then give away the car he drives in
the *Nuthin' But a 'G' Thang* video as the prize in an MTV
contest? The answer's probably pretty simple: money," Cockrel concluded.[170]

Money is the motive, too, for the more corporate-minded
rap artists who are interested in enhancing their status and
bank accounts with business endeavors. Russell Simmons par-
layed his fledgling enterprise into a megabuck empire, gener-

ating $33 million in 1992. His Rush Communications was ranked thirty-second among black-owned corporations in America. Puff Daddy, fired by André Harrell and his Uptown Entertainment complex, is, at twenty-two, one of the youngest record company presidents in the business. Mary J. Blige and Jodeci are among his clients. And twenty-three-year-old Queen Latifah, with a string of platinum albums around her throne, has recently set up her own operation, Flavor Unit Records and Management Company, in Jersey City, New Jersey. Having doffed her customary crown hats, the Queen is still the queen as she reigns over a fiefdom of some seventeen recording artists, including Naughty by Nature, Black Sheep, Fu Schnickens, Nikki D, Simple Pleasure, and Freddy Foxx.

THE ICE PEOPLE COMETH
—

AMONG THE VARIETY of rapsters are those like A Tribe Called Quest, X Clan, and Brand Nubians, who are in the Afro-centric camp, proudly involved with resurrecting the glorious African past and the nationalistic fervor of African-American history. Afrocentricity, or an outlook, lifestyle, or attitude that is African-centered, may be a novel concept for a lot of today's rappers, activists, and intellectuals, but it's an old idea refashioned in Kente cloth and bravado. It is both theory and practice, states Molefi Kete Asante, chairperson of the Department of African-American Studies at Temple University in Philadelphia, who has written a book on Afrocentricity. "In its theoretical aspect it consists of interpretation and analysis from the perspective of African people as subjects rather than as objects on the fringes of the European experience," Asante explained.

The term resounds most stridently in the corridors of academe where it is often voiced in connection with "multiculturalism" and the "curriculum of inclusion." It is also mistakenly viewed by some administrators as a replacement for the standard "Eurocentric" focus of most school syllabi and curricula. Afrocentricity, Asante continued, "is not an idea to replace all things European, but to expand the dialogue to include African-American information."[171] In other words, the stress should be placed on inclusion, and not the exclusion of anything, although, given that everything cannot be covered, something has to be left out. The multicultural perspective developed by the New York school system and the series of essays written for the Portland, Oregon, schools are good examples of how a balance can be maintained to show the contributions of many ethnic groups to American society.

Unfortunately, much of the value and significance of Afrocentricity is obscured by controversy promulgated in many instances by opponents of change, and sometimes by its most passionate disciples. That is, there are a few promoters who have unwittingly given the term a bad name, prompting charges of "reverse racism" and anti-Semitism. "There is a degree of anger because we feel left out," said Jawanza Kunjufu, a highly respected educational consultant. "And the sentiment is, it was intentional."[172]

European intentions and the entrenchment of white supremacy are prime concerns of such scholars as Dr. John Henrik Clarke, Dr. Yosef ben-Jochannan, and Dr. Leonard Jeffries, although it is perhaps unwise and unfair to lump them without noting their differences. If there is an elder statesman, the supreme *griot* of African and African-American history, Professor Clarke deserves that honor. The Legendary Dr. Ben ranks right up there with him, but usually defers to his senior partner.

Dr. Jeffries, who is their equal in grit if not in publications, has been the epicenter of debate since he took over the Department of Black Studies at City College of New York in the late 1960s, and began lecturing about the evil "ice people" (Europeans) and gracious "sun people" (Africans), a typology perhaps appropriated from a white Canadian scholar. His latest joust with the university administration stems from a speech he gave in Albany in July 1991 in which he claimed Jews and Italians had collaborated in Hollywood to degrade blacks, and more unsettling, that Jews had financed the slave trade. It made little difference that Jeffries's remarks were mangled by the media, especially reporters at the rabidly reactionary *New York Post*; the good doctor had made the mistake of mentioning Jews in the same breath as the slave trade, and he should have known it would trigger a strong response. It did. And soon he was put on probation by the college trustees and later stripped of his chairmanship. Since he was a tenured faculty member, they could not fire him altogether. Dr. Jeffries sued the college for $25 million.

City College had picked on the wrong man, or at least, according to some legal experts, it had leveled the wrong charges. In May 1993 Jeffries was awarded $400,000 in damages after a federal jury concluded that college administrators and trustees had violated his constitutional privilege of free speech in removing him. Three months later Jeffries had the whole ball of wax when Judge Kenneth Conboy reinstated him as chairman of the Black Studies Department, ruling that the college, in stripping him of his position, had violated his First Amendment rights. In rendering his verdict, Judge Conboy chastised the college's officials and their handling of the case, blasting them for incompetence and irresponsible behavior. The administration is appealing the decision.

Dr. Jeffries's victory and reinstatement were reminiscent of Judge Alcee Hastings's resurrection. Hastings, the first black federal judge in Florida, was impeached by the Senate in 1989, although a jury had exonerated him of bribery charges. Three years later the exceedingly charismatic Hastings was elected a congressman from Florida, and placed right in the middle of those who had dispatched him. The old popular adage in the black community about "what goes 'round comes 'round" was never more apt.

Congressman Hastings is not one to miss an opportunity to invoke the rhetoric of Afrocentricity. In his speeches he often talked about the necessity to get back to blackness and to honor our proud African heritage. On the black middleclass circuit from which he raised money after being impeached, Hastings took advantage of the increasingly potent wave of black nationalism sweeping the country. This tidal wave would reach its crest by the fall of 1992 with the release of Spike Lee's *Malcolm X.*

SOUND BITE

"I don't see any American dream; I see an American nightmare. I am a victim of Americanism."

—MALCOLM X[173]

CHRONOLOGY—1990

February—Songstress Anita Baker, of Detroit, who made such an amazing debut with her album *Rapture* (1986), took home the Grammy for the best R & B female vocalist for her tune "Giving You the Best That I Got." She won two Grammys in 1989.

February 23—Arthur A. Fletcher, sixty-five, was named by President George Bush to succeed William Barclay Allen as chairman of the U.S. Commission on Civil Rights. Previously Fletcher, a successful businessman, had served under Bush when he was U.S. ambassador to the UN in 1971. In 1978 Fletcher lost a Washington, D.C., mayoral contest to Marion Barry.

March 3—Twenty-year-old Carole Gist of Detroit was crowned "Miss USA" in Wichita, Kansas. A graduate of Cass Technical High School and a student at Northwood Institute, Gist became the first black American to win this title. She received prize awards of more than $200,000.

April 3—Vocalist Sarah Vaughan, affectionately known as "Sassy," succumbed to lung cancer at her home in the Los Angeles suburb of Hidden Hills. For nearly fifty of her sixty-six years, she was a fixture on the jazz scene, and her melodious voice and interpretative skills were the standard by which most singers of her generation and the succeeding ones were measured. Coaxed into a amateur contest at the Apollo Theatre in 1942, Vaughan walked off with the top prize and caught the eye of Billy Eckstine, who recommended her to Earl "Fatha" Hines. The rest is a beautiful music history that includes her stellar performances of "Misty" and "Send in the Clowns."

April 25—Dexter Gordon, one of the leading tenor saxophonists in the history of jazz, died of kidney failure at Thomas Jefferson University Hospital in Philadelphia. Gordon, who was sixty-seven, had been suffering from cancer of the larynx. Though he was recognized as the star of the movie *Round Midnight* (1986) in his last years, Gordon's real reputation was earned in the jazz realm, where his distinctive sound and elegant manner placed him among the all-time great personalities in jazz. For many years he resided abroad, mostly in Sweden, where he was a national treasure. He will always be remembered among jazz lovers for his remarkable duet with tenor saxist Wardell Gray on their rendition of "The Chase."

May 16—Sammy Davis, Jr., arguably the most versatile performer in the history of entertainment, died of complications from throat cancer. He was sixty-four. Practically all of Davis's life was spent in show business, beginning as a child star in vaudeville with his father and his uncle Will Mastin. Davis excelled as a dancer, singer, actor, comedian, musician, and entrepreneur. In *Mr. Wonderful* (1956) and *Golden Boy* (1964), he demonstrated his prowess on the stage; on the screen his portrayal of Sportin' Life in *Porgy and Bess* (1959) was engrossing; and as a vocalist, his version of "That Old Black Magic" (1955) rivaled Billy Daniels's. His ability as a tap dancer was seen for the last time on-screen with Gregory Hines in *Tap* (1989).

June 6—Harvey Gantt, a North Carolina architect and mayor of Charlotte, won his state's Democratic nomination for the U.S. Senate. Gantt, forty-seven, was the first black in the state's history to receive such a nomination. He was also the first black student at Clemson University in South Carolina, and Charlotte, North Carolina's, first mayor.

August 17—Pearl Bailey, noted for her lively wit and engaging personality, died in Philadelphia of heart failure at seventy-two. She had a history of heart disease. But she also had a history of being a brassy, upbeat entertainer whose effervescence seemed inexhaustible. After her stage debut on Broadway in *St. Louis Woman,* in which she won the prestigious Donaldson Award for best new actress, Bailey was lured to Hollywood, where she continued to reveal her multidimensional talent. But her most unforgettable role was as Dolly Levi in an all-black production of *Hello, Dolly* (1967). Bailey's versatility extended beyond the stage, and for several years she was a cultural delegate to the United Nations.

October 16—Art Blakey, seventy-one, percussionist and band leader, died in New York City of undetermined causes. As the founder and leader of the Jazz Messengers, Blakey was a veritable musical academy. Practically all of the prominent hard bop musicians either played with him or were influenced by his robust, driving style behind his arsenal of cymbals and drums. With a perpetual smile on his face, Blakey could be a demanding accompanist, getting every ounce of creative juice out his cohorts. But he was also a sensitive musician and a fine composer.

November 27—Author Charles Johnson won the 1990 National Book Award for fiction. Johnson's novel, *Middle Passage,* continues the author's mixture of humor, history, and the anachronistic. He was the first black male writer to win the award since Ralph Ellison won it in 1954 for his picaresque novel *Invisible Man.*

THE YEAR OF THE X
—

HARDLY INVISIBLE TWO years later in 1992 was Malcolm X. In fact, Malcolm's image and legacy were never more visible as his face and name were scrawled on calendars, posters, billboards, books, magazines, newspapers, T-shirts, hats, and even potato chips. Spike Lee's biopic of Malcolm's life was the centerpiece of this revival, and save for a few lapses, it resonated with the same intensity as the hype that preceded it. Except for the phenomenal success of Terry McMillan's *Waiting to Exhale,* for which a sizable stand of trees would be needed to supply the paper for the number of books she sold, this was the year of the X.

Under fire from a faction of malcontent Malcolmites and black nationalists led by writer/activist Amiri Baraka, who didn't trust Lee with their precious icon, the director told the insurgents that he was going to make the kind of film he wanted to make. "This movie will not be made by a committee," Lee snapped uncharacteristically, "and I will not be intimidated by Baraka and others. What right have they to dictate to me?"[174] For several weeks Baraka and Lee assailed each other, providing the upcoming film with additional controversy, not that it needed any more.

Ever since Lee began campaigning to direct the film, the project was a bone of contention. Marvin Worth purchased the rights to the film in the early 1970s, but his attempts to find the right script and director met with snag after snag. When Lee was signed to direct, there was still a problem with the script, with several writers failing to satisfy Lee and the producers. The situation was finally settled after Lee decided to revamp a script written by the late James Baldwin and Arnold Perl. "Because Elijah Muhammad [the founder and leader of the Nation of Islam] was still alive," Lee said, "there were some things they [Baldwin and Perl] could not deal

275

with. I have added that portion of the history to the script."[175]
The hype picked up a notch.

Before the release of the film there were so many "X"
items on the market—more than two hundred by the end of
1992—that Dr. Betty Shabazz, Malcolm's widow, was forced
to hire a licensing agency to protect the rights of the estate.
Even Lee, with all sorts of merchandise in his stores bearing
the "X" logo, had at first refused to comply with the agency's
stipulations. Lee was also at war with Warner Bros., the film's
distributor, who were demanding he cut a provocative scene
from the film's opening of an American flag burning into
the shape of an *X* and footage depicting Rodney King being
savagely beaten by the cops. Then came the financial problems: A completion bonding company was threatening to take
over the project after Lee had gone over budget. "Malcolm
X is a $32–33 million movie," Lee said in an interview with
Henry Louis Gates, Jr., for *Transition,* an international journal, "but Warner Bros. only put $18 million into the film.
And Largo bought the foreign rights for $8 million; so it's 6,
7 million over budget . . . So we went in knowing that somewhere down the line, we'd have to find some extra money.
But we had to get the film made then: it's been two decades,
and we had to seize the opportunity."[176]

When Warner refused to fork over more money, Lee took
his plight to the black megastars with megabucks. Bill Cosby,
Oprah Winfrey, Michael Jordan, Janet Jackson, Prince, and
Magic Johnson were among those who raised the additional
funds needed to complete the film. According to statements
from Lee, the donors kicked in more than $5 million, al-
though several music trade magazines doubted this claim, sug-
gesting instead that Warner capitulated to Lee's demands.
Whatever the case, the bonding company was kept at bay,
even if the media were unable to resist rushing madly after
Lee's ongoing hype parade. His dazzle apparently blinded a
few reporters who he said misquoted his statement about
black children skipping school to see his film. "I never said
young black Americans should skip school," Lee countered.
"But it's important for families to take their kids early, because this is the most amount of money ever spent on a movie

in black history, and we had to fight to get the amount we got.''[177]

This piece of attention was followed by a disclosure that Lee and Warner Bros. would not be previewing the film at the Apollo Theatre in Harlem, where Malcolm X gained international acclaim. Lee was again on the defensive. Eventually, though, a compromise was reached, allowing the Apollo to have a benefit screening two days after the film's world premiere at the Ziegfeld Theatre in midtown Manhattan.

From the first provocative images to the last exhortations of Arrested Development over the credit crawl, *Malcolm X* is a powerful film. Denzel Washington falls just short of capturing Malcolm's full allure, that magnetic appeal that dazzled his worshipers and intrigued his enemies. And Lee did a good job of answering the lingering question of who killed Malcolm X. In graphic terms he showed the plotters at work, although the deeper machinations of the murder, whether it was ordered by Elijah Muhammad or facilitated by the FBI, remain as tangled and murky as the conspiracy theories surrounding JFK's assassination. The conjecture that Gene Roberts, the undercover cop who was Malcolm's bodyguard, rendered the final fatal shot does not add up, since keeping Malcolm alive was germane to his livelihood. Roberts would later infiltrate the Black Panther party and testify against them during the Panther Twenty-one trial in New York City.

If Lee had given but a tad more attention to the last year of Malcolm's life, the film might qualify as a great one, but at more than three hours in length, it seems remiss to have only a fleeting scene of those remarkable episodes that comprise his last year, a year in which Malcolm traveled to Africa and visited with all the progressive heads of state, including Nasser of Egypt, Obote of Uganda, Nyerere of Tanzania, Kenyatta of Kenya, Azikiwe of Nigeria, and most important, Nkrumah of Ghana. It was in these final hours that Malcolm's anti-imperialist, pro-Socialist leanings were sharply emerging, and some of this perspective is clearly evident in the Organization of Afro-American Unity (OAAU) documents, which, to a large extent, must stand as Malcolm's last will and statement. It would have been rewarding to experience Malcolm in this last incarnation, when the Nigerian students renamed him Omowale, or the "son who has come home."

Except for *Time* magazine, most of the major publications and their critics praised the film; it was an overwhelming success, despite many dissenters who claimed it was not "X-traordinary" but "X-crement." Social commentator Michael Eric Dyson found some value in the division. "No matter how [Malcolm] is pigeonholed, his stature derives as much from his detractors' exaggerated fears as from his admirers' exalted hopes," Dyson declared. "He has become a divided metaphor: For those who love him, he is a powerful lens for self-perception, a means of sharply focusing political and racial priorities; for those who loathe him, he is a distorting mirror that reflects violence and hatred."[178]

And there were many who kept Malcolm in a human context, willing to accept his virtues without losing sight of his foibles. There were even some rushing to claim his legacy when they denounced him in the flesh. "I think Malcolm X was essentially a black Republican by today's standards," TV commentator Tony Brown told Juan Williams in *GQ* magazine. "I use two basic criteria to come to that conclusion. Number one, Malcolm was for individual opportunity. Number two, he was for self-help. This is a Republican philosophy. It is right in line with [Marcus] Garvey, Elijah Muhammad, Booker T. Washington, and most of all, Malcolm X. And that philosophy stands in contradiction to those who believe in integration and in the government as the first and last resort of the black man."[179]

What Brown and others of his ilk obscure in this reclamation effort is that Malcolm was also a man of principles and integrity who saw the family as crucial in community stability. The conservatives can claim him on these grounds if they choose, but these values alone, though pertinent, do not constitute a full-blown philosophy. To say that he was a proponent of self-help and individual opportunity does not, in and of itself, make him a Republican. What about Malcolm's opposition to racism, capitalism, and imperialism? What about his stance on self-defense and his strong identification with things currently labeled Afrocentric? Any one of these factors is more salient to one's philosophical makeup than self-reliance and individuality. Malcolm, to his death, was a revolutionary black nationalist and this alone should be enough to give him considerable distance from the conservative or neoconservative tar brush.

To date the film has made well over $50 million, but according to Lee's office, it is still short of what was expected, although there remain the tabulations from foreign distribution and videos. Indeed, the money is important, but not as significant as the movie's impact on black youth, who now possess at least some inkling of Malcolm's life and commitment. No longer can they say with innocence, "Who is Malcolm the Tenth?" And there are scheduled even more projects about him such as the documentary by Henry Hampton and Blackside Productions, and Manning Marable's biography. These and other works will help chip away the myth and mysticism and allow us to view the man and his essence.

CLINTON'S POSSE

ANOTHER THING IGNORED by those who assert that Malcolm is a Republican by today's standards is the reality of change, and change was something that Malcolm was constantly undergoing. Which is to suggest that he might even have run for political office. He certainly would have no argument with some of the more radical voices among members of the Congressional Black Caucus (CBC) such as Ron Dellums and the group's chair, Kweisi Mfume, a representative from Maryland.

In September 1993 when the CBC convened its twenty-third meeting in Washington, D.C., it had grown to forty members and expressed a political clout and unity heretofore unknown. An example of this new assurance and power was the appearance of Minister Louis Farrakhan of the Nation of Islam at the convention. He was invited to participate on a panel on race relations in the United States. And what about the backlash from Washington and the Clinton administration? Mfume said that he was too old to worry about criticism. Members of Congress would make their own decisions. Earlier in the summer, in yet another demonstration of its new defiance, the CBC rebuffed President Clinton when he called for a meeting shortly after he had withdrawn the nomination of Lani Guinier to head the civil rights division of the Justice Department. Malcolm X would have been proud.

Conference delegates also voiced objections to certain bills proposed by Clinton on crime and health care, and they accused the president of failing to combat rising racism in the nation and said he lacks a sound civil rights policy. And Clinton's abandonment of Lani Guinier was still something that remained stuck in the craw of most CBC delegates, who were apparently not mollified by the number of black appointees brought in by the president.

Since his first weeks in office, Clinton had been pointing with pride at the number of blacks in his administration, among whom were Ron Brown, secretary of commerce, Mike Espy, the agriculture secretary, Hazel O'Leary, secretary of energy, Jesse Brown, secretary of veterans' affairs, Lee Brown, director of the Office of National Drug Control Policy, Alexis Herman, White House public liaison director, Margaret Williams, chief of staff for Hillary Rodham Clinton, Surgeon General Jocelyn Elders, and Mary Frances Berry, chairwoman of the United States Civil Rights Commission. Berry had already been a senior member of the commission, so there was nothing surprising about her appointment. Elders was the only Clinton appointee of several blacks who had served on his transition team, which listed Vernon Jordan, Marian Wright Edelman, Barbara Jordan, and William Gray III, who recently relinquished his congressional post to become a special envoy.

President Clinton seems committed to having African-Americans at all levels of government, in all departments. The White House in late summer 1993 released a report stating there were 329 African-Americans in top political positions within the administration. Some White House watchers say this is a gross exaggeration, and that many of those counted were really special assistants and various confidential secretaries in federal departments.

Appointments are one thing, but "jobs, justice, and peace" was the cry of thousands who gathered in Washington, D.C., to commemorate the historic march in 1963. Some marchers at this thirtieth anniversary celebration were upset that neither President Clinton nor Vice President Al Gore found time to attend; Attorney General Janet Reno represented the president. The complaint registered by most speakers was familiar, however, many of them noted that thirty years after the great march, things were worse. "Hope is down, the check has bounced insufficient funds," roared Reverend Jesse Jackson. "We march to put people first . . . to fulfill the covenant to put people back to work and to keep hope alive."

Coretta Scott King, Martin's widow, was warmly received by the crowd, and they listened raptly when she told them "Martin challenged us to march . . . There is still too much bigotry, homelessness, and violence," she said. "Today as in 1963 we have a new president, but leadership must ultimately come from the people."

Among the sharpest indictments of the president came from Reverend Benjamin Chavis, former executive director of the NAACP. "There's nothing wrong with taking a vacation," blasted Chavis, referring to Clinton's vacation on Martha's Vineyard, "but when you come back, there's another vineyard, and many people here can't take one."[180] Chavis might have been even more caustic, but perhaps he was mindful that the president had at least sent a videotaped message to the NAACP's annual convention held earlier in Indianapolis, Indiana.

BETCHA DIDN'T KNOW

At thirty, Representative Cleo Fields of Louisiana is the youngest member of the 103rd Congress. He also serves on the committee on small business.

CHAVIS AND LEWIS

—•—

REVEREND BEN CHAVIS was finally settling comfortably in his new role, which he had assumed in April 1993 after a heated contest. For several months prior to his selection, Chavis was a fourth or fifth choice, according to some reports, running well behind the leader of the pack, Reverend Jesse Jackson. It is difficult to analyze what factors proved decisive in turning things around for Chavis, but it may have been his ability to raise money for the financially beleaguered organization, or that he was the least contentious of the finalists. At the first convention under his leadership in Indianapolis, Chavis made good on his promise as he announced that the Reginald Lewis family had donated $2 million to the NAACP.

The Lewis family, it was later disclosed, was honoring a commitment Lewis had made before his death in January 1993 from brain cancer. He was fifty. Lewis was Chavis's lawyer during the Wilmington Ten days, and helped to get his client out of prison. The Wilmington Ten were arrested in 1972 for arson and conspiracy to assault during racial disturbances in Wilmington, North Carolina. The trouble stemmed from black students marching to protest what they felt were discriminatory practices in the city's recently desegregated public school system. Chavis was sent in by the Commission on Racial Justice to mediate the disturbances.

Over the succeeding years Lewis became one of the wealthiest black men in America. After graduating from Harvard Law School in 1968, Lewis spent two years at the New York law firm of Paul, Weiss, Rifkind, Wharton & Garrison. Five years later he established his own corporate practice, Lewis & Clarkson, specializing in venture capital. And venture, he did. In 1983 he started TLC Group with an eye toward buying and selling companies. That same year he bought McCall Pattern, a financially sluggish sewing company, and thoroughly revived it. By 1987 his company had revenues of $63 million.

Later, he sold McCall for $90 million, earning $50 million
in profits. His next target was the Beatrice International Food
Company, a vast operation with holdings in thirty-one countries. Lewis completed a leveraged buyout of the company in
1987 for $985 million, the largest LBO ever of overseas assets
by an American company. His company was now the first and
only black-owned company to ever eclipse the $1 billion bar-
rier. In 1988 TLC Beatrice became the top company on the
Black Enterprise list, and has held the spot for five years.

Prior to his death, Lewis had made arrangements for his
half brother, Jean Fugett, to succeed him as chairman. Lewis
was personally worth about $400 million, and his philan-
thropy was well known. In 1993 he gave Harvard Law School
a grant of $3 million, the largest grant in the school's history.
Some of the grant is earmarked for a law center to be named
in tribute to Lewis.

Meanwhile, Chavis, excited by the grant from the Lewis
family, now centered his attention on warding off the scuttle-
butt that he was surrounding himself with Marxists, Communists, and anti-Semites. The charges, primarily from the right-
wing press, were targeted at Chavis's new director of communications, Don Rojas, and his deputy director, attorney Lewis
Meyers. Rojas, a former press secretary to the martyred Grenadian leader Maurice Bishop, was the executive editor of the
New York Amsterdam News before joining Chavis. He was used
to the red-baiting tactics of the media and summed it up as
no more than "reactionary tripe." Meyers was labeled anti-
Semitic because he was at one time Louis Farrakhan's counsel, which would automatically defang the assertion since Farrakhan has a number of close Arab associates, and when we
last looked, Arabs were Semites.

"I hired these men because they are qualified to do the
jobs," Chavis told the press in Indianapolis during the convention. "I have the utmost confidence in their abilities to
perform and discharge the duties they have been assigned."[181]
Chavis also lanced another festering canker when he publicly
embraced the organization's president, Dr. William Gibson.
It had been rumored that the two top officials in the NAACP
were feuding. Chavis said that he and Dr. Gibson would con-

tinue to appear in public as long as it took to get the NAACP back on the right keel.

But Chavis's ship of state was abruptly grounded in August 1994, just 16 months into his watch when he was relieved of his stewardship after using NAACP funds to pay a former employee, Mary Stansel, who accused him of sexual harassment and job discrimination.

ASHE ASHÉ

THE BLACK COMMUNITY had hardly recovered from the shock of Reginald Lewis's death when word came that Arthur Ashe was dead, a victim of AIDS. Ashe gained his fame on the tennis courts, but he earned his glory as a determined civil and human rights activist. He had contracted HIV (human immunodeficiency virus) through blood transfusions during one of two open-heart operations in 1979 and 1983. In 1988 he was diagnosed with AIDS, after undergoing brain surgery.

Despite the setbacks and failing health, Ashe continued his research on blacks in sports, his autobiography, and the struggle against apartheid in South Africa and human rights violations in Haiti. Several months before his death, Ashe was arrested while protesting U.S. policy on Haitian refugees. He was also extremely devoted to his family, to his daughter, Camera, and to his wife, Jeanne, herself an award-winning photographer. The same zeal for perfection that made him such an intimidating opponent on clay or the hard court accompanied Ashe into the political arena. He lost his life, not his will.

Ashé, pronounced ah-*shay*, is the Yoruba word for "so be it"; it is a "spiritual command," the power to make things happen, and this embodiment of the word certainly applied to Ashe, Arthur. But it was also a term that gained currency at the end of the 1980s and was still widely used among devotees from Harlem to Los Angeles. In its most vital manifestation ashé is symptomatic of the growing Afrocentric movement, and its living avatars were increasingly involved in rites and rituals in Haiti *(voodoo)*, Jamaica *(pocomania)*, Trinidad *(shango)*, and Brazil *(candomble)*.

Ashé colorfully abounds at the street bazaars in Harlem, and not far away on the walls inside the Studio Museum and at Barbara Ann Teer's National Black Theatre. Ashé is really untranslatable; it is an ineffable quality of metabrilliance that only now and then takes on a human form. It is one's personal spiritual power, which, as Dr. Justine Cordwell summarizes in the foreword to *The Way of the Orisha,* by Philip John Niemark, "grows throughout life through a person's diligent application to doing good deeds, coupled with appropriate and calm behavior and with service to the gods in the form of sacrifice."[182]

In sports it might be akin to what Michael Jordan does in his most transcendent moments. He clearly has been otherworldly during his athletic career, and particularly over the last three seasons, each year leading his Chicago Bulls to the NBA championship. To the dismay of his fans, Jordan never pulled on his shorts for the 1993 basketball season after losing his father in July 1993. And Oprah Winfrey may have more than her share of ashé, as the talk-show diva garnered the biggest bucks in entertainment in 1993, and with an estimated $98 million over two years, has become the first woman to top *Forbes* magazine's annual list of the highest-paid celebrities. Actors and actresses Morgan Freeman, Alfre Woodard, Danny Glover, Angela Bassett, Avery Brooks, Will Smith, and Laurence Fishburne all possess that je ne sais quois. In 1992 Fishburne won the Tony Award in August Wilson's *Two Trains Running,* recently won an Emmy for his guest stint in the premiere episode of TV's "TriBeCa" series, and was nominated for an Oscar for his powerful portrayal of Ike Turner in the film *What's Love Got to Do With It.*

Trumpeter Wynton Marsalis, right from the cradle of *vodun* where the *orishas* of ashé are known to prosper, has been blessed with phenomenal talent, and is now testing his managerial gifts as artistic director of the prestigious Lincoln Center Jazz Series. Reverend Gardner Taylor, who recently stepped from the pulpit of Concord Baptist Church, where he pastored one of the largest congregations in the country, is obviously endowed with traces of ashé, though he would be the last to admit it. Like the late Reverend C. L. Franklin of Detroit, Reverend Taylor is in contact with another force at the height of his best sermons. Gordon Parks conveys a similar magic in his art, music, novels, poetry, and photography. Parks is cut from the same spiritual essence of a Paul Robeson, and he has lost none of that sly twinkle in his eye and brio that have sustained him into his eighties.

Track star Gail Devers and former astronaut Mae Jemison are ashé bearers, impressive young women of boundless talent who are nowhere near their peaks. Devers demonstrated her superb strength and endurance in the World Games of 1993, winning both the 110-yard hurdles race and the hundred-meter dash. Jemison, thirty-five, was the first African-American female astronaut to go into space on September 12, 1992. She was one of the shuttle *Endeavor*'s seven-member crew that launched into orbit the first cooperative mission of the U.S. and Japan. Among her duties on the space lab module was conducting fertilization studies on female frogs and to take part in an experiment to determine if biofeedback techniques affect space motion sickness. In 1993 Jemison, citing a desire to pursue other goals, resigned from the space program.

With Jemison off to test her potential elsewhere, there are five black astronauts left at NASA (National Aeronautics and Space Administration), with another scheduled to begin soon. Colonel Guion Bluford is the senior member, and he was the first black to fly in space in August 1983, after a Cuban of African descent had been in a USSR spaceship. He flew as a mission specialist whose primary duty was the deployment of a satellite from *Challenger*'s cargo bay. Major Charles Bolden, who flew more than one hundred sorties while assigned in Thailand in 1973, was selected as an astronaut candidate in 1980. He is now eligible to pilot future space shuttles. Air Force Colonel Frederick Gregory, a former test pilot who has flown more than forty different types of military and civilian aircraft, became an astronaut candidate in 1978. Like Bolden, he is also qualified to pilot space shuttles. Dr. Bernard Harris, Jr., became a full-fledged astronaut in 1991. He joined NASA's Johnson Space Center in 1987 as a clinical scientist and flight surgeon.

Another of the pioneering black astronauts was Dr. Ronald McNair, who perished aboard the flawed *Challenger* that exploded shortly after liftoff from Cape Kennedy and plunged into the waters off the coast of Florida in January 1986. There are other blacks assigned to NASA, among whom are Harrison Allen, a chemical engineer, who has written many technical papers and holds a patent on the ignition of solid propellant rocket motors; Dr. George Carruthers, a physicist responsible for the Apollo 16 lunar surface ultraviolet camera/spectrograph, which was placed on the lunar surface in April 1972; Lewis Andrews, a mathematician and chemist, who began his career in the field of environmental management as a space scientist at NASA's Marshall Space Flight Center, where he conducted research and managed studies on natural environmental parameters for space flight missions; and management technician Ruth Blair, who also started at Marshall Space Center. She works as a contract specialist. Ashé, ashé.

BETCHA DIDN'T KNOW

Rutgers University professor Shirley Jackson was the first black woman to earn a doctorate in physics from the Massachusetts Institute of Technology, in 1973.

NO EBONY IN THE IVORY TOWERS

As THE LATE musician Sun Ra was known to say, "Space is the Place," and blacks are right in the thick of things, poised as they have been on other frontiers, and ready to assist in the discovery of what lies within and beyond our galaxy. In several ways blacks are doing better in outer space than here on Earth, that is, here in the United States. Out in the universe, okay, at the university, not so hot. At least not at Duke University, where the administration is still far short of the hiring goals it promised to meet five years ago. In 1988, under pressure from students and some faculty members, Duke agreed to an initiative to add a black faculty member to each of its departments. The university missed its goal by a wide margin, hiring only eight new black professors. Duke's dilemma was symptomatic of the faculty problem prevalent in the ivory towers all across the nation.

Duke made an honest effort, said Samuel DuBois Cook, the university's first full-time black professor and currently president of Dillard University in New Orleans. "It didn't reach that goal, but the goal was a worthy one, and Duke should stick by its guns." To some extent the school did honor its commitment. While it hired twenty-five new black faculty members, seventeen others departed, raising the black total to thirty-nine among sixteen hundred full-time professors. "Duke made a commitment and didn't live up to it," said Shavar Jeffries, a student from Newark "If Duke can send [coach] Mike Krzyzewski to Canada and Greece to find talented basketball players, it can send faculty and administrators wherever they have to go to get black faculty here."

To Duke's credit, the 2.4 percentage of blacks on its faculty is at the norm for major white institutions nationwide. Duke has also increased the number of black Ph.D. candidates from twenty-one to fifty-five, or 3.8 percent of all doctoral students at Duke. Several things handicap Duke and other universities who seek to bolster their black faculty numbers: Fewer than 1,000 blacks annually receive Ph.D.s, and half of these are in the field of education. Furthermore, top black students know they can command more money outside the university in business, medicine, or law.

Universities and colleges will have to offer more competitive salaries and find some way to retain existing black faculty members if there is going to be any appreciable change to an increasingly bad situation. And the already tiny pool to draw from shrinks a little more each year. In 1980 the number of blacks receiving Ph.D.s was 1,032; in 1991 the number was 933.

Unable to secure coveted positions at places like Columbia, where an unusually high 8 percent of the faculty is black, or at Rice with its exceedingly low percentage of 1.3, black professors look to the historically black colleges.[183] Dr. Darryl Roberts exercised that option when Duke denied him tenure a year ago. He now heads the political science department at Tuskegee University. Brothers and sisters, you can go home again.

WE'RE IN THE SAME BOAT NOW

ABOUT THE TIME black students at Duke University and the administration were dickering over the faculty disparity, residents of Crown Heights, Brooklyn—blacks versus the Lubavitcher Hasidic Jewish community—were on the verge of explosion once more. Since the early 1950s when a federal housing act paved the way for people of color to move into Crown Heights, the Hasidim have had to share their limited space with other groups. Eventually the size of Hasidic families who are determined to live in close proximity in order to ensure cultural coherence, and the scarcity of affordable housing created a problem with incoming residents from the West Indies, whose families were often just as large, and with a similar demand for shelter.

The partitioning of Crown Heights by the city fathers in 1976 and 1977 marked the beginning of Hasidic political ascendance. Andrew Cooper, editor and publisher of the *City Sun,* a Brooklyn-based black weekly, was there when the so-called melting pot began to boil. "Mayor Abraham Beame and City Councilman Theodore Silverman successfully argued for a separation of the community governing bodies—community boards, school districts, police liaisons," Cooper recalled. "In 1967, the Board of Estimate decided to keep all of New York City's communities intact except Crown Heights. The line was drawn down the middle of Eastern Parkway, dividing the community board and creating two 'nations,' separate and unequal. One community board's members were all black; on the other side, the Hasidim gained disproportionate power." The situation in Crown Heights was a classic encounter between the irresistible force and the immovable object. "Both groups," said Richard Wade, a specialist in urban affairs at the City University Graduate Center in New York City, "are locked into a unique historical struggle over a limited amount of space." They are, in the words of Professor Gerald Horne, chairman of the black studies department at the University of California at Santa Barbara, "living cheek to jowl," and unavoidably at each other's throats.[184]

With each passing year, as the two communities rubbed against each other, the possibility of raw hostility became more imminent. Increasingly, black residents resented the preferential treatment the Hasidim received, particularly the unequal distribution of police protection and city services. Things were tense, nerves rubbed raw, and the tinderbox was ready for detonation in 1991 when a speeding car driven by a Hasidic man ran a light, jumped the curb, hit and killed seven-year-old Gavin Cato and injured his cousin, Angela. The car was part of a special convoy escorting the Grand Rebbe, the spiritual leader of the Lubavitchers, who was returning from a weekly visit to his wife's grave site. Grand Rebbe Menachem Schneerson, a ninety-year-old, paralyzed rabbi, was viewed by his followers as the Messiah. Not until the "Messiah" gave the word—and he could barely speak during the last two years before his death in 1994, since he experienced a stroke in 1992—would the Lubavitchers consider relocating. "Schneerson," writes Lenni Brenner, a leftist Jewish scholar, "is a contemporary religious fundamentalist. For him, George Bush's victory over Saddam Hussein is a sign of the imminence of the coming of the Messiah."

Four days of outrage followed as black residents torched cars, broke store windows, and vented their frustration in a number of ways. The riot had its only human fatality when Yankel Rosenbaum, a visiting rabbinical scholar from Australia, was attacked by a group of young blacks and stabbed by one of its members. Lemrick Nelson, the only black arrested, was charged with the murder, tried, and acquitted, which further incensed the Hasidic community. Various efforts were made to cool things between the feuding factions, and a decisive step occurred in December 1992 when prominent civic leaders, at the invitation of Mayor Dinkins, Reverend Jesse Jackson, Congressman Charles Rangel, Peggy Tishman of the Jewish Community Relations Council, and financier Felix Rohatyn, head of the Municipal Assistance Corporation, assembled at the Apollo Theatre for a screening of *The Liberators,* a documentary about black troops rescuing Jews from Nazi concentration camps during World War II, made by Bill Miles and Nina Rosenblum, a black man and a Jewish woman, themselves the personification of the evening's overture toward healing.

Implicit in the evening's objectives was the understanding that the furor in Crown Heights did not exemplify the relationship between blacks and Jews. It should be noted that no member of the Lubavitcher sect attended the affair. Reverend Jackson's appearance was especially conspicuous, and he told the gathering during his moment at the podium that "Jews came from Europe in steerage and we were brought from Africa in chains in the bottom of ships, but we are in the same boat now." Jackson was extending yet another olive branch to the Jewish community, continuing the rounds of apology for his past mistakes. "While the walls of Berlin have fallen," Jackson preached, "we cannot allow walls to be erected in Crown Heights."[185]

There was not a dry eye in the theater when the houselights came up again after the film was over. The film had served as a reminder of the age-old relationship between Jews and blacks; it was time to recall those productive times when the groups were momentarily allied, and the more optimistic among them were quick to recount how devoutly Jewish abolitionists assisted runaway slaves, deemphasizing those Jews who held slaves and helped operate and finance the dreaded system. Indeed, Jews fought alongside John Brown in the battles over "Bloody Kansas." Harold Cruse, in his important book *The Crisis of the Negro Intellectual,* however, attempts to balance the record, noting "American Jews were no different from other individual American whites: They were pro-slavery, anti-slavery, slave-owners, slave-traders, pro-Union, pro-Confederacy, war profiteers, army officers, soldiers, spies, statesmen, opportunistic politicians or indifferent victims of intersectional strife of the Civil War."[186]

Then came the civil rights era, the hallmark of black and Jewish relations. Whenever the "alliance" between blacks and Jews is cited, this association, forged during the civil rights struggle, is the most common referent. Even the biblical Hebrews for worshipful black Christians, or the black/Jewish connection in radical and Communist groups of the thirties, cannot be compared to the camaraderie between the two groups on the southern battlegrounds, which has a useful "trinity" in the martyrdom of James Chaney, Andrew Goodman, and Michael Schwerner. "I think all of us need to stop romanticizing the fact there's been such a close relationship between blacks and Jews over the past thirty years and recognize like all people that we have worked together and do work together on occasion," was the sober response of Roscoe Brown, Jr., president of Bronx Community College.[187]

This conclusion is echoed time and again in Jonathan Kaufman's *Broken Alliance—The Turbulent Times Between Blacks and Jews in America.* Kaufman admits, though, that he had begun his research under the impression that the black/Jew relationship, especially during the civil rights period, was one of goodwill and idealism, but what he found was far different. "The alliance between blacks and Jews was never as strong as it appeared," he wrote. "It was rooted as much in the hard currency of politics and self-interest as in love and idealism. Even at those times when the alliance seemed strongest— when police unearthed the bodies of Schwerner, Chaney, and Goodman; when blacks and Jews worked side by side for the passage of the civil rights laws; when Jews in the North and West wrote checks to the NAACP, SCLC, and SNCC—the symbols of cooperation covered a cauldron of ambivalent feelings and conflicting emotions."[188]

At the same time that SNCC was actively adopting a "black power" plan of action and extricating whites from the organization—many of them Jews—the Jews in New York City, most notably the lower-class Jews, exacerbated the growing rift. In 1966, 55 percent of New York's Jews voted against a police civilian review board proposition endorsed by the vast majority of blacks. "These lower-class Jews," said Lenni Brenner, "saw the cops as their defenders against black lumpen males who were ripping them off to get money to buy heroin. They didn't see them as racial inferiors, as many other whites then did, and no one thought these muggers and burglars were anti-Semitic." If the significance of this development escaped all but the keenly observant, the New York teachers' strike the following year in 1967 was much too large and rancorous to ignore.

The bitter standoff over the community control of schools in the Ocean Hill–Brownsville section of Brooklyn was essentially between middle-class Jewish teachers and lower-class black parents. What the black parents viewed as a struggle for power and self-determination was seen by Jews as anti-Semitism. Nearly two years of argument and innuendo brought no satisfying results and what most people recall from the debacle is a radio show hosted by Julius Lester in which he invited a teacher, Leslie Campbell (Jitu Weusi), to read a poem written by one of his students that began: "Hey Jew boy, with the yarmulke on your head/You pale-faced Jew boy—I wish you were dead."[189]

These were some of the simmering episodes that formed the backdrop of the incidents in Crown Heights, and the city's leaders—blacks and Jews—who schmoozed at the Apollo were hoping the historic collaboration between the two groups, which, as Paul Robeson, Jr., observed, "derived from overriding common interests . . . and a common fear," was stronger than the discord threatening to split them irreconcilably.[190] Seven months later, in July 1993, the six-hundred-page, two-volume Crown Heights Report was released, and nobody was satisfied. The Hasidim assailed the Report, which found that Mayor Dinkins and then Police Commissioner Lee Brown did not hold back the police and thereby endangered the lives of the Lubavitchers. Black residents of Crown Heights were upset because the report had glossed over the death of Gavin Cato and, according to several community leaders, had failed to even interview anyone in the Cato family. Later, it was disclosed that attempts had been made to reach members of the Cato family, but they had declined to participate.

Overall Jewish response to the report was favorable, although many felt that Mayor Dinkins should have initiated the investigation, and not Governor Mario Cuomo. Both Jews and blacks rushed to Washington shortly after the report appeared, requesting Attorney General Janet Reno to investigate the unrest in Crown Heights for violations of Yankel Rosenbaum's civil rights on the one hand, and Gavin Cato's on the other. She decided to drop the case, finding that neither party presented compelling evidence. Dinkins and his supporters were obviously concerned about how the fallout from the report would affect his reelection bid. He had only narrowly defeated the Republican contender in 1989, and he could not afford to lose any of the Jewish votes that helped him over the top. It was not the election that occupied the minds of most citizens; they wondered if Crown Heights would explode again. Reverend Al Sharpton was among many community leaders who called for calm. And later, the swami of soundbite would muse: "How is it that blacks and Jews who share the covenant of the Old Testament cannot live together today in Brooklyn?"[191]

YOUNG HOT BLOODS

Joshua Redman is a 24-year-old tenor saxophonist who is exceptional with or without the horn in his mouth. As a student at Harvard University, Redman racked up several honors and graduated summa cum laude in urban studies. He decided to hang up his Phi Beta Kappa key and forgo a full scholarship to the Yale Law School for the uncertainties of the jazz life. But uncertainty is slowly fading as he moves to the top of his class on the saxophone. Within a year he won the hotly contested Thelonious Monk saxophone competition in 1991, inked a recording contract, and produced his debut album, which was an instant success. Influenced by John Coltrane, Hank Mobley, Dexter Gordon, and his father, Dewey Redman, himself a powerful saxophonist, Redman has completed his second album, *Wish,* which will only increase his following and growing reputation.

Anna Deveare Smith is so adept at slipping into characters that it is difficult to get a peg on the real Ms. Smith. In her one-woman show *Fires in the Mirror,* the dramatist portrays a neighborhood of characters, moving almost seamlessly from an angry black militant, to white housewife, to angst-ridden Hasidic Jew, to a bemused homeless person, to a fast-talking Rasta. This performance is an attempt to capture the human drama, the tension that brought Crown Heights into the national spotlight. Smith interviewed hundreds of people in the neighborhood, including several celebrities, and then distilled these interviews into biting cameos in her show. She is currently gathering raw material for a staging of the Los Angeles riots of 1992. Her impersonation of Rodney King should be a showstopper.

Ralph Wiley began his writing career as a sports journalist, shaping those totally absorbing profiles for *Sports Illustrated,* but with three books under his wing, Wiley is now the budding author. *Why Black People Tend to Shout* launched him, and then his collaboration with Spike Lee on his book about the making of the film *Malcolm X* made him an even hotter literary property. In his third book, *What Black People Should Do Now* (1993), a collection of essays, Wiley unloads his full analytical arsenal, discussing everything from the vagaries of the publishing industry to Clarence Thomas and Anita Hill, and always with his special perspective and clever way of cutting to the essence of an issue. Wiley is an entertaining social commentator who gets a kick out of telling it like it is.

Monie Love has a name that is a bit misleading for a twenty-two-year-old rapper with a social consciousness. On her first album, *Down to Earth* (1990), Love waxed poetic on advice to her homegirls. The social thrust gained momentum on her next album, *In a Word or 2,* where her rhyming info on the importance of dealing with AIDS and HIV virus ranks her among the most enlightened of the hip-hop horde. She also offers some insight on motherhood, about which she can speak with authority since her daughter is nearly two. As a maturing artist, Love enhances her performances and recordings with such stellar musicians as bassist Bootsy Collins and saxophonist Maceo Parker, Bel Biv Devoe, Johnny Gill, and Keith Sweat. When Monie talks or raps, she is serious business, and the crap takes a walk.

Andre Harrell is one of the music industry's most enterprising young executives. At thirty-two, Harrell is the CEO of Uptown Entertainment, a multifaceted empire encompassing record and movie divisions. He is a native New Yorker who was half of the early 1980s rap duo Dr. Jeckyll and Mr. Hyde. But with a sharp business acumen, Harrell quickly set the performing aside to pursue the managerial end. Now his Uptown Records includes a joint venture with MCA, and has placed him right at the cutting edge of black music. Heavy D. and the Boyz, Guy, Jodeci, Mary J. Blige, and Al B. Sure are a few of the chart-busters under Harrell's supervision.

BETCHA DIDN'T KNOW

Robert Maynard was the first black to own a major daily newspaper in America. In 1983 Maynard and his wife, Nancy, bought the financially troubled *Oakland Tribune*, and by 1989 the paper won a Pulitzer Prize for photographs of the Bay-area earthquake. Maynard died August 17, 1993, of prostate cancer. He was fifty-six.

CHRONOLOGY—1993–1994
●

June 16—Singers Otis Redding, Dinah Washington, and Clyde McPhatter were among seven musicians honored by the U.S. Postal Service with commemorative twenty-nine-cent stamps.

The stamps are issued in two formats: sheets of thirty-five stamps each and booklets of twenty stamps.

August 4—Sergeant Stacey Koon and Laurence Powell, convicted of beating Rodney King and violating his civil rights, were sentenced to meager terms of two and a half years. The judge said he imposed shorter terms because, in his opinion, King provoked the officers. He also concluded that the officers had endured a "specter of unfairness" after a jury failed to convict them in an earlier trial.

September 5–11—Upwards of 75,000 people attended the National Baptist Convention U.S.A., Inc., in New York City. The Convention, with its 7.8 million members, is the largest black organization in the nation. "The Convention is our political outlet, our social outlet, our economic outlet, along with its primary religious dimension," said the Reverend Timothy Mitchell, pastor of Ebenezer Baptist Church in Flushing, Queens.[192]

September 28—Jamal Mashburn, an all-American basketball player at Kentucky, donates $500,000 to a university scholarship fund. "I see this as my chance to give something back to the people who have helped me and to help those students who may not otherwise have a chance," Mashburn said.[193] Mashburn, who left the university after his third year, has not reached contract agreement with the Dallas Mavericks but did sign a five-year $5 million contract with Fila, an Italian shoe and sportswear company.

September 29—A federal court in Manhattan settled a lawsuit in the Yonkers desegregation case in which almost 1,000 black and Hispanic families will be offered apartments in predominantly white middle-class neighborhoods in Westchester County. The case stemmed from a suit filed two years earlier by seventeen black and Hispanic families, all of whom were holders of Section Eight certificates permitting them to live in private apartment buildings. The families charged that local agencies running the Section Eight program in Westchester County made no attempts to place them in predominantly white apartment buildings, guiding them instead to run-down sections of Yonkers. The settlement is certain to have national implications, affecting similar cases now on the docket in several states.

October 1—A report from the Treasury Department finds that law enforcement officials bungled nearly every aspect of their plan to apprehend David Koresh, the leader of the heavily armed cult near Waco, Texas, and then misled Congress and investigators about their mistakes. The report deals only with the original raid on the compound, February 28, 1993, in which four agents and six cult members were killed. In a subsequent raid, April 19, federal agents assaulted the cult with tear gas, and fire consumed most of the cult members and the compound. Authorities said eighty-five people died in that fire, including seventeen children. There were several African-Americans among the casualties.

October 8—Toni Morrison, noted author of such books as *Beloved, Song of Solomon, Sula,* and *The Bluest Eye,* won the Nobel Prize in Literature. She is the first black woman to receive the prize. Her winning the award, said literary agent Marie Brown, "is a significant milestone for her personally, and for all of us who labor in the field."[194]

November 6—David N. Dinkins conceded the mayoral election to Republican candidate Rudolph Giuliani. Guiliani rejected the notion that the changing of the guard was anything other than a fair and forthright call for change.

November 29—Very few people were aware that the speech Khalid Muhammad of the Nation of Islam would give on this date at Kean College, New Jersey, would be the source of so much controversy for the rest of the year. In his speech, Muhammad castigated Jews, Catholics, and "Uncle Tom" black leaders.

December 17—Dr. Lorraine Hale was among ten child advocates recognized as "Champions for Children." Dr. Hale continues the mission of her mother, the late Clara Hale, caring for babies with AIDS, and who are addicted to drugs and alcohol. Gasby Greely, a popular TV commentator, was named national communications director of the International environmental organization Greenpeace. She will oversee the organization's public information and activist networks.

January 22—Angela Bassett won the Golden Globe Award for best actress in a musical or comedy for her role in *What's Love*

Got to Do With It. Bassett later received an Academy Award nomination as a leading actress for the same role.

January 30—Emmett Smith, running back for the Dallas Cowboys, was named the Most Valuable Player in the Super Bowl. Smith became the first player in NFL history to win the rushing title and the Super Bowl MVP in the same year. He was also named the MVP of the NFL.

February 5—A jury convicted Byron De La Beckwith, seventy-three, of murder in the 1963 death of Medgar Evers, who at that time headed the NAACP office in Jackson, Mississippi. Beckwith was sentenced to life in prison. This was the third time Beckwith was tried for the murder. Twice in 1964 all-white juries failed to reach a verdict. The jury that convicted him had eight black and four white members.

February 7—Songstress/actress Whitney Houston won seven American Music Awards. Her single "I Will Always Love You" topped both the pop/rock and R & B categories. Later, Houston won three Grammys.

February 18—Jake Gaither, longtime Florida A & M coach, died at a hospital in Tallahassee. Gaither, ninety, had been in failing health. During his twenty-five-year tenure at the school, Gaither compiled an enviable 203–36–4 record, an .884 winning percentage, and sent more than forty players to the NFL, including Bob Hayes and Willie Gallimore.

March 1—Ray Charles, Dr. Dre, Digable Planets, Janet Jackson, Toni Braxton and Whitney Houston were among African-American artists to win Grammys. Peabo Bryson and Regina Belle were also honored in the Pop Duo or Group Performance for their version of the theme from the film *Aladdin.* Curtis Mayfield and Aretha Franklin received Achievement Awards.

April 12—David Levering Lewis won the Pulitzer Prize in biography for *W. E. B. Du Bois: Biography of a Race: 1868–1919.* Lewis will also later receive the Parkham and Brancort awards in history. For one author to win all three coveted honors in one year is unprecedented.

April 16—Ralph Ellison, best known for his novel *Invisible Man* (1952), died in New York City. He was eighty. Ellison was also the author of two collections of essays, *Shadow and Act* (1964) and *Going to the Territory* (1986).

May 10—Nelson Mandela was sworn in as South Africa's first black president, in Pretoria. Mandela, an uncompromising freedom fighter, served twenty-seven years in prison before his release in 1990. Mandela and the ANC triumphed decisively in all but two of the country's nine provinces.

May 21—George Gregory, eighty-eight, the nation's first black all-American basketball player, died at his Manhattan apartment. The cause was colon cancer, said his wife, Helen Gregory. Gregory was the star center and captain of the Columbia University basketball team in 1930–31, and led the team to its first league championship.

June 12–14—The NAACP hosted a successful National African-American Leadership Summit, overcoming all the controversy centered on an invitation to Minister Louis Farrakhan of the Nation of Islam. More than eighty nationally recognized leaders attended the summit and discussed economic, community, and youth empowerment, as well as moral and spiritual renewal.

June 17—O. J. Simpson, famed football star and movie actor, surrendered to the law enforcement officials after being pursued by the police for sixty miles on the Los Angeles freeway. Simpson has been charged with the murder of his ex-wife, Nicole, and her friend Ron Goldman. With a history of abusing his ex-wife, Simpson pled not guilty to the charges and faces trial in late 1994.

July 13—Cornel West, the author and scholar, was at his eloquent best during an appearance at the Slave Theater in Brooklyn. West, who is moving from Princeton to Harvard University in the fall, dwelled on market forces and how they have deleteriously affected the nation's mores and values.

SOUNDBITE

"Free the land!"

—IMARI ABUBAKARI OBADELE,
FOUNDER AND SECOND PRESIDENT
OF THE REPUBLIC OF NEW AFRIKA[195]

THIS LAND WAS OUR LAND

THERE IS ANOTHER issue of land facing black Americans, but it is much larger than thousands of Crown Heights. That land sprawls across the South, across the endless farms, creeks, and byways once known as Dixie, where half the black population of America still dwells. Half of the nation's thirty to forty million African-Americans may live in the South, but their ownership of land diminishes by the moment. Black farmers lose land at an average of 160,000 acres per year, almost as fast as the rate of the world's shrinking rain forests.[196]

Most black farmers, according to the Atlanta-based Federation of Southern Cooperatives and Land Assistance Fund (FCC/LAF), own fewer than one hundred acres. "Between 1920, when black farmers numbered nearly a million, and 1982," writes Toni Joseph in *Emerge* magazine, "almost 94 percent of all black-owned farms were sold or lost. At last count, fewer than 22,500 blacks farmed less than 2.5 million acres."[197] Hoping to stifle this accelerating loss of land, the FCC/LAF has organized 15,000 black farmers into thirty-five agricultural cooperatives throughout the South, with technical assistance offered for specialty crops and animal problems while helping to secure the latest managerial skills and find commercial markets. They also help facilitate a limited number of small loans for the farmers.

The bulk of land formerly owned by blacks was lost during the migrations following World Wars I and II when thousands of blacks dropped their hoes, sold the mules, and answered the siren call from the North. Many of them needed no beckoning to say good-bye to Jim Crow, the debilitating boll weevil, night riders with their lynch ropes, the drudgery of sharecropping, and, much later, the unscrupulous property sales and transfers. But despite the persistence of poverty and inequity, many blacks sought to hold on to their meager plots of land, resisting—and sometimes fighting—even the tempting offers from land developers. Residents of the Georgia and South Carolina Sea Islands have been battling encroachment from white developers for years, but futilely.

In Daufuskie, South Carolina, popularized as one of the remaining sectors where African retentive Gullah or Geechee culture flourishes, the land has been precipitously slipping into the plans and schemes of developers. One land-grabbing company, eager to expand its holdings, constructed luxury homes over an ancestral burial ground. This desecration has a northern counterpart in downtown New York City. For several years dispute raged over the "Negro Burial Ground," which was dated as an early eighteenth-century site, and unearthed during the construction of a federal office building. More than four hundred skeletal remains were torn from the gravesite. In the summer of 1993 it was finally agreed, after endless rounds of debate, that the remains would be turned over to Howard University and placed under the supervision of the school's anthropologist, Dr. Michael Blakey. The bones disinterred in Daufuskie never had the opportunity to be salvaged. They were reportedly thrown into the river by the white developers.

Also in 1984 the same company bought up to 720 acres of Daufuskie for $6.5 million. A plantationlike private club was established, complete with "Members Only" signs and the closing of a road leading to one of the town's most radiant beaches. Similar development tracts are popping up in and around Charleston, and on Hilton Head and Sapelo Island, another vital Gullah enclave. On Sapelo the indigenous population has dramatically decreased twofold. Long-standing local landmarks and schools have been closed, and the fishery has been taken over by large-scale mainland operations. Residents are powerless to stop the advance. It is either go with the flow, and accept a job that comes with the new golf course where once a pasture of cows grazed, or pull up stakes. Most of the younger blacks in the vicinity are steadily leaving their homes for better opportunities elsewhere. Those who stay and fight the invasion draw inspiration from their Geechee ancestors who, after the end of the Civil War, mustered out of the army, kept their rifles, and returned to their land, vowing not to concede one inch to former slaveholders.

SOUNDBITE

"But when the battles are over, Negroes and white people must live together in the United States. To forget this is the great betrayal of the future."

—HOWARD THURMAN (1900–1981),
AUTHOR AND THEOLOGIAN[198]

PAST IS PROLOGUE

AFRICANS WERE BROUGHT to the so-called New World to work the land, to be drawers of water and hewers of wood, to ease the burden of their slave masters and provide them with a smooth conduit to wealth and prosperity. Not only were these tasks fulfilled with skill and alacrity, Africans also found time to tend to their own personal needs, which, while doing so, was another way they contributed mightily to American society. Africans began as captives but soon captivated their governors, providing ringing chorus after chorus of enthralling melody, enriching the repertory of dance, lifting drama, poetry, and literature to singular heights of American originality, without misplacing those values and a lifestyle so vital to their African experience or a love so necessary to their well-being. This was an "ethos," scholar Sterling Stuckley has noted, "which prevented them [African captives] from being imprisoned altogether by the definitions which the larger society sought to impose."[199] In this context steel-drivin' John Henry shared his sweat without sacrificing his dignity, Br'er Rabbit the trickster told the tale without losing his own, and Michael rowed the boat ashore, and still had energy left to cut a nasty, high-steppin' cakewalk. Yes, Mae West, Beulah peeled your grape and endowed you with soul, style, and grace at the same time!

Thus, from slave ship to spaceship, blacks have played a central part in the creation of this nation. Each rivet, each nail, each plank, is baptized in black blood. Without black labor, the infrastructure of the past would crumble. Without the black spirit and morality, America would be a hollow shell, a soulless, vapid nation with only greed and plunder to mark its passage. "In other words," writes Ralph Ellison, "had there been no blacks, certain creative tensions arising from the cross-purposes of whites and blacks would also not have existed. Not only would there have been no Faulkner; there would have been no Stephen Crane, who found certain basic themes of his writing in the Civil War . . . there would have been no Hemingway, who took Crane as a source and guide. Without the presence of Negro American style, our jokes, our tall tales, even our sports, would be lacking in the sudden turns, the shocks, the swift changes of pace (all jazz-shaped), that serve to remind us that the world is ever unexplored, and that while a complete mastery of life is mere illusion, the real secret of the game is to make life swing."[200]

In both a literal and figurative sense, blacks have given America "soul," that sometimes inexplicable force which is akin to ashé and is among the permanent claims this country can make when the final roll call of nations resounds. Now, if anybody asks you who made up this song, tell 'em it was ＿＿ done been here and gone . . . gone on down the glory road!

NOTES

1. Bell, Derrick. *Faces at the Bottom of the Well—The Permanence of Racism,* Basic Books, New York, 1992, p. 194.

2. Quarles, Benjamin. *The Negro in the Making of America,* Collier, New York, 1964.

3. Carew, Jan. *The Fulcrums of Change—Origins of Racism in the Americas and Other Essays,* Africa World Press, Trenton, New Jersey, 1988, p. 3.

4. Wright, Richard R. "Negro Companions of the Spanish Explorers," in *The Making of Black America,* eds., August Meier and Elliott Rudwick, p. 32.

5. Jackson, John. *Introduction to African Civilizations,* Citadel Press, New York, 1990, p. 119.

6. Cowley, Malcolm and Daniel Mannix. *Black Cargoes—A History of the Atlantic Slave Trade 1518–1865,* Viking Press, New York, 1962, p. 106.

7. Bayliss, John F. *Black Slave Narratives,* Collier Books, London, 1970, p. 44.

8. Higginbotham, A. Leon. *In the Matter of Color—Race and the American Legal Process: The Colonial Period,* Oxford University Press, New York, 1978, p. 151.

9. Bennett, Lerone. *Before the Mayflower,* Penguin Books, Middlesex, England, 1982, p. 182.

10. Jordan, Winthrop D. *White over Black—American Attitudes Toward the Negro 1550–1812,* Penguin Books, Baltimore, 1968, pp. 450–451.

11. Viola, Herman J. *After Columbus—The Smithsonian Chronicle of the North American Indians,* Smithsonian Institution, Washington, D.C., 1990, p. 145.

12. See recent bio on Jefferson.

13. Brent, Linda. *Incidents in the Life of a Slave Girl,* Harcourt Brace Jovanovich, New York, 1973, p. 29.

14. Bayliss, p. 196.

15. Franklin, John Hope. *From Slavery to Freedom: A History of Negro Americans,* Alfred A. Knopf, New York, 1980, p. 193.

16. Du Bois, W. E. B. *John Brown,* International Publishers, New York, 1962, p. 347.

17. McPherson, James M. *The Negro's Civil War,* Ballantine Books, New York, 1965, pp. 188–189.

18. Du Bois, W. E. B. *The Souls of Black Folk,* The Blue Heron Press, New York, 1953, p. 82.

19. Stuckey, Sterling. "A Last Stern Struggle: Henry Highland Garnet and Liberation Theory," in *Black Leaders of the Nineteenth Century,* eds., Leon Litwack and August Meier, University of Illinois Press, Urbana and Chicago, 1988, p. 146.

20. Dittmer, John. "The Education of Henry McNeal Turner," in *Black Leaders in the Nineteenth Century,* eds., Leon Litwack and August Meier, University of Illinois Press, Urbana and Chicago, 1988, p. 270.

21. Dittmer, p. 271.

22. Nalty, Bernard C. *Strength for the Fight—A History of Black Americans in the Military,* The Free Press, New York, 1986, p. 87.

23. Nalty, p. 73.

24. Du Bois, p. 41.

25. *Three Negro Classics,* Avon Books, 1965, p. 148.

26. Du Bois, p. 43.

27. *Three Negro Classics,* p. 140.

28. Du Bois, p. 43.

29. Du Bois, p. 51.

30. Hughes, Langston and Milton Meltzer. *A Pictorial History of the Negro in America,* Crown Publishers, New York, 1956, p. 217.

31. Morgan, Anne Hodges and Rennard Strickland, eds. *Oklahoma Memories,* University of Oklahoma Press, Norman, 1981, p. 18.

32. Katz, William Loren. *Black Indians: A Hidden Heritage,* Atheneum, New York, 1986, p. 145.

33. Davis, John P., ed. *The American Negro Reference Book,* Prentice Hall, Inc., Englewood Cliffs, 1966, p. 782.

34. Davis, p. 783.

35. Du Bois, W. E. B. "Commentary," *Dial,* July 16, 1901, p. 53.

36. Davis, p. 59.

37. Du Bois, "Editorial," *The Crisis,* 1, No. 1 (November 1910), pp. 10–11.

38. Du Bois, "Close Ranks," *The Crisis,* 16 (July 1918), p. 111.

39. Little, Arthur W. *From Harlem to the Rhine,* Covici-Friede, New York, 1936, p. 71.

40. Lewis, David Levering. *When Harlem Was in Vogue,* Oxford University Press, New York, 1981, p. 5.

41. Haywood, Harry. *Black Bolshevik—Autobiography of an Afro-American Communist,* Liberator Press, Chicago, 1978, p. 81.

42. Briggs, Cyril, ed. *The Crusader,* Volume IV, 1921.

43. Garvey, Marcus. *The Philosophy and Opinions of Marcus Garvey,* edited by Amy Jacques-Garvey, Antheum, 1994, p. 310.

44. Cruse, Harold. *The Crisis of the Negro Intellectual,* Quill, New York, 1984, p. 36.

45. Boyd, Herb. *African American History—Quote A Day,* Longmeadow Press, Stamford, 1993.

46. Gayle, Addison, ed. *The Black Aesthetic,* Doubleday Anchor, Garden City, New York, 1971, p. 167.

47. Survey Graphic, *Harlem Mecca of the New Negro,* March 1925, p. 631.

48. Kellner, Bruce. *The Harlem Renaissance: A Dictionary of the Era,* Methuen, 1984, p. 231–232.

49. Ellison, Ralph. *Shadow and Act,* Vintage Books, New York, 1972, p. 78.

50. Angelou, Maya. *I Know Why the Caged Bird Sings,* Random House, New York, 1969, p. 49.

51. Johnson, Howard. Interview with author.

52. Abernathy, Ralph David. *And the Walls Came Tumbling Down,* Harper & Row, New York, 1989, p. 7.

53. Denby, Charles. *The Indignant Heart—A Black Worker's Journal,* Wayne State University Press, 1989.

54. Giddings, Paula. *When and Where I Enter: The Impact of Black Women on Race and Sex in America,* William Morrow, New York, 1984, p. 237.

55. Peery, Nelson. *Black Fire—The Making of an American Revolutionary,* The New Press, New York, 1994, p. 30.

56. Null, Gary. *Black Hollywood,* The Citadel Press, Secaucus, New Jersey, 1987, p. 76.

57. Duberman, Martin Bauml. *Paul Robeson,* Alfred A. Knopf, New York, 1988, p. 342.

58. Robinson, Jackie. *I Never Had It Made,* Rachel Robinson, New York, 1972, p. 98.

59. Parks, Rosa. *My Story,* Dial Books, New York, 1992, pp. 113–116.

60. Williams, Juan. *Eyes on the Prize—America's Civil Rights Years, 1954–1965,* Viking, New York, 1987, p. 89.

61. Boyd, *African American History—Quote A Day,* 1993.

62. Williams, p. 145.

63. Smith, Jessie Carney, ed. *Notable Black American Women,* Gale Research, Detroit, 1992, p. 41.

64. Abernathy, p. 359.

65. Williams, p. 179.

66. Williams, p. 240.

67. Blackwell, Unita. Interview with author.

68. Forman, James. *The Making of Black Revolutionaries,* Open Hand, Washington, D.C., 1985, p. 236.

69. Forman, p. 145.

70. Forman, p. xiv.

71. Brown, H. Rap. *Die Nigger Die,* The *Dial* Press, New York, 1969, p. 144.

72. Haley, Alex. *The Autobiography of Malcolm X,* Ballantine Books, New York, 1973, pp. 191–192.

73. Haley, p. 390.

74. Boyd, *African American History—Quote A Day.*

75. Seale, Bobby. *Seize the Time,* Black Classic Press, Baltimore, 1991, p. 59.

76. Seale, p. 66–69.

77. Hilliard, David. Interview with author.

78. Brown, Elaine. *A Taste of Power,* Pantheon, New York, 1993, p. 261.

79. Gayle, p. 372.

80. Murray, Albert. *The Omni-Americans,* Avon Books, New York, 1970, p. 314.

81. Gayle, p. 382.

82. Kerner Report of the National Advisory Commission on Civil Disorders, Bantam Books, New York, 1968, p. 1.

83. Kerner, p. 282.

84. Garrow, David. *The FBI and Martin Luther King, Jr.,* Penguin, New York, 1981, p. 214.

85. Abernathy, p. 414.

86. Abernathy, p. 433.

87. Branch, Taylor. *Parting the Waters,* Simon and Schuster, New York, 1988, p. 10.

88. Wilmore, Gayraud S. and James H. Cone, ed. *Black Theology—A Documentary History, 1966–1979,* Orbis Books, New York, 1979, p. 21.

89. King, Martin Luther, Jr. *Why We Can't Wait,* The New American Library, New York, 1963, p. 77.

90. Terry, Wallace. *Bloods*, Ballantine Books, New York, 1992, p. 9.

91. Terry, p. xvii.

92. Allen, Robert. Letter in possession of author.

93. Alkalimat, Abdul. *Introduction to Afro-American Studies: A Peoples College Primer*, Twenty-First Century Books, Chicago, 1986, p. 140.

94. Allen, Ernie. "Dying From the Inside: The Decline of the League of Revolutionary Black Workers," in *They Should Have Served That Cup of Coffee*, ed. Dick Cluster, South End Press, 1979, p. 78.

95. Grant, Joanne, ed., *Black Protest*, Ballantine, New York, 1968, p. 548.

96. Marable, Manning. *Race, Reform and Rebellion*, University Press of Mississippi, Jackson, 1984, p. 131.

97. Marable, p. 132.

98. Staples, Brent. "Editorial," *New York Times*, September 6, 1993.

99. Clarke, John Hendrik. Interview with author, 1990.

100. Marable, p. 137.

101. Grant, Joanne. *Black Protest*, Fawcett Premier, New York, 1968, p. 522.

102. Marable, p. 150.

103. Marable, pp. 152–153.

104. Marable, p. 154.

105. Georgakas, Dan. "Bayard Rustin (1910–1987)," *Encyclopedia of the American Left*, eds. Mari Jo Buhle, Paul Buhle, and Dan Georgakas, Garland Publishing New York, 1990, p. 663.

106. Lanker, Brian, *I Dream a World*, Stewart, Tabori & Chang, New York, 1989, p. 31.

107. Marable, p. 112.

108. Marable, Manning. Interview with author.

109. Smith, Ronald. *Cosby*, SPI Books, New York, 1986, p. 110.

110. Smith, p. 43.

111. Smith, pp. 55–56.

112. Smith, p. 65.

113. Bogle, Donald. *Blacks in American Films and Television,* Garland Publishing, New York, 1988, p. 225.

114. Hornsby, Alton Jr. *Milestones in 20th Century African-American History,* Visible Ink Press, 1993, p. 229.

115. Hauser, Thomas. *Muhammad Ali: His Life and Times,* Simon & Schuster, New York, 1991, p. 136.

116. Wolper, David with Quincy Troupe. *The Inside Story of TV's "Roots,"* Warner Books, 1978, p. ii (preface).

117. Haley, Alex. *Roots—The Saga of an American Family,* Doubleday, New York, 1974, p. 679.

118. *Black Enterprise,* June 1992, p. 230.

119. Billingsley, Andrew. *Climbing Jacob's Ladder,* Simon & Schuster, New York, 1991, p. 308.

120. Boyd, *African American History—Quote A Day.*

121. Churchill, Ward and Jim Vander Wall. *The Cointelpro Papers,* South End Press, Boston, 1990, p. x.

122. Durden-Smith, Jo. *Who Killed George Jackson?,* Alfred A. Knopf, New York, 1976, p. 292.

123. Shakur, Assata. *An Autobiography,* Lawrence Hill, New York, 1987, p. ix.

124. Hughes and Meltzer, p. 82.

125. Rampersad, Arnold. *The Life of Langston Hughes,* Volume II, *I Dream a World,* Oxford University Press, New York, 1988, p. 123.

126. Marable, Manning. *How Capitalism Underdeveloped Black America,* South End Press, Boston, 1983, p. 126.

127. Staples, Robert. *The Urban Plantation,* The Black Scholar Press, Oakland, 1987, p. 113.

128. Marable, p. 127.

129. Lusane, Clarence. *Pipe Dream Blues—Racism and The War On Drugs,* South End Press, Boston, 1991, p. 14.

130. Madhubuti, Haki. *Black Men—Obsolete, Single, Dangerous?*, Third World Press, Chicago, 1990, p. 45.

131. Abernathy, p. 594.

132. Boyd, Herb. "The Black Left In Struggle—1980–1985," in *The Year Left 2*—An American Socialist Yearbook, eds. Mike Davis, Manning Marable, Fred Pfeil and Michael Sprinker, Verso Press, 1987, p. 21.

133. Boyd, p. 26.

134. Boyd, p. 27.

135. Boyd, *African American History—Quote A Day.*

136. George, Nelson. *The Death of Rhythm and Blues,* E. P. Dutton, New York, 1998, p. 190–191.

137. Boyd, *African American History—Quote A Day.*

138. Hernton, Calvin. *The Sexual Mountain and Black Women Writers,* Anchor Press, New York, 1987, p. 16.

139. Boyd, "The Black Left In Struggle," p. 31.

140. Barboza, Steven. *American Jihad—Islam After Malcolm X,* Doubleday, New York, 1994, p. 110.

141. Rojas, Don. Interview with author, 1990.

142. Rojas, Don. Interview with author, 1990.

143. Boyd, "The Black Left In Struggle," p. 28.

144. Boyd, "The Black Left In Struggle," p. 28.

145. Goode, W. Wilson with Joann Stevens, *In Good Faith,* Judson Press, Valley Forge, 1992, p. 210.

146. Goode, p. 230.

147. Moore, William. "Dance," *Black Arts Annual— 1987–1988,* ed. Donald Bogle, Garland Publishing, New York, 1989, p. 130.

148. Boyd, *African American History—Quote A Day.*

149. Mandela, Nelson. *The Struggle is My Life,* Pathfinder Press, New York, 1990, p. 214.

150. Mandela, p. 271.

151. Boyd, Herb. *Amsterdam News,* June 27, 1991.

152. Robinson, Randall. Interview with author.

153. Dash, Julie. *Daughters of the Dust,* The New Press, New York, 1992, p. xii.

154. *New York Times,* July 26, 1992.

155. Simmons, Charles. "The Los Angeles Rebellion: Class, Race Misinformation," in *Why L.A. Happened—Implications of the '92 Los Angeles Rebellion,* ed. Haki Madhubuti, Third World Press, Chicago, 1993, p. 144.

156. Dinwiddie, Michael. Interview with author.

157. Daniels, Ron. Interview with author.

158. Chrisman, Robert and Robert Allen, eds. *Court of Appeal: The Black Community Speaks Out on the Racial and Sexual Politics of Clarence Thomas vs. Anita Hill,* Ballantine Books, New York, 1992, p. xii.

159. Chrisman and Allen, p. 274.

160. Boyd, *African American History—Quote A Day.*

161. Jemison, T. J. Interview with author.

162. Primm, Beny J. "AIDS: A Special Report," in *The State of Black America, 1987,* National Urban League, New York, 1987, p. 159.

163. Primm, p. 162.

164. Baldwin, Elaine. Interview with author.

165. Welsing, Frances Cress. *The Isis Papers,* Third World Press, Chicago, 1991, p. 295.

166. Madhubuti, p. 55.

167. Hildebrand, Lee. *Hammertime,* Avon Books, New York, 1992, p. 115.

168. *Vibe,* September 1993.

169. Butts, Reverend Calvin. Interview with author.

170. Cockrel, Ken Jr. *Metro Times,* Detroit, 1993.

171. Asante, Molefi. *Afrocentricity,* Africa World Press, Trenton, New Jersey, 1988, p. 1.

172. Kunjufu, Jawanza. Interview with author.

173. Breitman, George, ed. *Malcolm X Speaks,* Grove Weidenfeld, New York, 1965, p. 26.

174. Lee, Spike. Interview with author.

175. Lee, Spike with Ralph Wiley. *By Any Means Necessary,* Hyperion, New York, 1992, p. 27.

176. *Transition,* Oxford, Issue 56, p. 187.

177. Lee, Spike. Interview with author.

178. Dyson, Michael Eric. *Reflecting Black,* University of Minnesota Press, Minneapolis, 1993, p. 115.

179. *Gentlemen's Quarterly,* December 1992, p. 192.

180. *New York Amsterdam News,* March 20, 1993.

181. Chavis, Ben. Interview with author.

182. Niemark, John. *The Way of the Orisha,* Haprer/Collins, New York, 1993, p. xii.

183. *New York Times,* September 19, 1993.

184. Cooper, Andrew, Richard Wade and Gerald Horne. Interviews with author.

185. *New York Amsterdam News,* March 20, 1993.

186. Cruse, Harold. *The Crisis of the Negro Intellectual,* Quill, New York, 1984, p. 478.

187. Brown, Roscoe. Interview with author.

188. Kaufman, Jonathan. *Broken Alliance: The Turbulent Times Between Blacks and Jews in America,* New Ameircan Library, New York, 1988, p. 17.

189. Brenner, Lenni. Interview with author.

190. Robeson, Paul Jr. *Paul Robeson, Jr. Speaks to America,* Rutgers University Press, New Brunswick, New Jersey, 1994, p. 170.

191. Sharpton, Al. Interview with author.

192. Mitchell, Timothy. Interview with author.

193. *New York Times,* September 29, 1993.

194. Brown, Marie. Interview with author.

195. Obadele, Abubakari Imari. *Free the Land!,* House of Songhay, Washington, D.C., 1987.

196. Joseph, Toni. "The Forty-Acre Dream Dies Hard," *Emerge,* February 1993, p. 59–62.

197. Joseph, Toni. p. 59–62.

198. Thurman, Howard. *The Luminous Darkness,* Friends United Press, Richmond, Indiana, 1965, p. 59.

199. Stuckey, Sterling. *Slave Culture,* Oxford University Press, New York and London, 1987.

200. Ellison, Ralph. *Going to the Terriotry,* Random House, New York, 1986, p. 109–110.

INDEX

HERB BOYD has taught African and African-American history at Wayne State University in Detroit, his hometown, and ethnomusicology at Oberlin University. He was music consultant for Time-Life's *Voices of Triumph* series. His articles on jazz have appeared in numerous publications, including *Downbeat*. An award-winning journalist, his byline has appeared in *Emerge*, New York *Amsterdam News*, *Black Enterprise*, the Detroit *Metro Times*, and elsewhere. He is the author of *African History for Beginners* and co-editor with Robert Allen of *Brotherman: The Odyssey of Black Men in America—An Anthology*. Boyd has traveled extensively in Africa and the Caribbean, and lives with his wife in New York City, where he teaches at the College of New Rochelle, Manhattan Campus, and New York City Technical College.

THE AFRICAN AMERICAN EXPERIENCE
from Avon Books

BULLWHIP DAYS   70884-1/ $14.00 US/ $19.00 CAN
edited by James Mellon
In their own voices, an oral history of the personal memories of the last survivors of American slavery.

CELIA: A SLAVE   71935-3/ $10.00 US/ $12.00 CAN
by Melton A. McLaurin
An account of a landmark courtroom battle that threatened to undermine the very foundation of the old South's most cherished institution.

PRIDE OF FAMILY   71934-7/ $10.00 US/ $12.00 CAN
by Carole Ione
The story of four generations of American women of color.

GROWING UP BLACK   76632-9/ $9.00 US/ $11.00 CAN
edited by Jay David
From slave days to the present—25 African-Americans reveal the trials and triumphs of their childhoods.

Coming Soon

PUSHED BACK TO STRENGTH
by Gloria Wade-Gayles   72426-X/$10.00 US/$12.00 CAN

DOWN THE GLORY ROAD
by Herb Boyd   77523-9/$12.50 US/$15.00 CAN